India

# Ram Mohan Roy

# Ram Mohan Roy

## Social, Political and Religious Reform in 19th Century India

### S. CROMWELL CRAWFORD

Paragon House Publishers
*New York*

Published in the United States by
Paragon House Publishers
2 Hammarskjold Plaza
New York, New York 10017

First published in 1984 by Gulab Varizani
for Arnold-Heinemann Publishers (India).

**Library of Congress Cataloging-in-Publication Data**

Crawford, S. Cromwell.
  Ram Mohan Roy.

  Bibliography:
  Includes index.
    1. Rammohun Roy, Raja, 1772?–1833.  2. Rammohun Roy, Raja,
1772?–1833—Ethics.  3. Reformers—India—Biography.  I. Title.
DS475.2.R18C73  1986  954.03'1'0924 [B]  86–91442
ISBN 0–913729–15–9

*FOR THE SADGUNNS*

*Marjorie*
*Archiebald*
*Jean*
*Sandra*

# Contents

# Foreword

It is an honor to contribute a Foreword to this work, even though there is no need at all for such an appendage. Nonetheless it is worthwhile to answer a certain question which may well be posed by readers: Since there is an overload of excellent writing on Ram Mohan Roy, can we expect this book to expand our knowledge or deepen our perception? The answer is that Professor Cromwell Crawford's approach to his theme is an outreach of his uniquely original thinking and, because of that, his work stands apart in the isolation of its own individual category. Here is an achievement that has no common ground of comparison with the mass of materials in the field. While the author possesses the full arsenal of a researcher and makes strident use of his tools, his success stems, in the final analysis, from something which is not tangible. Inspiration shapes his methodology. And that inspiration, a dynamic inner resource, is just another term for self-identification—in a special way.

To rescue my meaning from its shroud of vagueness, I have to recall the historical setting of the Crawfords themselves—their deep-thrust root in the Indian scene. The author has done some hard research into archival documents to uncover those roots buried in the earth of some centuries. We learn from his findings that his "great–great–great–grandfather," Henry Crawford, arrived in India at the time of Warren Hastings to join the East India Company's civil service. When he retired in 1800, Ram Mohan was young and yet unknown. "At any rate," says our author, "here was a member of my family who participated in the shaping of the forces in whose matrix Ram Mohan Roy lived and labored." Next, there was Henry's son, Charles, an official in London's India House, and it is highly probable that he met the distinguished visitor from India who spent three years in Britain. There is also every likelihood that Ram Mohan Roy was known personally to Henry's daughter, Frances, who resided in Calcutta with her husband. Finally, it must be noted that Ram Mohan was buried in the city of Bristol, at a site a couple of miles away from the manor house in which our author's great–grandparents lived.

"All of this weaves a web of closeness which permits me vicariously to reach out to the hero of this book through my more fortunate for-bears."

Mark the words: "My more fortunate forbears." The fact, however, is indisputable that Cromwell Crawford has been closer—in spirit—to Ram Mohan Roy than any of those named above. His narrative carries the feeings that he has lived in the closest association with Ram Mohan Roy, sharing thoughts, values, visions, and struggles; driving together in the city streets to attend meetings; and always ready to offer the man he so deeply admired whatever scholarly assistance was needed.

This feeling gets dramatized in the ecstatic words he scribbled at the back of a snapshot he sent me from Bristol not long ago. The snapshot is of the mausoleum of Ram Mohan Roy, built under the direction of Dwarakanath Tagore. It is easy to imagine Cromwell Crawford, as he is gazing wide-eyed at the monument, feeling overwhelmingly that time, since 1834, has come to a stop and he is reliving the days gone by with Ram Mohan Roy!

There are many pages in this volume which come to life with the same unique distinctiveness. That vests the writing with its most strik-ing characteristic: a glow of creativity. And that is what makes the work stand apart, isolated and splendid, from others of its genre.

BHABANI BHATTACHARYA

*Manchester,*
*MI*

# Preface

Raja Ram Mohan Roy was like any other man—only more so. This "moreness" has been viewed from diverse perspectives. Jeremy Bentham found him an "intensely admired and dearly loved collaborator in the service of mankind." For Sophia Dobson Collet, Ram Mohan presents "a most inspiring study for the New India of which he is the type and pioneer." Romain Rolland ranks him as a man who "ushered in a new era in the spiritual history of the ancient continent," and who was "the first really Cosmopolitan type in India." Brajendranath Seal credits him with having laid "the foundations of the true League of Nations in a league of National Cultures." Monier Williams salutes him as "the first earnest-minded investigator of the science of comparative religion that the world has produced." For Sarojini Naidu, he was "the first great modern International Ambassador." Dr. Sarvepalli Radhakrishnan calls him "a philosophic modernist, a progressive religious thinker anxious to emphasize the essentials of religion." And Mahatama Gandhi saw him as "the father of advanced liberal thought in Hinduism." For each of these authorities, the life of Ram Mohan Roy added up to *something more* in some particular field of endeavor—religion, social welfare, education, politics and internationalism. My purpose in this book is to advance the research by exploring the element of "moreness" in its ethical dimension; a task I hope to accomplish with the aid of historical analysis. Excellent books have been written on Roy, but the area of ethics has not yet received the attention it deserves.

The notion of "moreness" enables us to do justice to the Raja's greatness without producing a pious piece of hagiography. Unfortunately, writers past and present have tended to apotheosize the man, either directly or indirectly. In the first category belong such giants of the "Bengal Renaissance" as Rabindranath Tagore, Ramananda Chatterjee and Brajendranath Seal. Even as late as 1933 when the centennial of Ram Mohan's death was being commemorated, these gifted souls looked at history through heroic eyes.[1] In a moving oration entitled, "Rammohun Roy: The Universal Man," Sir Brajendranath says:

To him, all mysteries were unveiled, and all idols broken. He was the peer of the Voltaires and the Volneys, the Diderots and the Herders across the seas; and he had seen and travelled beyond them all, a modern Ulysses, voyaging in the land of the setting sun, and descending—not once, not twice, but many times—into the dark under-world, to bring messages from the old prophets in the Night of Ages.[2]

By 1972 when the two hundredth anniversary of his birth was celebrated, there was a growing disillusionment over the prospects of modernization, and frustrated scholars, unable to perpetuate the heroic view of history held by their forbears, challenged the so-called myth of the "Renaissance" and Ram Mohan's role in it as a modernizer. They concluded that the mythographers were premature in their "eagerness to find a father figure for modern India in Rammohun Roy and a radical break with the past in Bengal in the beginning of the nineteenth century."[3] These sentiments are conveyed through the pungent remarks of Ramesh Chandra Majumdar, "On Rammohun Roy":

> The pertinent question in the present context is "what was the extent of his success in laying thereby the foundation of the present Bangasamaj and dispelling the darkness by light?" The reply is written large in blazing letters upon the illuminated gates of two thousand Durga Puja pandals in Calcutta whose loud-speakers and *Dhak* or trumpets proclaim in deafening noise, year after year, the failure of Rammohun to make the slightest impression from his point of view on 99.9 percent of the vast Hindu Samaj either in the 19th or in the 20th century.[4]

Ironically, the debunkers of Roy are little different from his deifiers because they implicitly and indirectly attribute to him qualities which could belong only to divinity. In faulting his programs and policies, the full ramifications of which could only have been known to Hanuman or hindsight, they unwittingly ascribe to him a certain omniscience. In ridiculing his reforms that went awry, they claim for him an omnipotence which would have enabled him to control subsequent events in Bengal from his grave in Bristol. Perhaps Majumdar might have thought differently had he read Jesus' parable of the sower. Sometimes, says the great story–teller, the good seed falls on stony ground and perishes; sometimes it chokes among thorns and thistles; and sometimes it falls on good ground and bears fruit. Jesus' own religious movement died on Palestinian soil, for it must be remembered that Christianity is really the product of St. Paul and took root in Hellenistic soil. Judged by Majumdar's success criterion, Jesus was a failure!

The fact of the matter is, as our notion of "moreness" suggests, Ram Mohan was far ahead of his times. Even now, some one–hundred–and–fifty years after his death, the Indian soil is not ready for the seed he sowed. No wonder the germination process has been so slow, and the fruits of modernization so few. One would hope that historic realism would make contemporary critics ask themselves whether, perhaps, the problem after all, is not so much with the *seed* as with the *soil*. It is not that Roy failed, but that he *was failed*.

This book is divided into two parts: Era and Ethics. The two parts are closely linked. The era is the matrix in which the ethics takes shape, and the ethics is what molds the matrix. In the one we look at the person; in the other, we look at the principles. The person lends credibility to the principles, and the principles make us want to believe in the person.

Quantitatively considered, there is an obvious imbalance in the treatment of each part—an imbalance which may question the justification of the work being entitled *His Era and Ethics*. However, since the historical matter serves as a sort of quarry out of which we mine precious metal, quantitative comparisons do not apply for enormous data are required to supply the long, linear evidence from which we extract the fine elements of ethical content. There is mass, and there is metal; but the mass must be gauged by the metal, not the metal by the mass.

There are two reasons in particular why we devote so much volume to the historical setting in Part One.

First, there is the problem of demythology. When Ram Mohan pleaded for the need to get behind the Christ of faith to the Jesus of history, little did he realize that historiographers would be confronted with similar problems in his own biographical resurrection. Our concern is to get behind the mythological figures who have arisen over the past two hundred years. Many of these figures are the fabrications of followers and represent their own ideological needs and projections. As David Kopf states:

> The historical problem of evaluating Rammohun's place in the Renaissance has been complicated by a continuous shift in his historical image in the minds of successive generations. Of all the major figures in the modern Indian intelligentsia, Rammohun Roy is perhaps the most universally appropriated by all the different religious communities of South Asia as well as by the non-theistic. Hindus and Muslims, Christians and Brahmos claim him as one of their own. Others much less religiously inclined deny his theism and laud his humanism and rationalism. And which other Indian intellectual besides Rammohun has ever been so warmly treated historically by nationalists, relativists and universalists?[5]

The process of demythologizing can only take place by critically examining the biographical literature; by seeing in the interpretations a reflection of the *situation* in which later writers find themselves; and by constructing a history of the "histories." Though not articulated, this methodology has been assumed in the writing of this book. Critics will differ from our recapitulation of the historic picture, but it will not be because of a lack of effort to discover an historical integrity among the man, his milieu, his mission, and his message.

A second reason why history is emphasized is because only by knowing the historical context can we evaluate the moral quality of the reformer's words and actions. Ram Mohan's ethics were situationally oriented. Unlike the ethical legalists of his day, both Hindu and Christian, who found in their holy books principles codified as laws, Ram Mohan treated general rules as "illuminators" rather than "directors," and subordinated law to the dictates of love, guided by reason, common sense and the best in tradition. Though responsibility was relative to historical circumstances; responsibility *in* in those circumstances was always *absolute*.

In view of this situational approach, it is necessary that we, at all times, delineate the historical matrix in which his ethics take concrete shape. For instance, as long as India was socially and economically backward, Ram Mohan considered it expedient to welcome the British as agents of modernization; but *had* India *been* strong, united, and enlightened, love of freedom and fatherland would have made him forcefully resist the flying of the Union Jack on Indian soil. However, ethical expediency in this case does not warrant the judgment that he was a lackey of the British. Similarly, he believed there was a time to commend his people, and a time to condemn. The two moral judgments are contradictory, but the apparent contradiction is reconciled within the situation.

So, in the first part I say to the reader: *Ecce Homo!* Take a close look at this man. Hear what he said and see what he did as we recreate the *total* historical environment in which he lived and labored. What emerges then are the lineaments, not of a saint or a sycophant, but of a man whose moral profile stirs our humanity to relish the many challenges that life holds out for each of us. The narrative makes it clear that history has made the man; but there is *more*—the man has made history! This is why scholars can criticize him—*and they should*; but none can ignore him.

The second part of the book deals with ethics—normative ethics, to be precise. This subject matter represents a somewhat new trend. Until a decade or so ago, moral philosophers were preoccupied with the so-called problems of metaethics. "They were concerned with such things as the analysis and examination of the way moral concepts and moral arguments worked and, sometimes, the development of general theories about the meaning and characteristics of fundamental moral ideas. Their philosophical inquiries were about ethical statements and judgments."[6]

The distinction between metaethics and normative ethics is not cut-and-dried, but our concern is with the latter. Ram Mohan dealt with moral issues which, in principle, are still very much alive today, both in India and abroad. We try to show the religious and philosophical background against which he formulated, if only in an implicit way, a system of ethics by which he differentiated between "good" and "evil" modes of behaving with respect to specific moral problems. Whatever freed the individual on all levels of human awareness and helped build harmonious structures of society, were deemed "good;" and all forms of bondage that enslaved the humblest peasant or the nation-at-large, were looked upon as "evil."

It will be observed that, in chapters 6 through 11, a great deal of space is devoted to the issues of free press, education, economics, politics, immigration, etc., all of which is in keeping with the Era and Ethics approach we have chosen. However, it may sometimes appear difficult to discern any direct relation to religion, keeping in mind the fact that Roy's ethics is religous ethics. It is therefore incumbent upon us to remind the reader that one of the hallmarks of the Hindu tradition is the integration of the social and religious realms. Social order (*dharma*) cannot be separated from religious practice. For more details I refer the reader to my work *Evolution of Hindu Ethical Ideals*.

The concluding chapter is a salute to this pioneer of modern India in whose greatness lies her own. The sentiments expressed by James Russell Lowell in "The Present Crisis" are a fitting summation of Ram Mohan's era and ethics.

> When a deed is done for Freedom, through the broad earth's aching breast,
> Runs a thrill of joy prophetic, trembling on from east to west,
> And the slave, where'er he cowers, feels the soul within him climb
> To the awful verge of manhood, as the energy sublime
> Of a century bursts full-blossomed on the thorny stem of Time.
>
> Through the walls of hut and palace shoots the instantaneous throe,
> When the travail of the Ages wrings earth's systems to and fro;
> At the birth of each new Era, with a recognizing start,
> Nation wildly looks at nation, standing with mute lips apart,
> And glad Truth's yet mightier man-child leaps beneath the Future's heart.[7]

As a footnote to this study, the history I have researched has been personalized for me by virtue of members of my family who were closely connected with the governance of India in Ram Mohan's times.

First, there was my great-great-great-grandfather, Henry Crawford, H.E.I.C.S., who first came to India as a writer in 1761. An editorial of the *London Daily News* November 26, 1885) paying a tribute to my great-grandfather, George Morland Crawford, points out that he was the grandson of Henry Crawford "who was associated with Warren Hastings and Robert Clive in their political and military achievements. He was given a liberal pension by the Hon. East India Company after he retired from the Governorship of Ganjam, and lived at Gunnersbury House, which he sold to the Princess Amelia."[8] Henry Crawford left the service of the company in 1800, which was about the time Ram

Mohan made his acquaintance with John Digby of the Bengal Civil Service. In other words, Ram Mohan was not yet in the public light, so the possibility of the governor knowing him was nil. At any rate, here was a member of my family who participated in the shaping of the forces in whose matrix Ram Mohan lived and labored. We may also assume that Henry Crawford kept in touch with what was happening in the land to which he dedicated himself for a quarter of a century, and may thus have come to know of Ram Mohan during the years of his retirement.

Next, there was Charles Venner Crawford, son of Henry. In the book, *Half-Lights on Chelsfield Court Lodge*, a section is devoted to "Crawford of Chelsfield" in which we are informed that Charles Venner Crawford held office "at India House in the Department of the Auditor of India Accounts, which he held from 1822 to 1834, when, with a reorganization of the staff he dropped out."[9] The dates of his service indicate he may have come into contact with Ram Mohan. By now Ram Mohan was a prolific publisher, a formidable polemicist, and an ardent social reformer whose skills and knowledge were utilized by the governor-general. On his visit to London, he was the toast of the town, and received the highest acclaim when he was received by the King.

There can be no doubt that from his conning tower in India House, Charles Venner Crawford must have come to know of Ram Mohan Roy very well indeed. It is also highly probable that the two had met at one of the business or social meetings arranged by the East India Company in connection with the Raja's visit.

Similarly, there is every likelihood that Frances Crawford, daughter of the governor, had some personal acquaintance with Ram Mohan by way of family connections and interests in Calcutta. She took up residence in the city when she married Henry Money, and is buried there. On the other side, the Raja is buried in the city of Bristol, a couple of miles from the Manor House in which my great-grandparents dwelt.

All of this weaves a web of intimacy which permits me vicariously to reach out to the hero of this book through my more fortunate forbears. If only the Crawfords had used their considerable journalistic skills to record what they had seen and heard, this work would be presented with fewer apologies to my kind readers.

This book has been written in solitude, but it is the product of numerous social relationships which I gratefully acknowledge.

At the University of Hawaii my thanks go to Lynette Wageman, Librarian; Professor Jagdish Sharma, Department of History; Gayle Yoshida, Journals Editor; Gail Dwight who proficiently prepared the entire manuscript; and Janet Cooke who proofread the manuscript and made important suggestions.

In England I greatly appreciated the help and hospitality of the Archiebald Sadgunns while conducting research in London and Bristol.

In Bombay my thanks go to Dr. M. S. Gore, Director, Tata Institute of Social Sciences, and to Dr. P. K. Muttagi for inviting me, during my sabbatical leave, to work on my manuscript in this prestigious centre of learning. The faculty and students provided me with warm friendship and helpful suggestions. In the Gateway city it was also my pleasure to meet Mrs. Bansari Sheth, Honorary Secretary, Asiatic Society, who supplied me with important sources through the Central Library.

In Delhi I received the support of the Supreme Court Advocate, Buchoo Shroff, and his lovely wife, Veena, who introduced me to important consultants. Chief Justice S. K. Das, Supreme Court (ret.), reviewed several chapters and shared insights from his own writing and from his vast experience in the Brahmo Samaj.

In Calcutta it was my good fortune to meet Professor Dilip Kumar Biswas to whom I was already indebted for his excellent co-editing of Sophia Dobson Collet's, *The Life and Letters of Raja Rammohun Roy*. With similar care he read long portions of my work and expanded my knowledge of the Raja. I was also enriched by the observations of Dr. B. N. Dasgupta whose work on Roy was in the press. Scholars at the Rabindra Bharati Museum and University were most generous with offers for research assistance, especially Samar Bhowmik, Curator, S. M. Ganguly, Librarian, and Professor Sabita Mukherjee.

I am especially grateful to novelist Bhabani Bhattacharya for taking time from his immense literary labors to write the Foreword for this book.

Finally, for their continuous cheer and inspiration, I express my thanks to my daughters, Suzanne and Christine.

CROMWELL CRAWFORD

*Honolulu, Hawaii*

 *PART ONE*

# THE ERA OF
# RAM MOHAN ROY

# CHAPTER 1

# The Preparatory Years

*The Oxford History of India* describes Ram Mohan Roy as "the greatest creative personality of nineteenth century India."[1] The man's greatness has been studied from many angles by distinguished historians and social scientists. The purpose of the present work is to view him, in the finest tradition of the Gita, as an agent of *dharma* (righteousness), a doer of ethics, a champion of love, liberty, and justice against all that is cruel and irrational in the world.

If we were to historicize the *Gita's* concept of *adharma* (unrighteousness) in some particular period of Indian history, the declining years of the Moghul empire would starkly qualify. Mid-eighteenth-century India was in a state of general malaise.

Politically, the Moghul empire in the north, stretching all the way from the Punjab, Sindh, and Kashmir to Bengal, "still presented an imposing front to the world," but close observers could see "how far the inevitable dry rot of decay had advanced."[2] Farther south, the decline was more advanced. In the west Maratha power was poised as a dynamic threat to Moghul supremacy.

Economically, the general standard of life plummeted as the mounting costs of military operations siphoned off declining revenues. "There was increasing concentration on the effort to keep things as they were rather than on improvement or development."[3]

Culturally, the erstwhile patrons of the arts were preoccupied with their own political and economic survival, and therefore had little time or resources to extend their patronage. There still were master masons and craftsmen, but their skills went begging. Moghul architecture, immortalized in such earlier edifices as the Jama Masjid, gradually declined, first in means and then in taste. Muslim and Hindu art also deteriorated for want of recognition. "Exquisite work could still be done, but patronage was erratic and the flashes of brilliance transitory."[4]

3

Socially, education was limited to children of the elite, while common people were schooled only in the basics. Elements of Hindu society which were quiescent in more stable times, began to rear their ugly heads. "Suttee, frowned upon by the Mughuls, revived as their power declined. Infanticide was encouraged by economic stringency as security diminished. Such customs as *purdah* or female "seclusion" tended to increase among Hindus as well as Muslims for the same reason."[5]

In the field of religion, we walk in the graveyard of men and movements that flourished in bygone ages. The fifteenth to the seventeenth-centuries witnessed the rise of new cults such as the *bhakti* (devotion) movements, but only their ghosts survived. "Syncretistic movements like that of Guru Nanak, the founder of *Sikhism*, or the *Kabirpanthis*, the followers of Kabir, had either developed into military bodies whose sword was their creed or become bodies of quietists in the process of being transmuted into new castes. Indeed, the one sign of positive development in this field was the tendency of ascetics to develop into military bands. Groups of armed ascetics, valiant for their Lord, roamed and often terrorized the countryside, specially in the north."[6]

In every sector the glory that was India had vanished and darkness was upon the land. "There was energy, ability, and intellect in abundance, but they were directed to mutually contradictory ends or wasted in sterile endeavours. In Chinese phrase the signs were many that for the Mughuls in India the Mandate of Heaven was exhausted."[7]

The British were "Heaven's" instrument in removing the "Mandate." The British period of Indian history has been reckoned as beginning from various dates, but the one that seems most appropriate for us is 1774, when Warren Hastings assumed the new position of governor-general established by the Regulating Act of 1773.[8] The same legislation set up a new Council and a Supreme Court in Calcutta, all of which heralded the political supremacy of Britain over Bengal.

At the same time when India's destiny was being linked with the foremost power of the West, a man was born (1772) who was the very embodiment of Hindu *dharma* (moral duty), and yet one who, through understanding and appreciation of the values of the West, became a living link between the two cultures. This man of multiple aspects was Raja Ram Mohan Roy. He belongs to the lineage of India's moral heroes who have set their country's faltering feet back upon the ancient course of *dharma*.[9] It is a tribute to his labors that India was delivered from the grip of medieval darkness. In the poetic words of Rabindranath Tagore:

> He shed radiance all over the land; he rescued us from the penury of self-oblivion. Through the dynamic power of his personality, his uncompromising freedom of the spirit, he vitalized our endeavour, and launched it into the arduous adventure of realization. He is the great pathmaker of this century who has removed ponderous obstacles that impeded our progress at every step. . . .[10]

Not only was the timing of Ram Mohan's birth historically auspicious, so was its place and pedigree. He was born in the village of Radhanagar, Hooghly District, in the province of Bengal. Had his birth taken place outside of Bengal, there is doubt whether Ram Mohan could have achieved his mission with equal success. The fact of the matter was that the British were integral to Ram Mohan's reforms, especially in the key area of education. From 1757 to 1911, Bengal was the center of British India, and it was in Bengal that the Indian Renaissance got its start. Ram Mohan's birth in this dynamic province was therefore highly propitious.

Pedigree was equally important as place. Ram Mohan was born into an Orthodox *Brahmin* family. In a caste-ridden age had he been born less than a *Brahmin*, it would have been impossible for him to be heard, let alone to move in influential circles. That is why, despite his egalitarian predelictions, Ram Mohan was prudent enough to recognize the advantageous leverage proffered by caste, and, therefore, maintained the sacred thread until his death. This is a highly controversial matter which I have addressed frankly in appropriate sections.

Caste standing gave him the necessary social standing. During the reign of Emperor Aurangzeb, Ram Mohan's great-grandfather, Krischnachandra Banerji, joined the service of the Nawab of Bengal and was honored by him with the title "Raya Rayan," later contracted to Roy. Ram Mohan recalls that his grandfather, Braja Benode Roy, was "chief of different districts during the administration of His Highness the Nawab Mohabut Jung" of Murshidabad. His father, Ram Kanto Roy, held landed property and "rented a farm from Government, the revenue of which was lakhs of rupees."[11] Later he became *zamindar* to the royal family of Burdwan, an arrangement which landed him and his sons in malicious litigation.

Ram Mohan also inherited high moral and religious traditions. Though his ancestors had abdicated the hereditary profession of their *Brahmanical* class when they took service under the Moghul government, nevertheless, they were "all renowned for their great piety and orthodoxy."[12] His father, a Vaishnavite, was especially "noted for his quiet and retiring disposition and his great devotion to the religion of his ancestors."[13] His mother, Tarini Devi, "a woman of strong character and fine understanding," belonged to the rival sect of the *Shaktas*, but in the interests of religious unity in the home, joined the *Vaishnav* cult.[14]

The lad grew up with a profound reverence for *Vishnu*. The story has it that he would not partake of water before reciting a chapter of the *Bhagvata Purana*. Perhaps it was this single-minded devotion to *Vishnu* which later served as the basis for his theism.

Child-marriage was the custom, so Ram Mohan was wed to a little girl who, sad to say, died in childhood. By the age of nine, he was married successively to two wives in keeping with the practice of *Kulin*

*Brahmins*. The first wife bore his children and died in 1824. His second wife survived him.

Ram Kanto's affluent status enabled him to secure the best education available for his son. In the local *patshala* (school) he received a Bengali education, and under the village *moulvi* (religious scholar) he studied Persian, the language of the court.

In his ninth year Ram Mohan was moved to Patna, a famous seat of Islamic studies. Here he was groomed for a career in Muslim courts. He studied Arabic translations of Euclid and Aristotle. He considered the logic of the Arabians as "superior to every other," and was later to make efficient use of this knowledge in his polemics. Of greater impact was his study of the *Koran* in Arabic. Its unequivocal monotheism began a revolution in his mind, and he was awed and inspired by the character of its Prophet. Arabian and Persian poetry fascinated him, especially the works of Hafiz, Sadi, and Shiraz. He was equally intrigued by the mystical philosophy of the *Sufis* and the doctrines of the *mutazilas* (freethinkers). He also studied Islamic law and jurisprudence.

The Muslim influence became such a part of Ram Mohan that throughout his adult life it was evident in his manners, dress, and food.

At the end of three years, the lad was moved to Benares, the most hallowed seat of Sanskrit learning. He was brought to the holy city at the insistence of his maternal relatives, all of whom were priests by profession. For the next three years he mastered Sanskrit and delved into the treasures of the *Vedanta* and *Upanishads*. He also studied the *Smritis*, the *Tantras*, and the *Puranas*, though there is doubt in regard to his knowledge of the *Vedic Samhitas*.

At the close of these six years of intense diverse studies, Ram Mohan returned home. But in a radical sense he could not go home again. The new knowledge of *Sufi* philosophy reinforced by the *Vedanta*, had alienated him from the popular Hinduism represented by his family's altar.

The clash between father and son is captured in this memorandum of Mr. Adam (1879):

It is not often that we get an insight into Hindu family life but his [Ramkanta Roy's] son gave me a slight glance at least in referring to the amicable differences that arose between himself and his father on the subject. I inferred from what R. R. said that he always left it to his father, as head and most venerable member of the family, to open the question which he thought fit to moot, and when he had finished his immediate argument, he was generally willing to listen to his son with patience, which sometimes, however, forsook him. The son's response after the necessary preliminary admissions, usually began with the adversative particle "But" (*kintu* ). "But not withstanding all this, the orthodox conclusion you aim at does not follow." The father complained of this, and on one occasion, at least, burst out in the tone of remonstrance, as of an injured party: "Whatever argument I adduce you have always your *Kintu*, your counter-statement, your counter-argument, your counter-conclusion to oppose me." The son recounted this to me with half a smile on his lips and a touch of humour in his voice, but without any expression of disrespect to his father.[15]

At about the age of sixteen this budding scholar composed a manuscript questioning the validity of idol worship. This "produced a coolness" between Ram Mohan and his immediate kindred, whereupon he proceeded on his travels, finally reaching Tibet.[16]

In none of extant writing is there any specific mention of his visit to Tibet, but Dr. Lant Carpenter vouches that he heard Ram Mohan hark back to it on two occasions, which is strong testimony for his having spent some time in the Himalayan kingdom between 1788 to 1790. The Reverend K. S. Macdonald affirms that while in Tibet Ram Mohan "spent two or three years disputing daily with the worshipper of the living Lama, who frequently passed from quiet ratiocination to angry abuse of the stranger." However, Ram Mohan received a good deal of kindness from the women, "a kindness which, forty years after, he said, had made him always feel respect and gratitude toward the gentle sex."[17]

By 1791 Ram Mohan was back in his ancestral home of Radhanagar, but not for long. A year later his father moved his joint family to a new house in the neighboring village of Langulpara. On December 1, 1796 Ram Kanto Roy divided his immovable property among his three sons. The new house at Langulpara was bequeathed to Jagamohun and to Ram Mohan. A house with a pond at Jorasanco in Mauja Calcutta was also deeded to Ram Mohan.

The idolatrous lifestyle of his father's home took its toll on Ram Mohan's endurance. In September of 1797 he did the only honest thing he could do; he left home. In evidence presented in the aforementioned Burdwan lawsuit, Ram Mohan testified that "so far from inheriting the property of his deceased father, he had, during his life-time, separated from him and the rest of the family, in consequence of his altered habits of life and change of opinions, which did not permit their living together."[18] Entrusting his wives to his mother, Ram Mohan departed Langulpara for Calcutta.

## CHAPTER 2

# Coming of Age

An entirely different side of Ram Mohan's diverse personality was revealed when he went into the business of money-lending in Calcutta. Quoting Brajendra Nath Banerji, Ram Mohan "maintained a lively business interest, in spite of his religious preoccupations." His clients included several eminent civil servants of the East India Company. Business was so lucrative that on July 12, 1799, Ram Mohan purchased two *taluks* (estates) in the Burdwan district which gave him a handsome return of Rupees 5,500. Simultaneously, he employed himself in "the business of dealing in Company's Papers."[1]

Toward the end of 1797, he took a short trip to Patna, Benares, and points north, returning to Calcutta by late 1800. This was also the year of the birth of his son, Radhaprasad.

Ram Mohan was in some official capacity closely associated with the Sadar Diwani Adalat and the College of Fort William. It was in Calcutta, in 1801, that he met John Digby. He early established a scholarly reputation with the chief Kaji of the Sadar Diwani Adalat and the *moulvis* of Fort William College. These scholars "had a high opinion of his character and abilities."[2]

Thomas Woodforde, Collector of Dacca-Jalalpore (Faridpur), was quick to recognize his expertise and hired him as *diwan* (govt. revenue officer) in March of 1803. The position was terminated in three months by Ram Mohan's departure for Burdwan to be by the side of his dying father. Reverend William Adam describes the deathbed scene:

> He had stood by the deathbed of his father, who with his expiring breath continued to invoke his God—Ram! Ram! with a strength of faith and a fervour of pious devotion which it was impossible not to respect although the son had ceased to cherish any religious veneration for the family deity.[3]

9

Jagamohun inherited his portion of the estate, but Ram Mohan received "no portion of his father's property."[4]

By 1804 Ram Mohan was back in the service of Woodforde who was now Registrar of the Murshidabad Court of Appeal. Here he published his *Tuhfat' ul muhwahhiddin*.[5] In the opinion of some scholars, this first published pamphlet of the Raja "stands out as one of the most, if not the most, significant publications in India during the first half of the 19th century."[6] Below is a synopsis of the work:

He starts by pleading for an objective study of religion based upon the premise that while true religion is rooted in human nature, much that goes in the name of religion is merely the product of habit. To be able to make the distinction between nature and habit is admittedly a difficult task, but not to be avoided for that reason.

Nevertheless, most religious leaders, seeking their private glory, appeal to supernaturalism in order to support their invented dogmas. The masses are mesmerized and are piously deceived. Instead of relying upon their own moral sense, these sheep-like creatures abdicate their powers of discrimination in deference to the revelatory claims of their leaders. So blind is their faith that even atrocities against nature are proclaimed as virtuous. Imagining that faith in their leaders is the cause of salvation from their sins, they perpetrate all manner of heinous crimes that are destructive of society, and reinforce this faith by reading legendary accounts of their leaders, past and present. Tales of miraculous happenings legitimize the rule of authoritarianism which the people happily accept because it is believed that God somehow has a hand in it.

Should the voice of reason accidently be heard, the true believer considers such doubt to be the voice of Satan and is quick to recant for fear of future punishment. The psychology of such belief is that people have been taught so thoroughly, as children, to accept and believe the folklores of their culture that, by the time they have matured, they are unable to perceive what is palpably nonsensical and absurd.

Superstitions are compounded when these specimens of conditioned behavior develop pretensions of becoming *mujtahids* (religious expounders) and, in the bargain, concoct new fantasies to bolster their faith. Their converts, with bias drummed into their heads, use these fallacious arguments to support their imagined superiority.

Should someone imprudently question any articles of faith, his co-religionists will either attack him with the spear of the tongue (slander) or with the tongue of the spear (kill him), depending on opportunities available.

The influence of the leaders upon their followers is so complete that they can incite them to kill or be killed even out of devotion to inanimate objects.

To strengthen the articles of faith, the *mujtahids* lay aside honesty and fairness and "invent passages in the form of reasonable arguments."

All religious creeds and injunctions have been invented in order to afford their protagonists the exercise of social control. Though there is no way to prove the truth concerning the existence of the soul and a future life, one may excuse belief in these articles of faith because of their beneficial effects upon society, namely, keeping the flock on the straight-and-narrow. However, hundreds of useless privations have been added to these two doctrines so that they are the cause of more harm than good. This illustrates the genius of religious leaders to make life burdensome by legislating strictures for the sake of communal control.

Despite the power of social conditioning, there is an "innate faculty" in man which is capable of viewing all religions rationally and justly, and discovering a common core, namely, belief in one God and the brotherhood of mankind.

On the other hand, religion, as commonly practiced, is imperialistic and arrogant, promising reward in heaven to those who think alike, while threatening damnation to those who differ. But, whereas such speculations belong to an unknown future, nature treats all men equally, regardless of religious labels.

Sectarian religion thrives on the propensity of people for the miraculous. Gaps in knowledge are filled by claims of divine intervention. The deity worshipped is a God of the gaps. But in nature there are no gaps; only the rule of unerring law. Everything in the world is causally connected, though some of the causes are not immediately apparent. Believers in miracles exploit the obscurity of these causes by substituting stories of divine activity.

Rational religion only accepts things as true which are consistent with the laws of nature and which can be personally verified.

When people act religiously they think they must turn off their critical faculties and let faith take over. Miracles would cease if people should become as vigilant of the causal nexus in the spiritual world as they are in the work-a-day world.

Rational inquiry into religion is often dismissed on the grounds that faith, not reason, is the key to understanding religious mysteries. "How could a matter which has no proof and which is inconsistent with reason be received and admitted by men of reason?"[7]

Sometimes it is argued that since God is omnipotent, all things are possible with Him, including those things which may confound reason. "But this argument does not prove anything but probability of occurrences of such things while they have to prove real occurrences of miracles of their ancient religious leaders and the modern mujtahids."[8]

Inasmuch as the so called super-human powers of their ancient leaders cannot be verified by contemporary followers, much is made of the long line of witnesses who attest through history to the authenticity of what first took place. But tradition is only as good as its bearers. It should therefore come as no surprise that the bearers of tradition closest to us in history are the ones whose credentials are most often questioned. By the opposite token, those most revered are those farthest removed from us. But several traditions are in the business of invoking divine origins, and since their claims are often in mutual conflict, it follows that their reports are to be regarded with healthy skepticism.

The supernatural prowess of the prophets are figments of pious imagination as exercised by their devotees. It is slightly incongruous that those who insist that with God all things are possible, make him precariously dependent on intermediaries. And yet, the instrument of God, for one group, is the instrument of the devil for another group.

Attempts are made to explain the discrepancies in precepts of different religions on the analogy that just as rulers modify the laws of their predecessors to do justice to present exigencies, so also, God establishes different religions in different places and causes one to be superseded by the other in keeping with his divine wisdom. The analogy does not hold because, whereas men are fallible and must therefore constantly revise their plans, God is infinite in wisdom and must therefore do what is best from the beginning.

Hindus consider they are being true to the precepts of God by worshipping idols. Muslims consider they are being true to God by waging war on all idolators. "Are these contradictory precepts or orders consistent with the wisdom and mercy of the great, generous and disinterested Creator, or are these the fabrications of the followers of religion?"[9]

Doctors of religion often quote a saying to make faith sound reasonable. They say, if faith be false, there is nothing lost for the believer; but if faith be true, everything is lost for the disbeliever. Thus, they try to make religion into a good wager, but the reasoning is only convincing to those who are easily persuaded. It cannot be admitted that even if a belief be false there is no harm in believing it. "Putting faith in the existence of such things which are remote from reason and repugnant to experience, is not in the power of a sensible man." Besides, "in case of having faith in those things, it may become the source of various mischiefs and troubles and immoral practices owing to gross ignorance and want of experience, i.e., bigotry, deceit, etc."[10]

Another argument that is popularized is that we should obediently follow the faith of our forebears, and renounce whatever deviates from it. The argument is fallacious because it is equally applicable to the founders of new religions which have subsequently attracted vast followings, as to "those who after receiving the doctrines of their leaders, have deviated from the old ways of their forefathers."[11] History shows that shifting religious allegiances has been a common practice. "Besides, the fact of God's endowing each individual of mankind with intellectual faculties and senses, implies that he should not, like other animals, follow the examples of his fellow brethren of his race, but should exercise his own intellectual power with the help of acquired knowledge, to discern good from bad, so that his valuable divine gift should not be left useless."[12]

Opponents of deists discount their validity because they are in the minority. But this makes truth dependent on numbers, which is contradicted by the religious admonition that one must seek the truth against all odds. Going back to the beginnings, the major religions of today were the minor religions of yesterday.

In sum, mankind can be divided into four categories:

1. Firstly—A class of deceivers who, in order to attract the people to themselves, wilfully invent doctrines of creeds and faith and put the people to troubles and cause disunion amongst them.

2. Secondly—A class of deceived people, who, without inquiring into the fact, adhere to others.

3. Thirdly—A class of people who are deceivers and also deceived; they are those who having themselves faith in the sayings of another induce others to adhere [sic.] to his doctrines.

4. Fourthly—Those who by the help of Almighty God are neither deceivers or deceived.[13]

The essay is brought to a conclusion on an ethical note with a quotation from the *Sufi* philosopher, Hafiz: "Be not after the injury of any being and do whatever you please. For in our way there is no sin except it (injuring others)."[14]

Ram Mohan states that the detailed arguments of this treatise may be found in another writing entitled, *Manazarat' ul adyan (Discussion of Various Religions)*. It is our loss that this work, either in print or in manuscript form, has not been located.

We now take a brief, critical look at the work we have just paraphrased. The *Tuhfat' ul muwahhiddin* is written in Persian with a preface in Arabic. Had it been written in Bengali, it might have become an original classic of Bengali prose; or were it written in English, it could have been "ranked with the rational treatises of the age of enlightenment in Europe."[15] The essay is written in an abstruse oriental style, but this is a poor excuse for the translation not being put into straightforward English at the hand of Obaidullah El Obaide.

The title is misleading, giving the impression that it is a *moulvi's* diatribe against Hindu idolatry. But the writer is a rationalist who considers all priests and prophets as tarred with the same brush. The essence of religion is simple belief in "One Being." All the rest is so much window-dressing to attract gullible people. Virtue resides in "giving comfort to the hearts of men," and there is "no sin except" injury to others. It is clear that for this free-thinker, universal morality is "the only true divine doctrine."

The tenor of the treatise shows the campaigning zeal that possessed Ram Mohan from his early days, making him a tireless opponent of all forms of irrationality and injustice.

It is quite evident that by this time (1803–1804) Ram Mohan had a firm grasp of other religions, otherwise he could not have composed such a piece. He freely draws upon a background of information. The influence of the Patna training is very much in evidence with quotations from the Koran and Muslim poets.

His main source seems to be a Persian work, *Dabistan mazahib* or *School of Religions*, composed in 1645. William Jones, introducing it to Orientalists, described it as "a rare and interesting tract on twelve different religions."[16] Native scholars were also acquainted with it through the several manuscript copies that were in circulation. It would have been rather odd if this work had escaped the notice of Ram Mohan, considering his keen interest in comparative religion and his knowledge of Persian. Had there been some oversight on his part, fellow scholars who were working with this tract, such as Francis Gladwin of the Fort William College, and *moulvi* Nazr Ashraf of the Sadar Diwani Adalat, would surely have drawn his attention to it.

Common themes between the *Dabistan* and *Tufhat* make the case for literary reliance even more convincing, especially with regard to the material found in the section dealing with the *Ilahi* faith of Emperor Akbar. Reason occupies a prominent role in both works. Since Ram Mohan's knowledge of English was quite rudimentary at this time, it is fair to say that his rational bias was not derived from Western sources, but was only reinforced by these later studies. The influence of the *Dabistan* is more formative. It emphatically denies any credibility to the prophets of any religion unless their message can be squared with reason. All appeals to miracles and the supernatural are proven absurd. Truth is free of contradictions; therefore the claims of each religion as possessing the whole truth are patently false. The peddlers of such piety are not worthy of following. "Why should we pay obedience to any person who belongs to mankind as ourselves, and who is subject to anger and lust, and avarice and passion, and love of rank and power, even more than ourselves?"[17] Reason is the only sure guide. It "renders it evident that the world has a Creator, all-mighty and all-wise."[18] Echoes of these and other themes are all found in the *Tuhfat*, as we have just seen.

Ajit Kumar Ray advances the intriguing theory that Ram Mohan had also based his second treatise, *Manazarat' ul adyan*, on the *Manazara* which is part of one section of the *Dabistan*. We have already stated that this work of the Raja is lost. Ray asks:

> Could it be that Rammohun was influenced by the *manazara* in the *Dabistan* and wrote his *Manazarat* in line with that of the *Dabistan*? In the absence of the actual work this is impossible to confirm, but if he did take

the idea and the theme from the *Dabistan*, it might solve a problem which puzzles many researchers: Why did some Zoroastrians take offence at his *Tuhfat*, which did not even mention their religion? The answer might be that the Zoroastrians did not take offence in the *Tuhfat* but in the *Manazarat*, which if it reflects similar, or somewhat similar views about Zoroastrianism to that of the philosopher in the *Dabistan*, would have been offensive to them.[19]

Setting aside our discussion of the *Tuhfat* for the time being, we are back in Murshidabad. In 1805 Ram Mohan left the city for Ramgarh where John Digby of the Bengal Civil Service was appointed Registrar of the Office of the Magistrate. Then in 1807 Digby went to Jessore to serve as Collector; and from Jessore he was transferred to Bhagalpur as Court Registrar. Ram Mohan accompanied him on these travels.

In Bhagalpur Ram Mohan had an altercation with Sir Frederick Hamilton, District Collector. Sir Frederick reprimanded him for riding before him in a palanquin. Muslim rulers had established a precedent whereby it was deemed disrespectful for a common person to go riding before a dignitary. Ram Mohan refused to comply with the custom and tried to reason with the Englishman. Unable to mollify his opponent, Ram Mohan rode on in his palanquin, leaving his lordship stewing in his dignity.

The matter did not end there. Ram Mohan considered the custom humiliating to every Indian and therefore petitioned Lord Minto for a ruling on this odious practice. Native honor was upheld as the haughty Englishman was duly censured. Ram Mohan's handling of this affair is a vivid disclosure of his sense of individual worth and dignity, and his readiness to act on the courage of his convictions.

In 1809 Digby was appointed Collector of Rangpur District. One of his first acts was to appoint Ram Mohan to the post of *diwan*—chief Indian officer of the Revenue Department. This was the highest an Indian could climb within the hierarchy of the East India Company. At first the Board of Revenue vetoed the appointment on the grounds that Ram Mohan lacked the experience and sureties, but the Board later reversed its decision. Ram Mohan's subsequent performance justified their trust.

Perhaps as early as 1809, but certainly in 1912 and 1815, Ram Mohan was delegated by the British Government to serve as its envoy for the settlement of border disputes between the kingdoms of Bhutan and Cooch-Behar. These missions "laid the foundation of Rammohun's subsequent reputation as a diplomat."[20]

Ram Mohan's tenure of government service did not extend much beyond the period of one year and nine months.[21] Discovery of this time frame has helped lay to rest certain insinuations that Ram Mohan "sold justice" while himself in the service of the Company, thus enabling him to become a *zamindar* (landlord) with an annual income of

Rupees 10,000 (about $1,000; handsome amount for that day). The suspicion could be entertained so long as it was calculated on the basis of ten years of government service, but the latest evidence shrinks that period to an untenable fraction.[22]

Aside from the time element the fact is that Ram Mohan was a man of means prior to his joining the East India Company. As previously noted, back in 1797, while in Calcutta, he had established a lucrative business in money-lending, and dealing in the Company's paper. By 1799 his finances were sound enough for him to purchase two *taluks* (estates) that brought him handsome rents. Over the next seven years (1803–1810), he added four more *taluks* to his burgeoning real estate. The annual income from these six *taluks* boosted his earning by a substantial Rupees 11,500 (current exchange: Rs.10 to the dollar).

Amid all these financial transactions Ram Mohan's record as a businessman was impeccable. As tribute to his moral integrity and fiscal astuteness, we read from "An account of a meeting for the formation of the Commercial and Patriotic Association in Calcutta" (February 4, 1828), that Babu Ram Mohan Roy was chosen among six other European stock holders to constitute the important "Committee of Management"; and "that Messrs W. Da Costa and Baboo Rammohun Roy be appointed Joint Treasurers to the Association, for the purpose of receiving monies, and making disbursements on account of it, under such rules as may hereafter be framed for their guidance."[23]

The above evidence, and absence of any to the contrary, proves that Ram Mohan was a businessman whose honesty was beyond reproach. Both Miss Sophia Dobson Collet and Mr. G.S. Leonard incorrectly construe the comments of Kishorychand Mitra as insinuating malfeasance on the part of Ram Mohan.[24] To the contrary they are testimony to Ram Mohan's exceptional character. Says Mitra, "If Rammohun did keep his hands clean and abstained, as in the absence of all positive evidence to the contrary, we are bound to suppose. . . that he must have been a splendid exception."[25] He was, indeed, an exception to the common practices of his times.

Along with Company service, Ram Mohan spent his days in Rangpur getting involved in philantropic projects, scholarly endeavors, and forming circles of concerned citizens to discuss social and religious issues. We have two reports.

In his article "Raja Rammohun Roy at Rangpur," Jyotirmoy Dasgupta says:

> At Rangpur he built a house near Mahiganje at Tamphat about 4 miles from the Court; . . . . At Rangpur Rammohun spent money for the public good also. A tradition is still current that the big tank near the local Court was dug at his cost. It is a well-known fact that he was a great Persian scholar, and at Rangpur he became known as a great Moulvi.[26]

Sophia Dobson Collet supplies us with a second report of his activities in Rangpur. She reports:

> It was during his residence in Rangpur that Rammohun first began to assemble his friends together for evening discussion on religious subjects, especially on the untenableness and absurdities of idolatry. Rangpur was then a place of considerable resort, and among its inhabitants were a good many merchants from Marwar and Rajputana, Jainas by faith. Some of these Marwaris used to attend Rammohun's meetings, and Mr. Leonard says that "he had to learn on their account the *Kalpa-Sutra* and other books pertaining to the Jaina religion."[27]

However, he was opposed by a scholar learned in Sanskrit and Persian who challenged him in a Bengali work entitled *Jnananjana*. The man was Gaurikanta Bhattacharya, a *diwan* to the Judge's Court. He tried to harass Ram Mohan by inciting crowds around him, but his tactics failed.

Ram Mohan's campaign against *sati* (widow-burning) also started in Rangpur, as we shall see later. This means that he did not wait on British initiative to undertake his social reform, as is sometimes believed.

The most formative development in Ram Mohan's personal and professional career was his mastery of the English language under the tutelage of John Digby. This was of paramount importance inasmuch as language was his link with Western civilization. Ram Mohan first undertook the study of English at age twenty-four, but five years later, when Digby made his acquaintance, his proficiency was minimal. Once their friendship grew, he began making rapid progress. Digby writes:

> By perusing all my public correspondence with diligence and attention, as well as by corresponding and conversing with European gentlemen, he acquired so correct a knowledge of the English language as to be enabled to write and speak it with considerable accuracy.[28]

The language study proceeded with accelerated speed because, for him, it was not simply a study of *words* but of *worlds*. Through print Ram Mohan peered into distant places and was excited by what he saw. It brought out of him a sense of common humanity, and stirred in him the love of universal freedom. Digby continues:

> He was also in the constant habit of reading the English newspapers, of which the Continental politics chiefly interested him and from thence he formed a high admiration of the talents and prowess of the late ruler of France and was so dazzled with the splendour of his achievements as to become sceptical as to the commission, if not blind to the atrocity of his crimes, and could not help deeply lamenting his downfall, notwithstanding the profound respect he ever professed for the English nation; but when the first transports of his sorrow had subsided, he considered that

part of his political conduct which led to his abdication to have been so weak, and so madly ambitious, that he declared his future detestation of Bonaparte would be proportionate to his former admiration.[29]

It is in the above context that we have the final resolution to the insinuation that Ram Mohan soiled his hands doing government service. The real motive behind his enlisting with the East India Company was not to amass money, because he was already wealthy, but in order to "learn the English language and study the English character."[30]

The above narrative of his sojourn in Rangpur makes it plain that "though employed in some of the most engrossing secular duties during these years, Rammohun never lost sight of the grand mission of his life, the religious reformation of his country, and was in fact preparing himself all the time for his great life-work."[31]

 *CHAPTER 3*

# The Impact of the West

## I. The New Attitude of Trusteeship

Two years prior to the Raja's arrival in Calcutta, the British Parliament passed the Charter Act of 1813 which stipulated that the sum of one *lakh* (one hundred-thousand) of rupees be anually "set aside and applied to the revival and improvement of literature and the encouragement of the learned Natives of India and for the introduction and promotion of the sciences among the inhabitants of the British Territories in India."[1]

The Charter Act stands out as a landmark legislation indicating a new attitude of the British toward India. It recognized that the government was obligated to "promote the interest and happiness of the native inhabitants."[2] Granted the initial impact was modest, and there was much official foot-dragging by government, but "the way was pointed to developments of the utmost importance."[3]

Two factors contributed toward the formation of this new attitude of trusteeship.

First there was the public indignation against the "nabobs"—the Company's officials who plundered the Indian economy during the time of Clive and Hastings. These *nouveaux riches* flaunted their ill-gotten gains through lavish living back home. Parliamentary investigations in the 1780s revealed what was suspected: corruption and mismanagement on the part of the East India Company from the directors on down. For Edmund Burke, the disorders were centered around Warren Hastings. Sparked with moral outrage, he asks:

Was there ever heard, or could it be conceived that a governor would dare to heap up all the evil practices, all the cruelties, oppressions, extortions, corruptions, briberies, of all the ferocious usurpers, degenerate robbers, thieves, cheats, and jugglers, that ever had office, from one end of Asia to another, and consolidating all this mass of the crimes and ab-

surdities of barbarous domination into one code, establish it as the whole
duty of an English governor?[4]

Burke was not only morally incensed by the plague the English traders had visited upon the deprived and defenseless Indians, he also saw
the constitutional threat that was posed to British politics by the power
of wealth now wielded by these mercantile moguls. Burke concludes his
impeachment of the governor-general by sounding this note of alarm:

> Today the Commons of Great Britain prosecute the delinquents of India:
> tomorrow the delinquents of India may be the Commons of Great Brit-
> ain. . . . Do you not know that there are many men who want, and indeed
> hardly wait, the event of this prosecution, to let loose the corrupt wealth
> of India, acquired by oppression of that country, for all the corruption of
> all the liberties of this?[5]

The net impact of Burke's speeches and the parliamentary investigations was the recognition of the need to regulate and reorganize the
British administration of India. This was accomplished through Pitt's
India Act of 1784, establishing dual control over Indian government
which was in effect until 1858.

Allied with the above was a second factor which moved the British to
consider themselves guardians and trustees of Indian interests. This
was the rise of humanitarian ideals in the eighteenth century accompanied by an eagerness for administrative reform. An important figure in
this movement was William Wilberforce (1759–1833). This friend of
the younger Pitt was not only a statesman, but a humanitarian. He secured passage of a bill abolishing the slave trade and worked toward
universal abolition of slavery. In the year of his death, slavery in the
British West Indies was abolished.

The humanitarian ideal also expressed itself in Burke's demand for
universal justice. Burke found an identity between the will of God and
the moral law—"One great, immutable, pre-existent law, prior to all
our devices and prior to all our contrivances, paramount to all our
ideas and all our sensations, antecedent to our very existence, by which
we are knit and connected to the eternal frame of the universe, out of
which we cannot stir."[6]

Thus, all men are cosmically bound to each other by the ties of responsibility. An implication of this is that there can be no legitimate
exercise of arbitrary power. Burke therefore attacks Hasting's "plan of
geographical morality" which discriminated between the rights of people. He declares before the House of Commons, "The laws of morality
are the same everywhere; and . . . there is no action, which would pass
for an act of extortion, of peculation, of bribery, and oppression in England, of bribery, and oppression in Europe, Asia, Africa, and all the
world over."[7]

The concerns for justice and welfare embodied in the above two factors were institutionalized in the Charter Act of 1813. In the thirteenth resolution on which the Act was based, Parliament resolved "that it is the duty of this country to promote the interest and happiness of the native inhabitants of the British dominions in India and that such measures ought to be adopted as may tend to the introduction amongst them of useful knowledge and of religious and moral improvement."[8]

## II. Three Views of Indian Administration

While Pitt's India Act provided the constitutional structure for administration, "it did not suggest any determining principles on which the establishment of order in India was to be based."[9]

The initiative to supply these principles came from Burke and his associates who were the architects of a Conservative theory of Indian government and society. The Conservative view was ascendant during Ram Mohan's early Calcutta years. By the time of his departure for England, the Conservative position was challenged and suerseded by the Liberals. Their chief advocate was James Mill. In between the Conservatives and the Liberals stood the great administrators who favored the principle of gradualism.

It must be noted that we are not talking about distinct schools of thought having party affiliations; rather, these were "tendencies in influencing those who determined policy whether in Parliament, the Court of Directors, or in the governing class at large."[10]

We shall now examine each of the above movements since all of them created the arena in which Ram Mohan conceived and carried out his reforming activities.

### The Conservative View

The cornerstone of the Conservative view of administering India was Burke's theory of the Indian constitution. Burke's political thinking commenced with the principle that the only just rule is the governance of a people in keeping with their specific character and circumstances. He therefore proceeded to marshal the facts with respect to Indian polity. His conclusion was that India's political order was a highly civilized one, consisting of laws, institutions and traditions that had been developed over time and which were in perfect accord with natural law. The Indian constitution was therefore to be respected, for even though it failed to rank with the British constitution which was informed by science and natural philosophy, the Indian constitution had the virtue of antiquity. Burke exclaims:

God forbid we should pass judgment on people who framed their laws and institutions prior to our insect origins of yesterday. With all the faults of their nature, and errors of their institutions, the institutions, which act so powerfully on their natures, have two material characteristics which entitle them to respect:—first, great force and stability; next, excellent moral and civil effects. . . . They have stood firm on their ancient base— they have cast their roots deep in their native soil; perhaps because they have never spread them anywhere else than in their native soil. Their blood, their opinions, and the soil of their country, make one consistent piece, admitting no mixture, no adulteration, no improvement: accordingly, their religion has made no converts; their dominion has made no conquests; but in proportion as their laws and opinions were concentrated within themselves, and hindered from spreading abroad, they have doubled their force at home. They have existed in spite of Mahomedan and Portuguese bigotry, in spite of Tartarian and Arabian tyranny, in spite of all the fury of successive foreign conquest, in spite of a more formidable foe—the avarice of the English dominion.[11]

The administrative policy Burke recommended on the basis of his respect for the Indian civilization was one that would prohibit any rash interference with the institutions, culture, and government of the people. Until 1813 Burke's Conservatism was the prevailing doctrine and remained as a force to be reckoned with up to 1828. Professor Eric Stokes assesses Burke's influence in the following tribute:

The resistance which liberalism encountered in India was not the ordinary inertia of the existing order. It encountered what in more intellectualized political tradition would be called a rival political philosophy. It encountered the spirit of Burke. The Liberal attempt to assimilate, to anglicize, was met by a generation of administrators, founded by Sir Thomas Munro, who possessed all Burke's horror at the wanton uprooting on speculative principles of an immemorial system of society, and shared all his emotional kinship with the spirit of feudalism and the heritage of the past. In the shaping of Indian policy this form of conservatism was to have a much stronger hold than in England, where the progress towards an industrial society was rapidly to empty it of content. In India, as the attitude of paternalism, it was able to make strong head against the reforming tides and to divide its opponents. It succeeded so far as to shift the emphasis of liberalism, by drawing out the latent authoritarianism that resided in its doctrine.[12]

The Conservative view was also supported by the research and publication of Orientalists. Removing the debris of medieval accretions, these scholars unearthed the cultural grandeur of India's past. And in so far as the values of their findings were permitted to penetrate the prevailing prejudice of the distant Englishman, they reinforced the Conservative position and legitimized the preservation of the Indian constitution. Figures who stand out are William Jones (1746–94),

Charles Wilkins (1749–1836), Henry Colebrooke (1765–1837), and Horace Hayman Wilson (1789–1860). From this illustrious company, Jones must be singled out as "one of the most brilliant men of the 18th century."[13] He is ranked a "key figure in the development of both the Oriental studies and the British policies of the eighteenth century."[14]

Professor Arthur L. Basham credits Jones and Wilkins as "the fathers of Indology."[15] Up to their time, Indology was an unexplored field. It offered vistas of high adventure because, unlike the civilizations of Egypt, Mesopotamia, and Greece, Indian civilization was preserved without any serious historical gaps. Along with China, India held the unique position among world cultures of maintaining unbroken links with antiquity.

Prior to the latter part of the eighteenth century, learned missionaries had made brilliant achievements in grasping certain Indian vernaculars and familiarizing themselves with the cultures of the people among whom they labored, but their scholarly interests did not reach out to India's past. This research was undertaken by Jones and his colleagues.

Jones arrived in Calcutta on September 25, 1783, after a six-month voyage aboard the frigate "Crocodile." He was appointed a judge of the Supreme Court under the governor-generalship of Warren Hastings. Jones was an exceptional linguist, having mastered twenty-eight languages. He independently discovered the affinity between Sanskrit and the Greek and European languages; but, contrary to widespread opinion, was not the first to make the discovery. That honor goes to Thomas Stevens (1583), an English Jesuit, and to Fillipio Sasetti (1585), an Italian merchant in Goa, who arrived at the same conclusion independently. However, Jones "put the idea of common origin in a dramatic and fascinating way, which easily captured the post Revolutionary European mind and stimulated further research on the subject."[16]

Jones introduced Sanskrit literature into Europe through several important translations of Indian works. In 1789 his translation of Kalidasa's *Shakuntala* appeared. It was followed by the *Gita Govinda* (1792), and the *Institutes of Hindoo Law* (1794, posthumously).

Jones's most abiding contribution was his founding of the Asiatic Society, January 15, 1784, which marked the birth of Indology. The Society's journal, *Asiatic Researches*, provided educated Indians and Englishmen with a telescope to peer into the remote reaches of Indian antiquity. In establishing the Asiatic Society, "Jones helped usher in the age of scientific specialization by forming a society which would study the Asians at close quarters and draw conclusions about their social, political, and economic institutions from the observations of its members."[17] Thus, Bacon's scientific methodology was extended to Oriental studies.

Jones's vast erudition made his assessments of Indian culture more credible for politicians back home. He was quoted as the supreme authority in the field.

First, he struck a sympathetic chord by demonstrating the resemblance between Sanskrit and classical European languages, and publicized this theory at a strategic time when the European mind was falling heavily under the influence of Romanticism. Europeans were charmed by the notion that their common roots lay in some far and unknown land. The famous passage in which Jones postulates his theory reads thus:

> The Sanskrit language, whatever its antiquity, is of a wonderful structure; more perfect than the Greek, more copious than the Latin, and more exquisitely refined than either, yet bearing to both of them a stronger affinity, both in the roots of verbs and in the forms of a grammar, than could possibly have been produced by accident; so strong indeed, that no philologer could examine them all three without believing them to have sprung from some common source, which, perhaps, no longer exists.[18]

Of all his translations, Kalidasa's *Shakuntala* captured the English imagination the most, going through five editions. Jones was astounded by the monumental creation of this "Indian Shakespeare." He argued that its greatness of style and decorum could only be the product of an intensely developed civilization. Regardless of when Sanskrit drama had its introduction in India:

> It was carried to great perfection in its kind, when Vicramaditya, who reigned in the first century before Christ, gave encouragement to poets, philosophers, and mathematicians at a time when Britons were as unlettered and unpolished as the army of Hanumat: nine men of genius commonly called the nine gems attended his court and were splendidly supported by his bounty, and Calidas is unanimously allowed to have been the brightest of them.[19]

Jones not only used Sanskrit drama to prove the antiquity of Indian civilization, but also to demonstrate that the literary achievements of ancient India were on par with those of the ancient progenitors of European culture.[20]

Jones had words of high praise for India's contribution to human civilization. The game of chess was an invention of the Indians. He also saw the "fertile and inventive genius" of the Indians at work in their sublime architecture, elegant poetry, and magnificent epics. He had similar praise for "their innumerable works on grammar, Logick, Rhetorick, Musick, all of which are extant and accessible."[21]

Even in the sciences the Indians had made notable progress. He offered evidence that the principles of gravitation were known to their ancient forbears and that their scientific speculations anticipated Newton.

His appreciation for the Indian religion, philosophy, and ethics grew with the years, though he abhorred the sordid accretions of popular priestcraft. He brought added authority to the traditional theory that Pythagoras and Plato were philosophically indebted to Indian metaphysics. And as for ethics, Indians possess lofty notions of their own, which called for caution on the part of missionaries. He remonstrates:

> Our divine religion, the truth of which (if any history is true) is abundantly proved by historical evidence, has no need of such aids, as many are willing to give it, by asserting that the wisest men of this world, were ignorant of the two great maxims, that we must act in respect of others, as we would wish them to act in respect of ourselves, and that, instead of returning evil for evil we should confer benefits even on those who wish to injure us.[22]

For the time being the Conservative cause which Jones advocated in respect to culture and polity prevailed. This is to admit that Jones played a more determinative role in shaping British thinking about India than historians have generally acknowledged.

One more figure must be introduced in the Conservative camp. If Jones was the father of the Asiatic Society, Warren Hastings was the godfather. A scholar in his own right, Hastings was a patron of all aspects of Oriental art and learning. Wilkins recognized his patronage in the following dedication of his first work to the governor-general: "As it was by your immediate counsel I undertook to translate this very curious relick of Hindu antiquity, I think it is my duty thus publicly to acknowledge such a distinguishing mark in your favour."[23]

Following Burke's principle that a people must be ruled in keeping with their "concrete character and circumstances," Hastings sought the preservation of Indian institutions. The British Empire could then be assured the success of the Roman empire which governed and flourished by the same principle.

Thus, Burke, Jones, and Hastings represent the Conservative effort to help rid the British public of its ignorance and prejudice regarding the culture and constitution of India. For a time they succeeded in stemming the tides of change. But few Englishmen seemed to possess their capability or inclination for appreciating insights and values. Though lacking popular support, the Conservatives nevertheless were always on hand to protest governmental interference in religious matters such as caste, *sati*, and the Jagannath festival; in economic matters pertaining to agriculture and manufacture; and in political matters such as territorial annexations. Until Ram Mohan departed India's shores, the Conservative voice could be heard; but with the reforming activities of Bentinck, this voice was muted.

## The Liberal View

William Bentinck had come under the influence of Bentham and Mill, leaders of the rationalistic wing of a second school of thought known as the Liberals. Humanitarians and Evangelicals also belonged to this movement. Their common goal for India was westernization. Whereas the Conservatives wished to move as slowly as possible, the Liberals were in a hurry to institute innovations along Western lines.

The Liberal movement was spawned in England by the Enlightenment. This eighteenth century phenomenon, following in the wake of the scientific revolution of the seventeenth century, gave rise to rationalist liberal, humanitarian, and scientific trends of thought. All Europe was astir with the ideas of the Enlightenment which had now taken hold of Britain.

By contrast with this new surge of life in the West, India seemed paralyzed and moribund. The Liberals, therefore found the position of the Conservatives wholly untenable and charged that their respect for India had no support in reason.

First we shall examine the attitudes of the Rationalist wing toward India. The leader of the philosophical radicals was Jeremy Bentham (1748–1832), famous for his ethical system of Utilitarianism. He and his group were primarily responsible for instituting major social and political changes in England, including changes in the criminal code. A strong advocate of democracy, he was opposed to monarchy and hereditary aristocracy at home, and to British imperialism in India. His chief ambition was to modernize the British system of jurisprudence, an enterprise which is reflected in the title of his famous work: *An Introduction to the Principles of Morals and Legislation.*

The basic principles of Bentham's utilitarian ethics was that pleasure was the *summum bonum* of life. It followed that the social test of a good action was the "greatest good of the greatest number." The method by which the moral character of an act was measured was by a hedonistic calculus.

Bentham demonstrated zealous interest in wanting to reform India's legal system. In 1793 he offered his services "as a sort of Indian Solon to Dundas," President of the Board of Control.[24] In his essay, "On the Influences of Time and Place in Matters of Legislation," he contemplated the changes that would be necessary with the indigenization of his system of jurisprudence in Bengal.

Bentham's utilitarian outlook was assured success in influencing British policy in India through the leverage of officials in high places. His writings were part of the syllabus in the East India Company's college at Haileybury. Legislators in the House of Commons were among his disciples. In India the spread of utilitarian ideas were guaranteed with the appointment of Bentinck as governor-general, for he had been fed "the pure milk of the Benthamite word."[25] The *Bengal Hurkaru* staunchly supported Bentham's ideas of rational law. And Ram Mohan Roy, "the bright morning star of new India, had long been catechized."[26]

Most importantly, utilitarian principles were guaranteed a role in Indian administration by the admittance of James Mill into the executive government of the Company in 1819. By 1830 he occupied the prestigious seat of Examiner. The importance of his office made him feel like a *raja*, and his pen felt mightier than a thousand swords. He describes his business with an element of awe.

> It is the very essence of the internal government of 60 millions of people with whom I have to deal; and as you know that the government of India is carried on by correspondence; and that I am the only man whose business it is, or who has the time to make himself master of the facts scattered in a most voluminous correspondence, on which a just decision must rest, you will conceive to what an extent the real decision on matters belonging to my department rests with the man who is in my situation.[27]

As to the desired shape of the kingdom which he now surveyed, Mill entertained no equivocation. It was to be Western. Prior to Mill, anglicization was chiefly *ad hoc* and accidental, such as the introduction of English law in Bengal, and the Permanent Settlement of Bengal. But with Mill, anglicization became conscious and deliberate.

Mill's views on the westernization of India are best studied in his *History of British India* (1817), a classic in the field of philosophical history. At the time he undertook this writing, Mill became a disciple of Jeremy Bentham. Utilitarianism provided him with a system through which he tried to explain history's lessons in terms of the rewards of virtue and the punishments of vice. He not only came to these philosophical conclusions, but made necessary administrative recommendations whereby his ethical and legal theories could be demonstrated in the Indian matrix.

Many of the recommendations were made into legislative acts by a generation of men who prepared for administrative positions in the Company's colleges where the *History* was part of the curriculum.

We shall now examine Mill's attitude toward Indian civilization as recorded in the above work. In his "General Reflections on the Civilization of the Hindus," Mill states the purpose of his study:

> To ascertain the true state of the Hindus in the scale of civilization, is not only an object of curiosity in the history of human nature; but to the people of Great Britain, charged as they are with the government of that great portion of the human species, it is an object of the highest practical importance. No scheme of government can happily conduce to the ends of government, unless it is adapted to the state of the people for whose use it is intended.[28]

The conclusion at which he arrives is that the state of Hindu civilization is an abject case of arrested development. Hindu civilization is so antiquarian that conversing with a contemporary Hindu is like speaking with "the Chaldeans and Babylonians of the time of Cyrus," and with "the Persians and Egyptians of the time of Alexander."

This being the case, Mill considers it absurd frivolity that eminent scholars on the order of William Jones should advance the hypothesis that Indian civilization, though inferior to European civilization in the terms of material wealth and military prowess, is, nonetheless, more than her equal in terms of the richness of her ancient culture. Jones had recommended that the attitude of the Englishman toward India be one of understanding, adaptation, and cooperation; but such forms of cultural interaction were as alien to Mill's utilitarianism as class cooperation was to Marx's dialectical materialism. And the reason is clear. Mill ponderously piles up Indian art, science, religion, and morality in the balance of utilitarianism; weighs the entire sum, and finds it worthless. The scale on which he weighs civilization is described thus:

> Exactly in proportion as *Utility* is the object of every pursuit, may we regard a nation as civilized. Exactly in proportion as its ingenuity is wasted on contemptible or mischievous subjects, though it may be, in itself, an ingenuity of no ordinary kind, the nation be denominated barbarous.[29]

The bastion of Hindu barbarism is its religion, for "everything in Hindustan"—laws, social classification, government, stages of life— "was transacted by the Deity."[30]

Mill says the *Vedic* account of the origin of the universe is all vagueness and confusion. "It is one of the most extravagant of all specimens of discourse without ideas." The daring propensity of an uncultivated mind to speculate ignorantly "never exhibited itself in more fantastic and senseless forms."[31]

With respect to the mode of creation, Mill found the Vedic description fantastic, wild, irrational; void of any intelligent design and contrivance, and therefore unmistakably the cosmogony of a people "whose ideas of the Divine Being were grovelling."[32]

He momentarily concedes "that human language does not supply more lofty epithets of praise than are occasionally addressed to their deities by the Hindus"; but such adulation is nothing other than flattery invented by the ingenuity of fear and desire.[33] Such is the linguistic progress, "not of knowledge and cultivated reason, but of rude and selfish passions of a barbarian"; and all these flowery epithets are coined by "men whose ideas of the divine nature are mean, ridiculous, gross and disgusting."[34]

Inasmuch as linguistic analysis can prove fallacious, Mill finds it necessary to investigate other religious phenomena which might clarify the Hindu's definition of divinity. These phenomena include services reputed agreeable to a divinity, and the laws which he is understood to have ordained. Since these do not correspond with ideas of infinite power, wisdom, and goodness, Mill feels fully assured that "the sublime language is altogether without a meaning, the effect of flattery, and the meanest of passions, and that it is directly suggested, not by the most lofty, but by the most grovelling and base ideas of the Divine Nature."[35]

Moving from Hindu religion to morality, Mill charges that ideas of right and wrong are ceremonially degraded. The saint is the one who is most bound by ceremonies. Among no other pople did the "ceremonial part of religion prevail over the moral" to a greater extent.[36]

Next, he turns to the literature of the Hindus for a clue to their position in the scale of civilization. The first phase of literature is poetry, the language of passion, for men feel before they speculate. "At this first stage of literature the Hindu has always remained," says Mill, because of his "habit of expressing everything in verse"—laws, sacred books, books of science, and even dictionaries.[37]

In his estimate of the two great poems, *Ramayana* and *Mahahharata*, Mill differed from Jones who considered them as having Shakespearean qualities. These fictions are extravagant, unnatural, and out of touch with the physical and moral laws of the universe.[38]

The root of all Hindu literature is the Sanskrit language, which sufficiently accounts for the literary backwardness. Orientalists had focused on the richness of Sanskrit—more copious than Latin; the mark of a refined and elegant people—but Mill thinks this celebration makes a defect into a perfection. "Redundancy is a defect in language, not less than deficiency."[39]

Of all the achievements connected with the Hindu society in the past, "nothing has called forth more eloquent expressions of eulogy and admiration than the astronomy of the Brahmens."[40] Mill wants to set the record clear. Contrary to Voltaire and others, he denies that the Hindus were scientifically sophisticated at a very early age. He draws this conclusion by reckoning from the chronology of the Hebrew scriptures.[41]

Mill admits that aside from European scholars, eminent thinkers in his native Scotland accept the scientific achievements of the ancient Indians. Mill considers the case open but not really debatable. "When an opinion is obviously contradicted by a grand train of circumstances, and is not *entirely* supported by the special proof on which it pretends to rest, it is unproved."[42]

Every shred of information currently available about the state of knowledge and civilization among the Hindus, unless astronomy be an exception, undeniably attests to the ignorance and low state of civilization among these people.

Mill not only attacked the society, government, and culture of the Indians; he also had some choice words for Parliament, the East India

Company, and the governors. British ignorance, aggressiveness, and imperialism were responsible for untold evils under which the natives of India suffered needlessly.

The upshot of the *History* was that a unique historical problem was posed by the accidental conjunction of a backward people and inept rulers. The solution to the problem must be worked out along Liberal lines. Indian institutions governed by European principles must be made to cater to the needs of the people. A just government based on good laws and light taxation should first tackle the problem of poverty. Participation of Indians in the administration is necessary, and the way to lift them to this level is for exemplary administrators to permeate the social matrix by their Liberal attitudes and policies. In brief, the solution to India's problem lay in westernization conceived along Liberal lines.

But the Liberalism of Mill was not always acceptable to the Liberal movement. What separated Mill from the mainstream British Liberal was his vast and complex understanding of the Indian scene. This caused him to differ from the other Anglicists on such issues as education; the desirability of a Utilitarian law code and courts; involvement of Indians in politics; and land ownership. He did not think the people needed rights *per se*, but they did need social and economic progress through a powerful and efficient administration. These differences aside, Mill's studies presented the nation with a system of the Liberal conception of India. "He made Britain aware of the Liberal programme, and he joined in the work of achieving this programme."[43]

The Utilitarians stood at the vanguard of the Liberal movement which was oriented toward westernization, and spearheaded the drive toward reform. Among their allies in this movement were the merchants, the manufacturers, and the missionaries. We shall select the last mentioned group for consideration because of their unique contribution and their later encounter with the Raja.

The Utilitarians and Evangelicals, though poles apart ideologically, were able to make common cause because of their mutual contempt for Indian society and because of their confidence in the efficacy of total reform if conducted upon Western lines. The dismal picture of Indian society which James Mill painted in his *History*, aimed at securing sanctions for the Utilitarian program of social reform, was reproduced by Charles Grant in his *Observations on the State of Society among the Asiatic Subjects of Great Britain.*

Originally written in 1792 to define the relationship between Britain and India as a basis for policy-making, the tract was widely propagandized on the eve of the Company's Charter renewal in 1813, and was quoted with decisive authority by the Evangelicals.

Grant commences his treatise with the Utilitarian premise that the happiness of the Indian people is morally incumbent upon the British policy-makers. His first line of reasoning is a candid appeal to self-interest. India has proven profitable to Britain and needs to be rewarded with good government "in order that we might continue to hold the advantage we first derived from them."[44] The second argument carries a moral appeal. Since the Company is "part of the Christian Community", it is duty-bound to promote "the general welfare of the many millions under its government."[45]

Grant next weighs the effect of British rule in a moral balance and finds it wanting, as compared with the "profound peace" Indians enjoyed under Aurangzeb.[46] The solution to poor economics was not the abdication of power but its improvement. Morally considered, British withdrawal could deliver the helpless natives into the corrupt hand of Indian or foreign adventurers. And from the point of political expediency, should the British renounce their claims on India, her enemies would become the beneficiaries.

Improved government would not only involve protection of the people from feudal and bureaucratic abuses, but would provide an analysis of the causes destructive of Indian society. Viewing the situation with Evangelical eyes, Grant thought that the root of all evil lay in the character of the Indian people which was inextricably related to their religion. Therefore, true improvement could only come through a radical alteration of the existing sysem. In support of his analysis, Grant gives a description of Indian society which vies with Mill's in its despicable characterization of the Indians. Quoting from Hindu sources and European travellers, Grant judges the whole Indian civilization as rotten to the core. His indictment reads like a chapter from the Doomsday book. Summarizing, he says:

> We cannot avoid recognizing in the people of Hindoostan, a race of men lamentably degenerate and base; retaining but a feeble sense of moral obligation; yet obstinate in their disregard of what they know to be right, governed by malevolent and licentious passions, strongly exemplifying the effects produced on society by a great and general corruption of manners, and sunk in misery by their vices, in a country peculiarly calculated by its natural advantages, to promote the prosperity of its inhabitants.[47]

For the Evangelical mind deliverance from this evil estate could not be brought about by legislation, but by a change in the inner man. The soul of India was bound through ignorance, but once this ignorance is dispelled, the people will see the error of their ways, accept new light, and build a new society.

"The introduction of light" which Grant proposed was first the introduction of Western education. Anticipating Ram Mohan Roy, Alexander Duff, and Thomas Babington Macaulay, Grant was the first to recognize the role of Western education and of the English language as catalysts for transforming Indian society. Once the process of education had accomplished its westernizing effects, the Indian character would be receptive to the light of the Gospel. Indians would then be converted, and the Christianization of India would bring prosperity to the land. This was exactly how William Wilberforce argued the case for Christianity in the course of the debates around the Charter Act of 1813. He claimed:

> Christianity, independently of its effects on a future state of existence, has been acknowledged even by avowed sceptics, to be, beyond all other institutions that ever existed, favourable to the temporal interests and happiness of man: and never was there a country where there is a greater need than in India for the diffusion of its genial influence.[48]

The material prosperity of the land would fulfill both the temporal and spiritual purposes of that act of Providence whereby India has been delivered into British hands. Grant asks concerning the Indians:

> Is it not necessary to conclude that they were given to us, not merely that we might draw annual profit from them, but that we might diffuse among their inhabitants, long sunk in darkness, vice and misery, the light and benign influence of the truth, the blessings of well-regulated society, the improvements of comforts or active industry?[49]

Grant's crusade for the Christianization of India through the missionary enterprise gained public support because of his alliance with William Wilberforce. "This participation by Wilberforce in Indian affairs was extremely important for it marked the beginning of the momentous association of the Clapham sect with social reform in India."[50]

The Clapham sect was composed of famous politicians and business men who were as distinguished for their piety as for their prosperity. Humanitarian in their practical orientation, they worked hard for the cause of abolition, but even harder for Indian missions. "What they did was to analyse the world in terms of their Evangelical religion and then set out to alter it."[51] At the time of the renewal of the Company's Charter in 1913, with the support of members of numerous other denominations and volunteer organizations, they pressed for the opening up of India for missions and succeeded in their quest.

The Charter of 1813 was thus a monument to the triumph of the attitudes held by Grant and the Evangelicals toward the character of Indian society and the consequent duty of the British government towards its "unenlightened subjects." Looking down the passage of time from the milestone of 1813, Professor Ainslie T. Embree comments that the success of the ideas contained in the *Observations* "was what Max Muller had in mind in 1882 when he deplored the fact that the young civil servants went out to India convinced that the people whom they would rule were not 'amenable to the recognized principles of self-respect, uprightness and veracity. . . never restrained in their dealings by any regard for truth, never to be trusted on their word'."[52]

The reason why Grant's views were so uncritically accepted, especially by men who had pretensions of morality, was that it gave them a righteous sanction to rule the land for profit. "A belief that Indian society was degraded, and that this was a reflection of the character of the people, was coupled with the equally strong conviction that it was possible for British power to change conditions or, at least, to provide a better framework for social justice than could rule by Indians." While this attitude was not blind to the blunders of British rule, "it meant that for those who believed in the need for improvement and change in India there seemed to be no alternative to the continuance of British control."[53]

### The View of the Great Administrators

We have thus far investigated the attitudes of two groups toward India, namely, the Conservatives and the Liberals. Between these two stood "a large group, both in India and Britain, with a foot in both camps."[54] The great administrators were prominent in this school of thought. "These were men who accepted the liberal or Christian gospels in varying degrees, desired to introduce western culture into India but preached patience and caution."[55] They took this stance because they were essentially pragmatists who generally did not allow political doctrine to come in the way of lessons learned through common experience.

Mountstuart Elphinstone stands out in this company. Coming to India in 1795, he served as an administrator and a diplomat before becoming Governor of Bombay in 1819. His *Account of the Kingdom of Cabul*, based on his experience as British envoy, shows that in his judgment a different culture is not a degraded culture. Like the Liberals, Elphinstone promoted reform, as his Bombay legal code attests. However, in a way quite uncharacteristic of the Liberals, he admits, "I doubt whether anybody could tell me what was good for the Mahrattas. I was certain that I could not, and therefore I wanted to be taught by time."[56]

Another administrator who took the middle path was Thomas Munro, who came to India in 1780. During his governorship of Madras (1820–27), he reversed Cornwallis' system of *zamindari* for his own of *ryotwari* whereby peasants became proprietors. But though he introduced Western concepts, he was not without traditional sympathies. His knowledge of Indian history and literature convinced him that many of the evils the Evangelicals attributed to Hinduism could be more correctly accounted for by the ravages of wars in recent times.

Thus, unlike the Conservative school, the administrators fostered gradual change. But contrary to the expectations of the Liberals who believed that Indian society could be changed rapidly by British control, the great administrators evinced diminishing confidence, especially after 1828. For example, Elphinstone's skepticism of Evangelical and Utilitarian hopes is reflected in the following remarks made in 1832: "An opinion seems rather to have grown in later years that it only requires a little enterprize to effect every change in [India] that we think desirable."[57] The governor thought otherwise.

Thus, the order of the day for these men is best summarized in Malcolm's dictum:

> Let us proceed on a course of gradual improvement, and when our rule ceases, as cease it must (though probably at a remote period) as the natural consequence of our success in the diffusion of knowledge, we shall as a nation have the proud boast that we have preferred the civilisation to the continued subjection of India. When our power is gone, our name will be revered; for we shall have a moral monument more noble and imperishable than the hand of man ever constructed.[58]

This concludes our examination of the different social forces which contended to define the direction which British welfare should take towards the Indian people. We have covered the ground in some detail with the expectation that the perceptive reader will find numerous points of contact between Ram Mohan's views and those we have surveyed. Sometimes the contact lies in reaction and difference rather than in attraction and similarity. In either case the British and all that they represented, constitute one area of impact in which the Raja did his thinking and carried out his reforms.

This emphasis is apropos because the impression often given by writers who hallow the memory of this great man is that somehow his ideas occurred in a cultural vacuum. But, as the adage has it, *ex nihilo nihil fit*. This is nowhere truer than in the case of Ram Mohan. Often the novelty his adulators ascribe to him is nothing except what has been forgotten, or not known, as the contribution of other men and movements.

The cultural assimilation was inevitable, given the synthetic and encylopedic character of the Raja's mind. Like a hungry man he devoured everything he read in the newspapers pertaining to European politics, society, and education. He incorporated the thinking of Western philosophers and was considered a member of the Benthamite school. He drew heavily on the research and translations of the Orientalists, and openly declared his indebtedness to Western religious influences, both of the Trinitarians and the Unitarians.

Thus, when Ram Mohan speaks, we must listen for the accents of Burke, Jones, Hastings, Bentham, Mill, Munro, and a host of others. It is *his* speech, but the stress and pitch of these personalities lend it peculiar prominence. We give no ground to his detractors who would reduce Ram Mohan to a retailer of knowledge. We hold that the man was a genius; at the same time we recognize that genius is a dependent quality. As William Cullen Bryant once said: "Genius cannot put forth its whole powers nor claim all honours without aid from the talents and labors of others."

While admitting the above, "the talents and labors" of all Western benefactors must be set in their proper time frame. Chronologically, they are subsequent to the two earlier influences of Persian and Vedantic thought. Only after he had drunk at the well of Perso-Arabic thought with its Islamic and Aristotelian blends, and had imbided the heady elixir of *Advaitic* monism, did he then turn to the fountains of the West. Rajat Ray correctly points out that "The three main influences in Rammohun's thought—Persian, Vedantic and occidental—were imbided by him successively, strictly in that chronological order, a fact which cannot be too often emphasized."[59]

## CHAPTER 4

# Ram Mohan's Response to the British Impact

The Raja's initial stroke of genius lay in his reaction to the challenge of Western civilization. In the words of the historian Vincent A. Smith:

> At the very time that Lord Hastings was completing the central edifice of British power in India, Ram Mohan Roy was tracing the lines of the first synthesis between East and West in India which was to transform that power by a process of internal development and finally peacefully to replace it.[1]

To appreciate Ram Mohan's response to the impact of the West, we must set it in the context of other Indian reactions.

First, there was the reaction of the aristocratic classes. Kings, princes, and nobility charged the British with wrongful seizure of their lands, their independence, and the disruption of traditional values. The revolt of 1857 was the last of several efforts by which the old order tried to retrieve its lost fortunes.

Then, there were the reactions of the new middle class which was organized around three groups—Orthodox, Radical, and Liberal.

The Orthodox group clung tenaciously to the old ways and traditions, avowing that political submission must not be followed by cultural submission. Hindu society, regulated by the caste system, was well suited to stand aloof from foreign encroachments. Of this outlook, M. E. Chamberlain states:

> The local nature of the loyalties and the all-pervasive social obligations of Hunduism, which had little to do with politics—to the Indian peasant politics in any case meant little more than the unwelcome obligation to pay taxes to somebody—ensured that there need be no direct interference with religious or social customs.[2]

37

The British knew and respected the Hindu fabric of society in the early days as evidenced by its restrictions on missionary activity. However, once missionaries were given free access, the Orthodox community rose to protect its culture.

The best-known guardian of the old ways was Radha Kanta Deb who crossed swords with Ram Mohan on more than one occasion. An eminent linguist and scholar, Radha Kanta belonged to several learned societies, and was known for his public service. In 1830 he formed the *Dharma Sabha* to combat the anti-*sati* legislation, spearheaded by Bentinck and assisted by Ram Mohan. He also secured the exclusion of Ram Mohan from membership on the Hindu College Committee. In 1851 he established the *Patitoddhar Sabha*, a society for the reclamation of converts to Christianity. He died in 1867. "His legacy was the revival of self-respect in the Hindu community and pride in its ancient culture.[3]

The Radicals, or "Young Bengal," were chiefly students at the Hindu College who had come under the influence of the young and dynamic Anglo-Indian educator, Henry Derozio, and other westernizers such as David Hare and Alexander Duff. Intellectuals all, the Radicals had drunk deep draughts of European rationalist thought. They sat at the feet of philosophers such as Locke, Hume, Reid, Stewart, Brown, and Bentham; scientists such as Dewey and Newton; social thinkers such as Tom Paine, Voltaire, and Adam Smith; and were "well read in English historians like Robertson and Gibbon, as well as romantic poets and prose writers.[4]

These Anglophiles considered Hinduism as productive of an effete culture which they renounced by receiving Christian baptism or joining beef-eating and beer-drinking clubs.

Such activities were too extreme and alienating to allow the radical movement to survive beyond 1840; even so, these young zealots managed to render some positive service. "By their integrity, dignified conduct and conscientiousness coupled with intellectual ability, they enhanced the self-respect and evaluated the moral stature of their society. They were men of honour in whom the nationalist sentiment—the love of India—first manifested itself."[5]

Raja Ram Mohan Roy was the chief architect of the Liberal response to the Western challenge. He rejected the cultural isolationism of the Orthodox and the cultural abdication of the Radicals. Instead, with the wisdom of the Buddha, he chose the middle path. He was joined on this course by a small but influential group of Indians who could no more eat beef than crawl into cultural cocoons. These he united in the cult of nationalism which had no precedent in Indian history. For this Indian to have brought about something so un-Indian, Ram Mohan has been deservedly described as "the greatest creative personality of the nineteenth-century India."[6]

In the span of time covering his Calcutta years, 1815 to 1830, he laid the blueprint for the Indian national movement. Of this, Vincent A. Smith states:

> His attitude towards the West was neither that of surrender, or withdrawal, or conflict. It was one of comprehension. The new world from the West was not to be a substitute but a supplement to the old. Synthesis, which is different from syncretism, was his remedy for the predicament of Hinduism.[6]

The means by which he sought to bring about this synthesis was reason. He discovered the principle of reason in the Upanishadic literature of ancient Hinduism. "Once this was accepted the western challenge could be met face to face. Western loans would not involve eastern apostasy; loyalty and reform could go hand in hand."[8]

By this scheme of genius, Ram Mohan was able to supply the rising westernized class with what they sorely wanted, but which neither the Orthodox nor Radicals could deliver, namely: to be westernized without being de-Hinduized. Whereas the Orthodox offered a past that had no future, and the Radicals offered a future that had no past, the Raja made possible a past that had a rich future and a future that had a rich past.

In view of the fact that the Raja's ethics was centered in his religion, the question may arise as to the justification for extended discussions of such non-religious topics as education and politics. The answer lies in the organic connection between the social and religious realms within the Hindu tradition. The central aspect of *dharma* integrates all areas of life, breaking down the familiar walls of sacred and secular. As a man of *dharma*, Roy believed that when you hallow this life in all its diversity, you meet the living God as its unconditioned source and depth. God is not to be met in some special church or temple but in the concreteness of the everyday. This means that religion as a special sphere of life is not real religion. The more real religion is, the more concerned it is with its own overcoming. Nothing is therefore profane. The profane is simply what has not yet been sanctified, for there is nothing so crass, base, or ordinary that it cannot become the material for sanctification. In the absence of this explanation, it is difficult to understand the Raja's reforming genius.

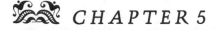 *CHAPTER 5*

# Religious and
# Moral Reform

## I. Campaign against Idolatry

First it must be pointed out that Ram Mohan's impulse to reform proceeded from his acute moral sense. In his introduction to the *Isha Upanishad* he draws attention to the contrast between a man's physical powers, which are limited, and his moral powers which possess the "capability of almost boundless improvement."[1] The endowment of these "extensive moral powers, together with the highly beneficial objects which the appropriate exercise of them may produce," often lead to feelings of sorrow and remorse when a person becomes "conscious of having neglected opportunities of rendering benefit to his fellow-creatures."[2]

Out of this sense of the moral structure of existence, Ram Mohan declares that though born a *Brahmin* and nurtured in all the *Brahmanical* principles, "being thoroughly convinced of the lamentable errors of my countrymen, [I] have been stimulated to employ every means in my power to improve their minds, and lead them to the knowledge of a purer system of morality."[3]

Thus, it was with a very strong sense of moral awareness that Ram Mohan launched his campaign against idolatry. His polemic was not merely theological, but practical. The issue was not simply one of polytheism versus monotheism, but of degradation versus dignity, and of superstition versus rationality. He says:

> Living constantly amongst Hindoos of different sects and professions, I have had ample opportunity of observing the superstitious puerilities into which they have been thrown by their self-interested guides, who, in defiance of the law as well as of common sense, have succeeded but too well in conducting them to the temple of idolatry; and while they hid from

41

their view the true substance of morality, have infused into their simple hearts a weak attachment to its mere shadow.[4]

The immorality of idolatry lay in its debasement of the people. Idol worship was the "source of prejudice and superstition and the total destruction of moral principle, as countenancing criminal intercourse, suicide, female murder, and human sacrifice."[5] It would be unfair to say that Ram Mohan was a rationalist who failed to understand the "real meaning" of idol worship because he was not concerned at this point with theological quibbling, but with social devastation.

The code of idolatry did have its definition of sin, but this was connected with "observances as to diet and other matters of form."[6]

Understanding the close connection between religion and morality, Ram Mohan decided that the only way to get the Hindus to change their lifestyle was by altering their popular modes of religious thinking. As long as the people were kept ignorant, it was but a natural inclination for them to worship objects resembling their own nature, and to become attached to "external forms of rites palpable to their grosser senses."[7] But, by elevating their religious sensibilities, their moral sights would also be raised.

The religion that Ram Mohan had in mind was not a new one or the invention of his mind, but the religion of the Hindus at the peak of their civilization. He based his claim not on some private revelation but on the basis of the most authoritative Hindu scriptures. These scriptures teach that "the sole regulator of the Universe is but one, who is omnipresent, far surpassing our powers of comprehension; above external sense; and whose worship is the chief duty of mankind and the sole cause of eternal beatitude; and that all that bear figure and appellations are inventions."[8]

The scriptures, such as the *Puranas* (collections of ancient tales) and the *Tantras* (texts of Tantric cults), do contain assertions respecting the worship of several gods and goddesses, but they reconcile these polytheistic assertions with their basic monotheism by affirming that:

> The directions to worship any figured beings are only applicable to those who are incapable of elevating their minds to the idea of an invisible Supreme Being, in order that such persons, by fixing their attention on those invented figures, may be able to restrain themselves from vicious temptations, and that those that are competent for the worship of the invisible God, should disregard the worship of idols.[9]

Unfortunately, the teachings of the authoritative Hindu scriptures have been concealed from the people because of the dark veil of the Sanskrit language. To remove the veil and to set the record straight, Ram Mohan decided to translate the principal portions of the Vedas from Sanskrit into native languages. He explains his strategy thus:

The greater part of Brahmans, as well as of other sects of Hindoos, are quite incapable of justifying the idolatry which they continue to practise. When questioned on the subject, in place of adducing reasonable arguments in support of their conduct, they conceive it fully sufficient to quote their ancestors as positive authorities! And some of them are become very ill-disposed towards me, because I have forsaken idolatry for the worship of the true eternal God! In order, therefore, to vindicate my own faith and that of our early forefathers, I have been endeavouring, for some time past, to convince my countrymen of the true meaning of our sacred books; and to prove, that my aberration deserves not the opprobrium which some unreflecting persons have been so ready to throw upon me.[10]

Between 1815 and 1819 Ram Mohan published and distributed, at his own expense, several works on the *Vedanta* in Bengali, Hindustani, and English.[11] For Hindu readers, Ram Mohan expressed the hope that "through Divine Providence and human exertions, they will sooner or later avail themselves of that true system of religion which leads its observers to a knowledge and love of God, and to a friendly inclination towards their fellow-creatures, impressing their hearts at the same time with humility and charity, accompanied by independence of mind and pure sincerity."[12]

Ram Mohan intended that his publications might assist European readers to understand Hindu theology. Their understanding would then be based on primary scriptures rather than on the "Puranas, moral tales, or any other modern works," or on "the superstitious rites and habits daily encouraged and fostered by their [Hindu] self-interested leaders."[13]

The *Government Gazette* (February 1, 1816) hailed the *Translation of an Abridgement of the Vedanta* as a phenomenon in the literary world. It regarded its singularity as arising chiefly from "its being the production of a learned Brahmin of great wealth and respectability, and whose acquirements in the language of Europe, as well as of Asia, add to the weight of his opinions, and importance of his name." Regardless of its theological merits, the *Gazette* noted the pamphlet "displays the deductions of a liberal, and intrepid mind."[14]

The *Calcutta Monthly Journal* (December 1817) stated on the occasion of the publication of the *Mandukya Upanishad* that the ceaseless efforts of this scholar to retrieve his countrymen from their delusion and ignorance, "deserve the highest praise; and although the success of his labours may not keep pace with his efforts—we are persuaded that in a short time he will perceive their beneficial effects."[15]

The *Journal* goes on to report a stirring among the educated classes:

Many well-informed natives, resident at this presidency, are now perfectly convinced, that Ram Mohun has reason and the *highest* Hindu authority, to support the opinions which he avows—and we firmly believe, are privately disposed to profess the doctrines, which his translations of the Shanscrit Scriptures inculcate.

However, due to the inveteracy of habit and prejudice, the *Journal* regrets that these Hindu intelligentsia are unable to profess what they believe in their hearts. "The dread of Brahminical excommunication, will perhaps prolong the period of their religious thraldom—and prevent that reformation, which as we have formerly said, will form the most important step to a much *higher* pinnacle of knowledge."[16]

The *Journal* continues that if the Hindu elite can be convinced that idolatry is inconsistent with scripture, the Hindu system of morality will be reformed and the citizens "will unquestionably become better men." Should these hopes be realized, the editor is confident that the intellectual exertions of the Raja will be gratefully remembered; and "if the labours of Luther in the Western world, are entitled to be commemorated by Christians—the Herculean efforts of the individual we have alluded to, must place him high among the benefactors of the Hindoo portion of mankind."[17]

News of Ram Mohan's campaign reached London where it quickly stirred Christian hopes for the evangelization of India. *The Missionary Register* (1816) states: "The rise of this new Sect, the zeal and subtlety displayed by its founder, with its obvious tendency to undermine the fabric of Hindoo Superstition, are objects of serious attention to the Christian Mind." The question of its informant is quoted, and upon it the *Register* rests its own hopes: "Who knows but this man may be one of the many instruments, by which God, in his mysterious providence, may accomplish the overthrow of idolatry?"[18]

Beyond England, Ram Mohan's fame reached all the way to North America. The *Calcutta Journal* (October 1818) reported receipt of an American review of the Raja's anti-idolatrous writings, and made this document available to the Bengal public, not only because of its literary novelty, but because the editor hoped that "it may also be conducive to nobler ends; and our personal knowledge of the virtuous and unsophisticated individual who has thus advocated the cause of truth, amidst obstacles from which any ordinary mind would have shrunk appalled, affords us an inexpressible pleasure in thus contributing our mite to his celebrity."

The review, entitled "Theology of the Hindoos," reads in part:

A considerable excitement has lately been produced in India by the attempts of a very wealthy and learned native, named Ram Mohun Roy, to restore the pure doctrines of the Vedas. He has translated several chapters of these sacred books into the Bengalee language, and circulated them among his countrymen. The parts which he has translated, are those which treat of a Supreme Being, his character, and the worship he claims. These have been entirely overlooked by the Brahmins. He seems to have just views of the absurd and wicked practices of his countrymen in their religious ceremonies, and a strong desire to wipe out so gross a stain in the human character. Already he is said to have many followers. Numbers, who knew nothing of the Vedas, except from the interpretation of their priests, are made acquainted with its true and most important doctrines.[19]

Thus, Ram Mohan's anti-idolatrous campaign for the moral and religious rejuvenation of his countrymen brought him early fame, but popularity had its price. His own family renounced him. In June 1817 his nephew, Govindaprasad, filed a suit in the Supreme Court laying claim to all of the movable and immovable property held by Ram Mohan. For two-and-a-half years the ugly business was dragged out until Ram Mohan finally won in December 1819. Sad to say, the prime mover in this sordid affair was not the nephew but Tarini Devi, his mother. She was probably alienated from him when he ceased supporting the idol worship in the family home.

The Orthodox section of Hindu society was also up in arms. Their traditional strongholds of self-interest being threatened, the *Brahmins* vented their anger on Ram Mohan with such epithets as "destroyer of religion," "renegade," etc. But to label Ram Mohan a destroyer of Hinduism was historically incorrect. Like Jesus, whom he admired, he came not to destroy but to fulfill. This, indeed involved destruction, but it was destruction of those alien accretions which had overlaid the religion and had deprived it of its former glory. To his critics Ram Mohan seemed the inventor of something new. That they could not recognize their own monotheistic past in his teachings, indicates how far removed they were from the original inspiration. What these critics saw was a new-fangled faith, whereas Ram Mohan was saying that monotheism should be the national religion of the Hindus. This ancient religion of his people was precisely what had earned for them the adulation of the civilized world, and "Rammohun's only passion was to see it re-established in the land, so that it might once again be the perennial source of all progress and comforts in their life, and all stigma that had been brought on the fair name of the once great Hindus might be removed once and for all."[20]

Without detracting from the moral courage of Ram Mohan in exposing the Orthodox practice of idolatry through a historico-critical investigation of the Hindu scriptures, credit must also be given to scholars associated with the Royal Asiatic Society, both Western and Indian, who were introducing Indian thought to the West through translations and critical commentaries. The publications of such men as Wilkins, Jones, Colebroke, and Wilson played a pioneering role in generating a lively interest in the critical inquiry of Indian history. "In one sense history was omnipresent in Hindu society but in another, in the sense of critical inquiry, it had never been prominent in Hindu scholarship. Too much had been overlaid by superstition. Indian nationalists were later to draw deep at the well of newly discovered knowledge about their past."[21]

Ram Mohan was among the first beneficiaries of this scholarship. In his preface to a translation of the *Isha Upanishad* he writes: "I must confess how much I feel indebted to Doctor H. H. Wilson, in my translations from Sanskrit into English, for the use of his Sanskrit and English Dictionary."[22]

Other national leaders followed in the reformer's trail. Mahatma Gandhi, for instance, traced the roots of his non-violence to the *Bhagavad Gita*, and acknowledged that this was made possible through the researches of Western scholars.[23]

The above findings illustrate a point made earlier, namely, that Ram Mohan's reformation did not take place in a vacuum. His movement presupposed a new spirit of inquiry and examination sparked by contacts with European civilization. In the absence of this climate of openness, Ram Mohan's various campaigns would have appeared only in the obituary columns of the Calcutta newspapers. But, whereas in the hands of the young Radicals, the torch of reason proved incendiary, in the hands of Ram Mohan it illumined the thinking of liberals of the new middle class.


## II. The *Atmiya Sabha*

Early upon his arrival in Calcutta (1815), Ram Mohan banded his non-conformist friends and well-wishers into the *Atmiya Sabha* or Friendly Association. The purpose of the *Sabha* was "the dissemination of religious truth and the promotion of free discussions of theological subjects."[24] The membership roster of these rich and influential personages which reads like a "Who's Who" of Bengali society, included Dwarkanath Tagore, Prasanna Kumar Tagore, Kali Nath, Baikuntha Nath Munshi, Brindaban Mitra, Kasi Nath Mullick, Raja Kali Sankar Gosal, Annada Prosad Banerji, and Nanda Kishore Bose, father of Raj Narain Bose who became president of the *Adi Brahmo Samaj*.[25]

These notables represent the inner circle with whose aid Ram Mohan founded the *Atmiya Sabha*. A host of other followers were more interested in the honor which company with the Raja conferred upon them; while some were drawn to him for his "wise counsel and ready help." The less resolute dropped off when Ram Mohan's movement became politically visible, causing the Orthodox community to step up its opposition against him. Ram Mohan loved all his disciples and took pleasure in addressing them as *beraders*, Persian for brothers.

There was great latitude in the religio-philosophical positions held by various members of the *Sabha*, with Hariharananda Tirthaswami representing the extreme Eastern side of the society, and David Hare, "the active and benevolent rationalist," representing the extreme Western side. Ideology apart, all members were bound by certain rules, one of which was that no member should participate in idol worship. It was this requirement that prompted Ram Mohan to terminate financial support for the maintenance of the family's idols, thus incurring their wrath.

The *Sabha* held weekly meetings at Ram Mohan's Maniktala residence. Below is an account of the nature and impact of these meetings, as reported by the *India Gazette* (May 18, 1819):

> We learn with great satisfaction that the meritorious exertions of Ram Mohun Roy, have already produced a most powerful effect on the Hindoos in Calcutta and its vicinity. An intelligent Correspondent has assured us, that an assembly of the followers of the Vedantic doctrines, took place. . . . The meeting was attended by some of the members of many of the families most eminent for wealth or learning amongst the Hindoo inhabitants. . . . There is no question that the leaven of religious reformation is now strongly fermenting, and that liberality of sentiment on general subjects is making most rapid progress amongst the natives of all classes.
>
> At the meeting in question, it is said, the absurdity of the prevailing rules respecting the intercourse of the several castes with each other, and of the restrictions on diet, etc., was freely discussed, and generally admitted —the necessity of an infant widow passing her life in a stage of celibacy— the practice of polygamy and of suffering widows to burn with the corpse of their husbands, were condemned,—as well as all the superstitious ceremonies in use amongst idolaters. Select pasages from the Oppunishuds of the Veds, in support of the pure Theistical system of worship were read and explained; and Hymns or songs were sung, expressive of the faith of the audience in the doctrines there taught.[26]

Members of the *Atmiya Sabha* did more than sing hymns, read scriptures, and rant over the evils of society. They believed in *karma yoga* (disinterested action) and actively espoused liberal causes and projects. The *Friend of India* gives an account of a new form of oath-taking by a member of the *Sabha*. Presenting his evidence in the Supreme Court, the native refused to swear on the waters of the Ganges because he did not believe in its imagined sanctity. Instead, in European fashion, he offered to be sworn by the *Vedas*. "This simple affirmation was taken, as practised in England by the society of Quakers."[27]

The English press diligently followed the activities of the *Atmiya Sabha* and published appreciative notices of its ameliorative efforts. The *Friend of India* observes:

> The attacks of Rammohun Roy on the polytheism of India, and the system of burning widows, have produced rejoinders and explanations, every multiplication of which tends to exhibit the weakness of the system;

and many who heretofore reposed the firmest belief in the dogmas of that faith which their ancestors have credited for ages, have now begun to waver.

The *Friend* goes on to express the hope that the "meritorious exertions" of the reformer are only the beginning of "an uninterrupted series of discussions which will issue in the final establishment of truth . . ."[28]

One notable confrontation in which the questions of truth were eloquently raised was the great debate which took place in 1819 between Ram Mohan and Subramanya Sastri, a *Brahmin* from Madras. Many of Calcutta's intellectual elite were present, including the leader of the Hindu Orthodox party, Radha Kanta Deb. The subject was idol-worship. It is reported that "by a rare display of erudition and forensic skill, Rammohun Roy is said to have vanquished his adversary."[29]

Soon after this debate the meetings of the *Atmiya Sabha* were terminated. The public impact of the Association during its brief span of four years was recognized by the *Friend of India* in its issue of September 1820. With a salute to its founder, the editorial states:

"He has done much; he has led the way in bringing to the crucible of public investigation, doctrines which have received the implicit credence of his countrymen from the remotest antiquity."[30]

## III. Controversy with the Serampore Baptists

The *Friend of India* was the organ of the Baptist Missionary Society headquartered in Serampore, some fourteen miles from Calcutta. The leader was William Carey who came under the influence of the great Evangelical revival inspired by George Whitefield and John Wesley. The specific brand of Christianity of this eighteenth-century movement is summarized in the biblical text, "Believe on the Lord Jesus Christ, and thou shalt be saved." Belief in Jesus Christ was the conviction that through his atoning death, the price of sin is paid, and by faith salvation is freely received.

As the founder of the modern missionary movement, Carey's contribution to Evangelicalism was the discovery of the universal dimension of the Christian gospel. Promoting this universalism, he could say with Wesley, "the world is my parish." Carey's epoch-making tract, "An Enquiry into the Obligation of Christians," signals "a distinct point of departure in the history of Christianity" because it made the Church aware of its missionary challenge.[31]

Carey landed in Calcutta on November 11, 1793, and was summarily rebuffed by the East India Company. Officials feared that the Christian gospel and Christian education would plant certain ideas in the minds of the natives which would bring about political unrest. Carey temporarily settled in North Bengal and worked as an indigo planter. He was to be joined by two other missionaries, Joshua Marshman, a school master, and William Ward, a printer. However, Charles Grant, then a Company Director, soon advised them to find refuge in Serampore which was under the Danish flag, and was hospitable to missionaries. On January 10, 1800, Carey was united with his two colleagues at Serampore which was thence known as "the cradle of modern missions."[32]

In Serampore the Baptists established their printing press which they considered a "wonderful engine" toward "weakening the spirit of eastern superstition." They also recognized a powerful anti-idolatrous spirit behind the publications of Ram Mohan, and this gave them hope that the next step in the life of this respected scholar would be the adoption of Christianity. They estimated:

> He is at present a simple theist, admires Jesus Christ, but knows not his *need* of atonement. He has not renounced his caste, and this enables him to visit the richest families of Hindoos. He is said to be very moral; but is pronounced to be a most wicked man by the strict Hindoos.[33]

For his part Ram Mohan enjoyed the company of the missionaries, engaged them in discussions, joined them in worship, and offered aid to their educational schemes.

Ram Mohan's initial efforts to understand Christianity were perplexing. He relates that for a long time he was unable to distinguish "amidst the various doctrines I found insisted upon in the writings of Christian authors, and in the conversation of those teachers of Christianity with whom I have had the honour of holding communication."[34]

Gradually, by laboring through the Bible in its original Hebrew and in Greek, and from his knowledge of comparative religions, the conviction dawned on him that the natural "law which teaches that man should do unto others as he would be done by," though partially taught "in every system of religion," is "principally inculcated by Christianity."[35]

He therefore decided to extract this basic message of Christianity from all doctrinal trappings and present it to his countrymen under the title of *The Precepts of Jesus, the Guide to Peace and Happiness*. He explains his rationale for limiting himself to the moral teachings of Jesus:

> I feel persuaded that by separating from the other matters contained in the New Testament, the moral precepts found in that book, these will be more likely to produce the desirable effect of improving the hearts and minds of men of different persuasions and degrees of understanding.[36]

The doctrinal passages are excised because of the questions they would raise in the minds of freethinkers. Also not included are the miracle stories which would carry little weight with Asians who were accustomed to narratives of an even more fantastic nature. On the other hand, moral doctrines are maintained because they are productive of harmonious relationships; are "beyond the reach of metaphysical perversion"; and are "intelligible alike to the learned and to the unlearned." These sample teachings are not only calculated to "elevate men's ideas to high and liberal notions of God," but are also well fitted "to regulate the conduct of the human race in the discharge of their various duties to themselves, and to society." For these many reasons Ram Mohan was confident that the publication of the *Precepts* would accrue to the benefit of many.[37]

Ironically, the very work that was intended to serve as *A Guide to Peace and Happiness* brought its author nothing but conflict and misery. The missionaries, whom Ram Mohan naïvely thought would be complimented by his work, declared open warfare on him. The first shot was fired by the Reverend Deocar Schmidt who, in his review of the book appearing in the *Friend of India*, speculated that the *Precepts* could "greatly injure the cause of truth."[38] The editor, Joshua Marshman, described Ram Mohan as "an intelligent heathen, whose mind is as yet completely opposed to the *grand design* of the Saviour's becoming incarnate."[39]

In the next issue of the *Friend*, Marshman released a volley of theological thunder against Ram Mohan, telling of how the announcement of the compilation by Ram Mohan for use by his countrymen excited much interest "in all who had witnessed his laudable endeavours to expose the folly of that system of idolatry universally prevalent."[40] The prospect of an intelligent Hindu commending Christian scriptures to be read by his countrymen, delighted all those who prayed for the Christianization of the heathen.

The publication of the *Precepts* dashed all these hopes to the ground. The editor charged: "Instead of exhibiting those precepts as a sample of the whole Scriptures, and representing them as affording indubitable proof of the authenticity of its narratives and the reasonableness and importance of its doctrines, [the precepts] were in reality separated from that gospel of which they form so important a part, and held up as forming of themselves the way of life." The whole idea was considered subversive, perverting "the grand design of the gospel," and frustrating "the grace of God in the salvation of men." It was patently clear that the editor was a very disappointed man.[41]

Disappointment turned to disaster when it was further learned that Ram Mohan, "instead of treating with reverence the other parts of the Sacred Oracles, unhappily tended to impugn them," telling the reader that the miracle stories would fail to impress the native mind and that some historical passages are liable to dispute.[42]

The editor pointed out that the Christian censure against Ram Mohan's compilation lay in his making the *Precepts* appear as the whole of the scripture when, in reality, they were only a part organically related to the whole. The religion Ram Mohan's texts deny by omission is the gospel which declares that men are saved by the atonement wrought on the cross by Jesus Christ; and the religion which it substitutes is that of moral merit. Such meritocracy is condemned by God's word, "for all have sinned and fallen short of the glory of God."

Thus, the editor marshalled numerous texts to prove that the gospel was like the seamless robe of Christ and that the moral teachings could not be separated from the doctrinal threads and the miraculous motifs which were woven into the fabric of the scripture.

Combining all these facts, Marshman argues that "Jesus *must* be regarded as God equal with the Father, expiating the sins of men," and concludes with an entreaty to the author of the *Precepts* "to weigh these things with the utmost care, not only for the sake of his countrymen, but from a regard to his own immortal interests, so deeply affected by that declaration of Jesus, 'no man cometh to the Father *but* by me.' "[43]

Ram Mohan felt "as much surprised as disappointed" by the incriminations of the Christian press. His response was made through *An Appeal to the Christian Public in Defence of the Precepts of Jesus*. Firstly, he takes exception to the unchristian and uncivil manner in which Marshman had adduced his objections to the *Precepts* by introducing personality and applying to him the epithet of heathen. Had the editor confined his inquiries to the evidence contained in the work, he could not have made such a gross violation of truth, charity, and liberality "which are essential to Christianity in every sense of the word."[44]

Ram Mohan asks by what definition could one who has avowed belief in "One God" and in "the Precepts of Jesus," be called a "heathen." He concedes that the editor cannot be accused of being the first Christian to use this unchristian phrase; numerous Christian sects use it liberally to stigmatize one another. "Very different conduct is inculcated in the Precepts of Jesus to John, when complaining of one who performed cures in the name of Jesus, yet refused to follow the Apostles: he gave a rebuke, saying, 'he that is not against us is on our part.' "[45]

For his part, Ram Mohan says he will give "preference to the guidance of those Precepts which justify no retaliation even upon enemies, to the hasty suggestions of human passions and the example of the Editor of the 'Friend of India'."[46]

Secondly, Ram Mohan examines the grounds on which the rebuttals of the editor are founded. Against the objection that the moral sayings of Jesus, independent of dogmas, are insufficient for salvation, he retorts that the reviewer has limited his meaning of the word "moral" to civil matters, whereas the intended meaning is inclusive of religious conduct. As previously stated in his Introduction, "This simple code is well fitted to regulate the conduct of the human race in the discharge of their various *duties to God*, to themselves, and to society" (italics supplied).[47]

In reply to the charge that it was presumption on his part, "independently of the Divine Teacher," to think himself qualified to know what sort of instruction is advantageous for the happiness of mankind, Ram Mohan pleads the support of Jesus. Quoting extensively from the four gospels, he cites such texts as: "Thou shalt love the Lord thy God with all thy heart, and with all thy soul, and with all thy mind. This is the first and great commandment. And the second is like unto it, Thou shalt love thy neighbour as thyself. *On these two commandments hang all the law and the prophets.*"[48]

Commenting on this great love commandment of Jesus, Ram Mohan notes:

> The Saviour meant of course by the words *Law* and *Prophets* all of the commandments ordained by divine authority, and the Religion revealed to the Prophets and observed by them, as is evident from Jesus' declaring those commandments to afford perfect means of acquiring eternal life, and directing men to follow them accordingly. Had any other doctrine been requisite to teach men the road to peace and happiness, Jesus could not have pronounced to the Lawyer, 'This do and *thou shalt live.*' It was characteristic of the office of Christ to teach men, that forms and ceremonies were useless tokens of respect for God, compared with the essential proof of obedience and love towards him evidenced by the practice of beneficence towards their fellow-creatures. The compiler, finding these commandments given as including all the revealed law, and the whole system of religion adopted by the Prophets and re-established and fulfilled by Jesus himself, as the means to acquire Peace and Happiness, was desirous of giving more full publicity in this country to them, and to the subsidiary moral doctrines that are introduced by the Saviour in detail.[49]

Thirdly, against the argument of the reviewer that the *Precepts* shed no light on two points indispensable for peace of mind, namely, obtaining favor with God, and having the strength to keep his commandments, Ram Mohan quotes Jesus. On the issue of the forgiveness of sins, he recalls passages such as the parable of the Prodigal Son which teaches that sincere repentance is the only prerequisite for winning the favour of God. As to finding strength to keep God's commandments, Ram Mohan stands on the gracious promise, "Ask and it shall be given you, seek and ye shall find, knock and it shall be opened unto you."[50]

Fourthly, Ram Mohan does not accept the reviewer's imputation that he has erred in "exalting the value of the moral doctrines above that of the historical facts and dogmas."[51] In the equation of the scriptures, duties towards man are tantamount to duties toward God. We are told in Matthew's gospel that on the judgment day the Son of Man will divide the sheep from the goats. To the former he will say, "come, ye blessed of my Father, inherit the kingdom prepared for you from the foundation of the world. For I was an hungered, and ye gave me meat: I was thirsty, and ye gave me drink: I was a stranger, and ye took me in:

naked and ye clothed me: I was sick and ye visited me: I was in prison, and ye came to me." Then the righteous shall ask their Lord when did they do all these things for him, and he shall answer them saying: "Inasmuch as ye have done it unto one of the least of these my brethren, ye have done it unto me."[52] St. Matthew's description of the day of judgment makes it clear that according to the divine calculus, love of God is shown by service to one's fellow creatures.

Fifthly, Ram Mohan defends what the reviewer has questioned, namely, "that the dogmatical and historical matters are rather calculated to do injury."[53] Looking abroad, he points to Christian countries which have been divided by wars inspired by dogmatic differences; at home, he shows how missionaries have completely counteracted their own benevolent labors by preaching dogmas which only move the natives to ridicule. Having witnessed this waste of human and material resources over a period of twenty years, Ram Mohan says he published the sayings of Jesus which were "best calculated to lead mankind to universal love and harmony," avoiding those matters which are really not essential, and which are open to diverse interpretations and dispute.[54]

Sixthly, Ram Mohan demonstrates that his action in selecting certain passages of scripture was by no means novel. Numerous Christian publications are composed of extracts from the Bible, and if their authors were questioned as to their object, their motives would not differ from his own, namely, to highlight "the superior importance of the parts so selected."[55]

Ram Mohan concludes his *Appeal* with a prayer which is as revealing as it is sincere: "May God render religion destructive of differences and dislike between man and man, and conducive to the peace and Union of mankind. Amen."[56]

Dr. Marshman responded to Ram Mohan's *Appeal* through his "Remarks" published in the *Friend of India* (May 1820). He labors to establish two points: the truth of miracles and dogmas; and the insufficiency of moral rectitude as a means to salvation, without benefit of the atoning sacrifice of God in Christ.[57]

Ram Mohan counters with a *Second Appeal to the Christian Public in Defence of "The Precepts of Jesus"* (1821). This treatise has two propositions: "That the Precepts of Jesus, which teach that love of God is manifested in beneficence towards our fellow-creatures, are a sufficient Guide to Peace and Happiness"; and that God, "who is the only proper object of religious veneration, is one and undivided in person."[58]

He begins with a general defense of the *Precepts*.[59] On miracles he avers that he does not doubt the "truth and excellence of the Scriptures" in which they are recorded. His exclusion of them was based on the assumption that they would not carry much weight with the Hindus whose legendary tales had accustomed their credulous minds to miracle stories of a more wondrous order. He himself had only contempt for these stories because they lacked moral content. Though the Christian miracle stories were morally and spiritually elevated, they lacked the appeal of sensationalism for his countrymen. Here, probably for diplomatic reasons, the rationalist philospher seems to have backed down from his position in the *Tuhfat*.

Further, he says that the dogmas found in the scriptures were excluded from the *Precepts* only on the grounds that they were "liable to the doubts and disputes of Free-thinkers and Anti-Christians." Again, we record our disappointment that the author of the *Tuhfat* has seemingly relaxed his rational rigor.

As to the second point urged by the editor, that salvation cannot be had by an adherence to the *Precepts* only but also by accepting the doctrine of the vicarious sacrifice of God in Christ, Ram Mohan replies with an astounding grasp of the New Testament.

The precepts have the highest scriptural authority—higher than Paul on whom the editor depends—the author of Christianity himself! When Jesus said: " 'On these two commandments [to love God and to love our neighbours] hang all the Law and Prophets,' he meant all divine commandments found in the Scriptures, obedience to which is strictly required of us by the founder of that religion."[60]

It goes against common sense to think that Jesus would have incited his followers to keep these commandments were they practically impossible, as Marshman urged.

Jesus clearly identified *love* to himself with keeping God's commandments: "If ye keep my commandments ye shall abide in my love." "But," says Ram Mohan, "if the observance of those commandments be treated as practically impossible, the love of Jesus and adherence to him must likewise be so considered, and Christianity altogether regarded as existing only in theory."[61]

While Jesus speaks at length on man's religious need to love God which must be expressed morally by love towards one's fellows, there is not "even a single passage pronounced by Jesus, enjoining a refuge in such a doctrine of the cross, as all-sufficient or indispensable for salvation." Repentance is the only prerequisite for the remission of sins, as the parable of the Prodigal Son touchingly illustrates.

After these general remarks, emphasizing what he had mostly stated in the *Precepts*, Ram Mohan gets down to specifics.

In his remarks, Dr. Marshman had advanced seven positions establishing what he considered the most important of all doctrines—the deity of Jesus Christ. Before considering these positions separately, Ram Mohan begins by showing that the "natural inferiority of the Son to the Father" is given in the scriptures. He grants that as the chosen Messiah, Christ had unique attributes and powers, but these were all derived from God. Christ clearly stated: "The Father is greater than I." Ram Mohan explains:

It would have been idle to have informed them of a truth, of which, as Jews, they would never have entertained the smallest question, that in his mere corporeal nature Jesus was inferior to his Maker; and that it must therefore have been his spiritual nature of which he here avowed the inferiority to that of God.[62]

Ram Mohan then examines seven arguments posited by the editor as confirming the deity of Christ. They are: (1) that Jesus possessed ubiquity; (2) that he declared that his nature was as mysterious as the nature of God; (3) that he possessed the power to forgive sins; (4) that he was all powerful; (5) that he would preside over the final judgment; (6) that he accepted the worship of men; and (7) that he considered himself part of the Trinity. Ram Mohan makes a careful exegesis of the texts on which these assumptions are based and demonstrates conclusively that the editor's interpretations are the product of linguistic and logical errors, and that he is constantly open to the "danger of resting an opinion on the apparent meaning of the words of insulated passages of Scriptures, without attention to the context.[63]

On ubiquity, Marshman quotes Jesus's words to Nicodemus: "No man hath ascended up to heaven, but he that came down from heaven, even the Son of man who is in heaven." He had taken these words to mean that Jesus was also in heaven at the time of his conversation with Nicodemus. Ram Mohan dismisses the claim, noting that the present tense is frequently used in a preterite sense, and hence the argument carries no weight.

On the mystery of Christ's nature, Marshman quotes: "No man knoweth the Son, but the Father; neither knoweth any man the Father, save the Son." He was resting his argument on two grounds: the incomprehensibility of God to man; and that incomprehensibility of nature belongs to God alone. From this the editor infers that Jesus, "knowing the nature of God, and being himself possessed of an incomprehensible nature, is equal with God."[64] Ram Mohan asks the editor if his definition of "incomprehensible" is total mystification, or mystery only in degrees. If the former, he denies total incomprehensibility of the Godhead because the passage cited declares God to be comprehensible both to the Son and to those who believe in him.[65]

On the forgiveness of sins, Marshman tries to prove that in exercising this prerogative peculiar to God, Jesus was thereby shown to be divine. Ram Mohan agrees that Jesus forgave men their sins, but held that this power was derived from God. Jesus clearly avows that God is the source of forgiveness "as appears from his petitioning the Father to forgive those that were guilty of bringing the death of the cross upon him."[66]

On the divine attribute of omnipotence, Marshman advances the position that Jesus claimed almighty power in an unequivocal manner. Here, too, Ram Mohan grants that Jesus possessed unusual powers, but these powers were derived from God.

On Jesus's role in the final judgment, Ram Mohan concurs with Marshman that the exercise of such an office requires divine qualification. At the same time, he considers it consistent with God's wisdom and omnipotence "to bestow wisdom equal to the important nature of this office on the first-born of every creature."[67]

On Jesus's acceptance of worship, Ram Mohan points out the word "worship" admits of two meanings: religious reverence paid to God, and civil respect due to superiors. In the case of Jesus and other biblical characters, the latter meaning is appropriate as the contexts show.

On Jesus associating his name with the Trinity, as in the baptismal formula; Marshman had taken it to mean a clear claim to divinity. Following much analysis, Ram Mohan concludes that the epithet "Son" found in the rite of baptism "ought to be understood and admitted by everyone as expressing the created nature of Christ, though the most highly exalted among all creatures."[68]

Having corrected Marshman's interpretations which would have presented Christ as divine, Ram Mohan inquires into the second important doctrine—the atonement. Marshman interprets the death of Jesus on the cross as a vicarious sacrifice, citing such verses as: "I am the living bread which came down from heaven: if any man eat of this bread, he shall live forever."[69]

Ram Mohan demurs. By the nature of the case the text must be understood figuratively, or else it would amount to gross absurdity. Jesus's mission on earth was not to die a substitutionary death but "to preach and impart divine instructions."[70] True, it is difficult and enigmatic to account for the savior's suffering. A clue may be found in the parable of the Wicked Husbandmen (Mark 12: 1–9) which Ram Mohan interprets as follows:

> This parable and these passages give countenance to the idea, that God suffered his Prophets, and Jesus, his beloved Son, to be cruelly treated and slain by the Jews for the purpose of taking away every excuse that they might offer for their guilt.[71]

The anti-Semitic bias in this explanation is unfortunate. It is quite out of character with the *Precepts*. It indicates Ram Mohan's uncritical deference to prevailing Christian attitudes and interpretations which would cast the Jews in the role of "Christ killers." He was capable of coming up with a more rational explanation of the sufferings of Jesus than resorting to warmed-over bigotry.

The question is raised as to whether Jesus, as God incarnate, suffered death and pain in his divine nature or human nature. If the former, it is highly inconsistent with the nature of God which is above being rendered liable to death or pain. If the latter, Ram Mohan perceives grave moral problems. The notion of an atonement for the offenses of others "seems totally inconsistent with the justice ascribed to God, and even at variance with those principles of equity required of men; for it would be a piece of gross iniquity to afflict one innocent being, who had all the human feelings, and who had never transgressed the will of God, with the death of the cross, for the crimes committed by others, especially when he declares such great aversion to it."[72]

In his effort to prove the atoning nature of the death of Jesus, Marshman had urged:

> Is he called the Saviour of men because he gave them moral precepts, by obeying which they might obtain the divine favour, with the enjoyment of heaven as their just desert? or because he died in their stead to atone for their sins and procure for them every blessing, etc.? If Jesus be termed a Saviour merely because he instructed men, he had this honour in common with Moses, and Elijah, and John the Baptist, neither of whom assumed the title of Saviour.[73]

Ram Mohan cites scriptures to show that other prophets are likewise referred to as "saviours." Of course, Jesus surpasses all of these other prophets inasmuch as he "instructed men in the Divine will, never so fully revealed."[74] For example, "it is true that Moses began to erect the everlasting edifice of true religion, consisting of a knowledge of the unity of God, and obedience to his will and commandments; but Jesus of Nazareth has completed the structure, and rendered his law perfect."[75]

To demonstrate the link between Moses and Jesus, Ram Mohan turns to the Sermon on the Mount where Jesus is cast in the role of the new Moses, having perfected the work of Moses. Having led his Christian opponent to the top of the mount on which Jesus delivered his precepts, Ram Mohan hopes that he may be justified in expressing his belief that "no *greater* honour can be justly given to any teacher of the will of God, than what is due to the *author* of the doctrine just quoted, which, with a power no less than standing miracles could produce, carry with them proofs of their divine origin to the conviction of the high and low, the learned and the unlearned."[76]

The third doctrine Ram Mohan tackles is that of miracles. As with other doctrines, he first defends his omission of miracles in his *Precepts* because, historically, they have been the basis of endless feuds and disputes. Secondly, miracles have been omitted because they are not essential to religion. The New Testament records show that "Jesus referred to his miracles those persons only who either *scrupled to believe*, or doubted him as the promised Messiah, or required of him some sign to confirm their faith."[77] Finally, the omission stems from his own experience. What drew him to Christianity was "the sublimity of the Precepts of Jesus," without the attraction of miraculous stories. He therefore omitted them from his compilation "without meaning to express doubts of their authenticity, or intending to slight them by his omission."[78]

The fourth doctrine Ram Mohan examines is the deity of the Holy Ghost. The editor had supported this trinitarian doctrine on the basis of the baptismal formula which tradition claims was enunciated by Jesus and in which the Holy Ghost is mentioned along with the Father and the Son (Matthew 28). For Ram Mohan it is preposterous that the mere association of names in a rite should be deemed tantamount to establishing the identity of their subjects.[79]

He proceeds to show on rational and scriptural grounds that the Holy Spirit cannot be thought of as a separate divine personality, but only as a guiding influence. God solely is the proper object of worship; the Son is the mediator; and the Holy Spirit is "that influence by which spiritual blessings are conveyed to mankind."[80]

The Raja warns that if this divine influence, metaphorically personified in scripture, is literally construed as a distinct personage within the Godhead, then the nature of Christian deity is no different than the polytheism which Christians condemn. A literal interpretation of certain key passages are also untenable because of immoral implications. There is the story, for instance, of how Mary conceived Jesus by the Holy Ghost which came upon her and overshadowed her (Matthew 1:11; Luke 1:35). If one interprets this story in a trinitarian sense, as does Marshman, "we should necessarily be drawn to the idea that God came upon Mary, and that the child which she bore, was in reality begotten of him."[81] The pure theist finds this notion revolting. He asks: "Is this idea . . . consistent with the perfect nature of the righteous God? Or rather, is not such a notion of the Godhead's having had intercourse with a human female, as horrible as the sentiments entertained by ancient and modern Heathens respecting the Deity?"[82]

The *Second Appeal* was met by a critical review by Dr. Marshman in the quarterly issue of the *Friend of India* (June 1821). Through one hundred and twenty-eight pages the editor tries to defend the bastions of Evangelical doctrine whose foundations were severely shaken by Ram Mohan's fire. Ignoring the canons of historical exegesis, he finds doctrines which had only emerged in the third and fourth centuries A.D., fully developed in the Old Testament era. So dogmatically is he convinced of the true nature of deity that he takes Ram Mohan's criticism of his conception as an arraignment of divine justice. Panting righteous despair, he prays that Ram Mohan's eyes be opened before "it be forever too late!"

Seven months later, Ram Mohan launched a biblical blitzkrieg against the two strongholds of Evangelical Christianity: the atonement, and the deity of Jesus. Whereas his Preface to the *Precepts* was a scant four pages, and his first *Appeal* twenty pages, the polemic became so heated that the *Second Appeal* covered one hundred and fifty pages, and the *Final Appeal*, two hundred and fifty-six pages!

The mounting tension was also evident on the side of the missionaries who now refused to publish Ram Mohan's *Final Appeal* at the Baptist Mission Press, as they had done his previous works. "It was thought in some sort a sanction of error, for the missionaries to have allowed any of the printing for Rammohun Roy to be done at their press."[83]

The ever resourceful Ram Mohan promptly purchased his own type, and with native help, published the *Final Appeal* on January 30, 1823.

Methodically, he removes the scriptural "proofs" on which the missionaries had built their Christological fortresses until he bares the humanity of Jesus. He denies anew that this man, no matter how exalted, ought to be worshipped, or that he has redeemed humanity by his "vicarious death." He makes his *Final Appeal* to the public in behalf of the *Precepts of Jesus*, against all claims of atonement, illustrating from scripture that his mission in the world was not to save men by dying in their place, but to offer them moral precepts, by obedience to which, through repentance and divine succour, they could receive peace and happiness.

Against insinuations of arrogance for presuming "to teach doctrines directly opposed to those held by the mass of real Christians in every age," Ram Mohan explains that entering into this theological controversy was not his idea. As a professed believer in one God, he was compelled to join the fray when "in reviewing the first appeal the Rev. editor fully introduced the doctrines of the Godhead of Jesus and the Holy Ghost, and of the Atonement as the only foundations of Christianity."[84]

With becoming sympathy he acknowledges that the views held by the missionaries, though no higher than the polytheistic faith of the Greeks and the Hindus, is not attributable to inferior judgment, but to early religious conditioning. Knowing fully the abiding effects of childhood impressions, he inists that the "unbiased judgment of a person who has searched the Scriptures only for a twelve-month with an anxious desire to discover the truth they contain, ought as far as authority goes in such matters, to outweigh the opinions of any number who have not thought at all for themselves, or who have studied after prejudice had laid hold on their minds."[85]

To rid the mind of the creedal cobwebs, Ram Mohan invites his critic to take a fresh look at the old doctrine of eternal punishment and see that it cannot stand on moral grounds. No matter how wicked a man is, he has done some good in his life. This means that "every man must be both guilty of infinite sin, and an agent of infinite virtue." Hence, "if we suppose that this very person is to be punished to eternity for the infinite sin he has committed, there will be no opportunity of his enjoying as infinite reward for his good work. But according to the position he must either be rewarded for his good or punished for his evil actions for eternity, while justice requires that he should experience the consequences of both."[86]

With the dispatch of the *Final Appeal*, Ram Mohan terminated this phase of his controversy with the Serampore missionaries.

Controversy shows character. A man reveals his true color in the heat of battle. What do we learn about this man, especially in respect to his moral fiber as he takes on the holy crusaders?

First, let us examine the charges brought against Ram Mohan by Dr. Marshman. There were three: that he was "depreciating the value of other parts of the inspired writings," considering them more capable of injury than inspiration; that he was attempting to invalidate the miracles of Christianity, categorizing them along with Hindu fables; and that his representation of Jesus was that of a mere teacher of morality, lacking the will or power to enforce his precepts.

All three of the charges were unjust and their proofs irrelevant.

In the first place, nowhere did Ram Mohan depreciate the value of other parts of scripture, and nowhere did he assert that the dogmatic and historical elements of the New Testament are productive of injury. In making his compilation, Ram Mohan was taking the same liberties with the scriptures as the missionaries who published scriptural tracts, and with the identical motives—to improve people morally and spiritually. Jesus himself selected two commandments: love of God and love of neighbor, and substituted these for all the Law and the Prophets. Ram Mohan was merely following in the footsteps of the Master when he compiled his *Precepts*, inclusive of the above commands and their subsidiary moral doctrines, to summarize the gospel.

In the second place, Ram Mohan did not invalidate Christian miracles, nor did he classify them with those of Hinduism. He merely said that Hindus would not take them very seriously because of their ignorance, prejudice, and familiarity with tales of exotic wonder.

Thirdly, he did not represent Jesus as a mere teacher of morality, no different from Mohammed or Confucius. As Son of God, he was "superior even to the angels in heaven, living from the beginning of the world to eternity . . . the Father created all things by him and for him."[87] He possessed special powers which were "received by him from the Father, as the Messiah, Christ, or anointed Son of God, and not solely in his human capacity."[88] His virgin birth was a mark of his special status.[89] In him "dwelt all truth."[90] As savior, he was "sent with a divine law to guide mankind by his preaching and example."[91] He did not destroy but fulfill the moral law given by Moses.[92] At the time of his trial and crucifixion he disavowed any claims to divinity. His present role is that of "Redeemer, Mediator and Intercessor with God, in behalf of his followers."[93]

The debate between Marshman and Roy produced more heat than light because both of them were arguing on two levels: the level of faith and the level of history. Whereas Marshman wrote in adoration of the Christ of faith, Roy was morally inspired by the Jesus of history. The very structure of the gospels lent to this confusion because the New Testament is itself written on these two levels. Furthermore, these two strands are not kept separate but are intertwined, and can only be taken apart, in some measure, through critical studies. Modern methodology is therefore the key to proper exegesis.

Marshman's methodology was inspired by his theology. He treated the whole Bible as having one "grand design" exemplified in the Evangelical doctrines of the atonement, the deity of Jesus, and the Trinity. He would bring the whole Bible to bear witness in support for these dogmas. Through Evangelical eyes, he could see King David singing psalms proclaiming the divinity of Christ; and he could watch the prophets as they predicted the sacrificial death of their Lord.

On the contrary, for Ram Mohan the Christian scriptures were historical documents which were to be examined critically. Following the historico-critical method up to a certain point, he could demonstrate how the Evangelical doctrines were products of elements alien to the tradition represented by Jesus.

The historico-critical method also guided his exegesis along the principles of contextualism. A text always spoke with a specific voice for a particular time and place. The prophets addressed their own people with a message relevant to their situation, and were not indulging in universalistic proclamations for other people in other times. The only universalism to be found in the Bible was the two-fold law of love of God and love to one's fellow men. However, as we shall see presently, Christological concessions sometimes marred methodological considerations.

Exceptions aside, his Christian biographer, Miss Sophia Dobson Collet, is correctly impressed by his modern approach to the scriptures. She observes:

> While the methods of exposition of the Hindu are more modern than those of his Christian opponent, many of his exegetical expedients are more apt to amuse than to convince a theologian of the present day. Yet the acquaintance which he shows with Hebrew and Greek and with expository literature is, considering his antecedents, little less than marvellous.[94]

Since these words were penned (1900), biblical scholarship has taken giant strides. Viewed from today's perspective, Ram Mohan's historical and literary approach to New Testament exegesis is better vindicated by contemporary biblical studies than the method of the missionaries. (It is indeed ironic that the author of the present work was first introduced to these studies in no place other than Serampore University itself! Here, for four years under the tutelage of educators of the Baptist Missionary Society, he was taught to investigate the Bible along historico-critical lines which better reflect the scholarly stance of Ram Mohan than the faith posture of the founders of the college!)

Apart from this, the ethical attitudes of the Hindu are different from those of the Christian.

From the commencement of their debate, Marshman failed to abide consistently by the issues and kept referring to Ram Mohan as a "heathen." This pejorative and patronizing phrase was prominent in the lexicon of the missionaries. It is hallowed in the popular missionary hymn of Bishop Heber of Calcutta, a contemporary of the reformer (1822–26). The hymn is entitled, "From Greenland's Icy Mountains," and includes the following verse:

> What though the spicy breezes
> Blow soft o'er Ceylon's isle,
> Though every prospect pleases
> And only man is vile.
>
> In vain with lavish kindness
> The gifts of God are strewn
> The heathen in his blindness
> Bows down to wood and stone.[95]

While use of the word heathen was common, it was unkind, injudicious, and inaccurate to use it in describing the author of the *Precepts of Jesus*. After all, the editor knew full well that Ram Mohan was eminently respectable, learned, and influential; and that he had endangered life and fortune to liberate his countrymen from the demoralizing effects of idolatry, and was trying to bring them to a knowledge of "One God who is the benevolent source of all creation."

Marshman also dabbled in insinuations, implying that the author of the *Precepts* was arrogant and vain. All of this brought "disappointment and vexation" to Ram Mohan who had gone out on a limb in order to generate an ecumenical appeal. Even so, he resolved early to conduct himself in the spirit of that man from Nazareth who counselled turning the other cheek. By such conduct, Ram Mohan shares with Mahatma Gandhi the peculiar honor of being one of two Hindus who have better exemplified the teachings of the Sermon on the Mount, in modern India, than all the professional purveyors of the precepts of Jesus!

The above sentiments were publically expressed through the press. "A Firm Believer in Christ" writes a letter to the *Calcutta Journal* in defence of the *Second Appeal*. He says the publication "will enable us to form some idea of his [R.R.] acquirements, and cannot fail of producing in every *Christian*, great regard for the Author, and a strong interest concerning so illustrious an Individual: and the more we learn of his conduct the more will he be raised in our estimation."[96]

Another letter from "A Christian" to the same paper refers to Ram Mohan as a "very remarkable person." The writer is aware of theological differences but recognizes "many able and excellent passages" in his pamphlet which he commends for public quotation. He signs off saying: "I cannot conclude without expressing my approbation at the candid and excellent temper shewn by Ram Mohun Roy."[97]

The editor of the *Calcutta Journal* appends a note to the above letter saying: "We agree entirely with our correspondent in the high praise due to Ram Mohun Roy for his temper and moderation, and we esteem highly his zeal and intelligence."[98]

Finally, from the vantage point of witnessing the entire controversy between the missionaries and the reformer, the *India Gazette* (May 17, 1824) editorialized its opinion. The statement speaks eloquently for the moral stature of Ram Mohan, and does justice to his formidable skills as a controversialist. The editor states:

> Though hitherto we have not in our paper, in any detailed manner, adverted to the labours of that distinguished Native, Rammohun Roy—still, we have been no disinterested spectator of them. *We say distinguished, because he is so among his own people, by caste, rank, and respectability; and among all men he must ever be distinguished for his philanthropy, his great learning, and his intellectual ascendancy in general.* As a man who has cut no mean figure in the republic of letters, and in the walks of philosophical enquiry, we have a right thus publicly to mention Rammohun Roy, and it is necessary that we should claim this right, lest it might be deemed indelicate in us to refer too pointedly to *a person whose great modesty of itself is an evidence of high genius, and certainly enhances its gifts.*

The *Gazette* then supports the editor of the *Unitarian Repository* in his taking exception to the attacks of the trinitarians. The editorial continues:

> We owe it to common sense and the cause of truth to declare that we entirely coincide in the Reverend Editor's opinion respecting *the attack on Rammohun, which really appears to us to have been about as injudicious and weak an effort of officious zeal as we ever heard of.* The effect of that attack was to rouse up a *most gigantic combatant in the Theological field*—a combatant who, we are constrained to say, has *not yet met with his match here* (italics supplied).[99]

The remarkable thing is that all of these eulogies were written by professing Christians. Indeed, Christians had good reason to be appreciative of the literary labors of this distinguished Hindu. Not only were his countrymen being benefited by an introduction to the ethics of the Christian system, Englishmen were being given back a part of Christianity which received short shrift in the preaching and publications of the Dissenters at Serampore. For instance, the Reverend Deocar Schmidt who had the dubious distinction of firing the first shot in this attack on the Raja, reduced Christianity, in his *Summary of the Scriptures*, to a somber "system of doctrines unencumbered with morality."[100] On balance there is much more doctrine in Ram Mohan's moral writings than there is morality in Schmidt's doctrinal writings.

Had the missionaries preached fewer of the doctrines and practiced more of the morality, they would have scored higher with the natives. A letter to the editor of the *Sambad Kaumudi* illustrates our meaning:

> Some days ago there was a Missionary Gentleman preaching the doctrines of Christianity to the Natives . . . . Desirous of hearing the discourse, I entered the bungalow, and found the gentleman engaged in a controversy with a Brahman on the subject of the Hindoo religion, which was conducted in a becoming manner, and with the use of polite language, asking him to corroborate his assertions by the authorities of the Shastru. In the course of this controversy, however, the Missionary gentleman thinking the Brahman had made a wrong quotation, said to him, "you are a low ignorant fellow," and made use of some other harsh expressions, which quite disheartened the poor Brahman, and frightened him into silence. The Missionary gentleman took this opportunity to dwell on the immoral character of the Hindoos. When he had done his preaching, I asked the favour of his answer to some enquiries I had to make respecting the Christian doctrines, and notwithstanding I repeated my request over and over again, he paid no attention to it, but silently stepped into his buggy and drove away.[101]

## IV. Collaboration with Unitarians and Presbyterians

The Baptists of Serampore were not the only Christians with whom Ram Mohan had dealings. We shall pursue some of these other relationships because they shed light on the question why Ram Mohan elevated Christian ethics above all other systems of ethics.

In 1823 Ram Mohan received a letter from the Reverend Henry Ware, Unitarian minister of Harvard College, requesting information on "the prospects of Christianity and the means of promoting its reception in India." One of Rev. Ware's questions is of special interest to us: "whether it be desirable that the inhabitants of India should be converted to Christianity, in what degree desirable, and for what reasons?" The reply is illuminating.

From the standpoints both of reason and the Bible, conversion to Christianity is not at all necessary, explains the Raja. The Bible plainly states that a simple belief in the unity of God accompanied by its appropriate expression in moral conduct is the only prerequisite for finding favor with God. He declares: "I am led to believe, from reason, what is set forth in scripture, that 'in every nation he that *feareth* God and worketh righteousness is accepted with him', in whatever form of worship he may have been taught to glorify God."[102]

However, Christianity does have a certain practical edge by virtue of its involvement with progressive movements in England and Europe; and "if properly inculcated, has a greater tendency to improve the moral and political state of mankind, than any other known religious system."[103]

By "properly inculcated" Ram Mohan meant the deemphasizing of doctrinal peculiarties so that pure theism is allowed to stand out. He welcomed Unitarianism because it was a branch of Christianity which had undergone this process of purification. He writes to Rev. Ware:

> It is impossible for me to describe the happiness I feel at the idea that so great a body of a free, enlightened, and powerful people, like your countrymen, have engaged in purifying the religion of Christ from those absurd, idolatrous doctrines and practices, with which the Greek, Roman and Barbarian converts to Christianity have mingled in it from time to time.[104]

In addition to his endorsement of Unitarians coming to labor in India, Ram Mohan also supported the Presbyterian Church of Scotland. He affixed his signature to a petition and memorial presented to the General Assembly of 1824 by Dr. Bryce, Church of Scotland Chaplain in Calcutta. The intent of the petition was to redirect "the attention of the Church of Scotland to British India as a field of missionary exertions."[105] Dr. Bryce acknowledges that he was encouraged by the approbation of Ram Mohan—"this eminently gifted scholar, himself a Brahman of high caste."[106]

Ram Mohan's own concurrence is stated thus:

> As I have the honour of being a member of the Congregation meeting in St. Andrew's Church (although not fully concurring in every article of the Westminster Confession of Faith), I feel happy to have an opportunity of expressing my opinion that, if the prayer of the memorial is complied with there is a fair and reasonable prospect of this measure proving conducive to the diffusion of religious and moral knowledge in India.[107]

Why did Ram Mohan support this petition of a trinitarian denomination? First, let it be noted that it was not without a reservation. The parenthetical disclaimer doubtlessly referred to the trinitarian articles of the Westminster Confession. But apparently both parties were prepared to make compromises in the interests of a working relationship —Ram Mohan on trinitarianism, and the Presbyterians on *Brahmanism*. This was probably the first true instance of ecumenism in India—not the narrower "ecumenism" that first led to the emergence of the Church of South India from among different Christian denominations, but a wider ecumenism which transcended the boundaries of two major faiths—Hinduism and Christianity.

The working relationship which Ram Mohan wished to cultivate was with the view to spreading Western education. Of all the demoninations it seemed that the Presbyterians were most adept in the field of education. Alexander Duff was an educator *par excellence*, but he had good support from his other Presbyterian colleagues. The Raja had hoped that if the Presbyterians kept their doctrinal instructions in a low key and got down to the chief business of educating Indian children in European learning and Christian morality, it would improve their hearts and minds, and the collaboration would prove worthwhile.

The above remarks should clarify Ram Mohan's courtship of Christianity. By extending the Hindu hand of fellowship, he had hoped to make India part of an extended family, indeed, the family of man, endowing the country with social and educational acquisitions which would boost the character of his people toward mobility and enlightenment.

## V. The Conversion of the Reverend William Adam

One of Ram Mohan's overtures won over the Reverend William Adam, well-reputed for his Oriental and classic acquirements and a member of the Baptist Missionary Society of Calcutta.

Ram Mohan had been busy translating the gospels into Bengali because he considered the two translations of Dr. William Carey and Mr. Ellerton "to abound in the most flagrant violations of native idiom."[108] Two missionaries, William Yates and William Adam, assisted him in the project.

Yates persevered with the translation until they came to the fourth gospel, chapter one, verse three. The problem was with the Greek preposition, *dia*. At first there was consensus that it be translated by the word "through," which made the text read: "All things were made through him." The next day Yates had a change of mind. He felt the translation smacked of Arianism and insisted that "through" be replaced with the preposition "by." Adam reports that during these discussions Ram Mohan "sat, pen in hand, in dignified reticence, looking or listening, observing all, but saying nothing."[109]

Yates dropped out of the group while he could. The force of erudition and personality emanating from Ram Mohan was an influence too potent to resist for very long. It was even rumored that Yates had left the Christian fold. This he hastily disclaimed by publishing his *Essays* in defence of important scriptural doctrines as a reply to the two *Appeals* (1822).

Adam, on the other hand, allowed himself to be led by reason into realms where "faith" feared to tread. The steps leading to his conversion are narrated by him in a letter addressed to N. Wright, dated May 7, 1821.

It is now several months since I began to entertain some doubts respecting the Supreme Deity of Jesus Christ, suggested by the frequent discussions with Rammohun Roy, whom I was endeavouring to bring over to the belief of that Doctrine, and in which I was joined by Mr. Yates, who also professed difficulties on the subject.[110]

The missionary community went into a state of shock when they learned of Adam's disavowal of trinitarian Christianity. It was a bitter pill to swallow: that a missionary who had come to convert the heathen was himself converted by one, *and that* while studying the Christian scriptures!

Feeling great insult to their pride, it was common for the missionaries to deride their erstwhile colleague as "the Second fallen Adam."

## VI. Unitarian Connections

The Unitarian sentiments shared by Ram Mohan, William Adam, and other seekers, led to the formation of the Calcutta Unitarian Committee in September 1821. These were not the first Unitarians in India. That honor goes to the South Indian Unitarians who organized a congregation on December 19, 1813, under the leadership of William Roberts, a "native of Carnatick." Unlike the southerners who came from poor, uneducated backgrounds and became full-fledged converts to Unitarianism, the Calcutta group comprised men who were peers of Ram Mohan in learning and wealth and, though staunch pillars of the movement, were not converts to Unitarianism. They all remained good Hindus. Their theism was broad enough to accommodate this movement from the West. The inclusive nature of this belief is clearly delineated by Ram Mohan in a tract, *Answer of a Hindoo to the Question, Why do you frequent a Unitarian Place of worship, instead of numerously attended established Churches?* Articles IX and X crystallize his answers:

> Because Unitarians reject polytheism and idolatry under every sophisticated modification, and thereby discountenance all the evil consequences resulting from them.

> Because Unitarians believe, profess, and inculcate the doctrine of the divine unity—a doctrine which I find firmly maintained both by the Christian Scriptures and by most of our ancient writings commonly called the Vedas.[111]

In line with these beliefs, the immediate aim of the Unitarian Committee was not "proselytism," but "to remove ignorance and superstition, and to furnish information respecting the evidences, the duties, and the doctrines of the religion of Christ."[112] It sought to accomplish this goal by "education, rational discussion, and the publication of books both in English and in the native languages."[113] The Committee hailed Ram Mohan as "one of our warmest supporters," and that with good reason. The Unitarian Press, the Anglo-Hindu school, and the Unitarian minister in the person of Mr. Adam, were all dependent on Ram Mohan for financial support. A true test of heart is money, and Ram Mohan generously invested both in the Unitarian cause.

Ram Mohan's swing towards Unitarianism made him the subject of international discussion with correspondents from England and America.

His English connections were such influential Unitarians as: Dr. Thomas Rees, Sir John Bowring, the Reverend Thomas Belsham, the Reverend W. J. Fox, Harriet Martineau, Robert Dale Owen, Dr. Lant Carpenter, and Dr. J. B. Estlin.

In a letter to Dr. Thomas Rees of London (1824), Ram Mohan thanks the Unitarian Committee for reprinting his compilation of the *Precepts* and the two *Appeals*, which he takes as a distinguished mark of their approbation. He exults that there are many friends in England and America who are "engaged in attempting to free the originally pure, simple and practical religion of Christ from the heathenish doctrines," and prays that the success of these gentlemen be as great as that of "Luther and others, to whom the religious world is indebted for laying the first stone of religious reformation, and having recommended the system of distinguishing divine authority from human creeds, and the practice of benevolence from ridiculous outward observances."[114]

He concludes his letter to Rees with appreciation for the gift of books to their library. Others, such as J. B. Estlin of Bristol, also donated books which were gladly received inasmuch as the Baptist library, heretofore relied upon by Ram Mohan, was now *verboten*.

Of greater interest to us was Ram Mohan's connections with America. Journals such as the *Monthly Repository* and *Christian Reformer* carried news across the Atlantic of this "East Indian apostle of Unitarianism." In his informative article, "Rammohan Ray and American Unitarians," Professor Bruce Robertson states:

> Ray's initial attraction was not simply the theological position taken in his translations from the *Upanisads* and in his *Precepts* and *Appeals to the Christian Public*, but also his self-tutored originality and the grand style of his polemic against his opponents. It reminded them of their recent pitch battle with the Calvinists. In Rammohan, they had both a fellow-laborer and a trophy in the battle for truth. Rammohan Ray and the American were brought together by a common adversary, and their friendship was cemented by common assumptions.[115]

We shall now examine some of the ethical elements of these assumptions as they appear in the correspondence available.

The Reverend Jared Sparks of the First Independent Church of Baltimore was the first known correspondent with Ram Mohan (letter dated March 3, 1822). He had literary, journalistic and educational interests, the last placing him in the presidency of Harvard from 1849–1853. A political liberal, Sparks was acquainted with several public figures including Thomas Jefferson, James Madison, John Quincy

Adams, Henry Clay, and Alexis de Tocqueville.[116] A liberal also in religion, Sparks was intrigued by the unitive character of Ram Mohan's theology as culled from tracts and reviews of his *Precepts* and his first *Appeal*.

Ram Mohan's reply to Sparks rings with optimism. With naive hope, he says he has every reason to believe that true Christianity, "hidden under the veil of heathen doctrines and practices," will soon emerge because "many lovers of truth are zealously engaged in rendering the religion of Jesus clear from corruptions."[117]

He comments on the missionary activity in India. He has praise for the missionaries' zeal and sense of duty, but disapproves of the means they have adopted. "They always begin with such obscure doctrines as are calculated to excite ridicule instead of respect."

From an ethical perspective, he finds the whole missionary enterprise unfair. If an organization plans to substitute its own values for the prevailing values of the land, it is duty bound to prove its own superiority. This, the missionaries have been unable to establish.[118]

At the same time he finds it of great satisfaction to his conscience that "the doctrines inculcated by Jesus and his apostles are quite different from those human inventions which the Missionaries are persuaded to profess, and entirely consistent with reason and the revelation delivered by Moses and the prophets."[119] He is therefore prepared to support the religion of Jesus at the risk of his own life. And then in words anticipating Gandhi, he says: "I rely much on the force of truth, which will, I am sure, ultimately prevail."[120]

He concludes his letter on a high note of morality, declaring that his view of Christianity in representing all mankind as the children of one eternal father, enjoins them to love one another, without making any distinction of country, caste, colour, or creed."[121]

Such zeal in the cause of truth delights Sparks, who assures him of his admiration for the firmness and ability with which he engages in the work of reformation.[122]

By this time, interest in India was mounting among the American Unitarians. The next few years saw the organization of a society for obtaining information respecting the state of religion in India (1825), and a fund was started for the British Indian Unitarian Association of Calcutta. An important figure in the proceedings was the Reverend Henry Ware, Sr., who held the Hollis Chair of Divinity at Harvard. A letter from William Adam to Channing (1823) was directed to Ware who initiated correspondence with Adam and Roy. He wanted to know the "prospects of Christianity and the means of promoting its reception in India."

Ram Mohan replied on February 2, 1824, giving candid answers to specific questions. In regards to the possibility of making real converts to Christianity and the efficacy of using Bible translations for this purpose, the answers are negative. The accounts of success by the Seram-

pore Baptists are incorrect and misleading. The few converts that exist
have come out of low castes, and their motives for embracing Christianity are often materialistic. It is difficult to proselytize Hindus due to
their reliance on the sanctity of their books and dread of losing caste.
Unitarians would have a greater appeal for the upper classes because of
the rational orientation of their beliefs; but among the lower classes,
their lot would be the same as that of the trinitarians.

Under these circumstances it is advisable that a few gentlemen, "well
qualified to teach English literature and science, and noted for their
moral conduct," should be employed to work with members of the
lower classes.

As for the respectable natives, there are many who thirst after European knowledge and literature, but who would be put off by the "mystical doctrines" of the missionaries. The appeal of an English education
is so great that "two-thirds of the native population of Bengal would be
exceedingly glad to see their children educated in English learning.
Christian educators of moral stature would not fail to impress every intelligent mind, provided their religion is represented "in its genuine
sense."

Throughout this long epistle, the ethical concerns of the writer are
uppermost. He is distressed by the padding of their statistics by the Serampore Baptists. He considers it farcical that missionaries not only con-
done, but seem to encourage Hindus and Muslims to become "rice
Christians" out of a vanity for large congregations. He bemoans the
sway of prejudice; the inability for openness; and winces at the tripe
peddled in the name of Christ which is as irrational as the creeds it crit-
icizes. Enlightenment that is born of the best known in Western art and
science, and tempered by morality, is the only way for securing comfort
and happiness for all classes to enjoy.

In anticipation of assurances of support from England and America,
the Unitarian Committee, spearheaded by Adam and Ram Mohan, organized a Unitarian Mission in Calcutta. Ram Mohan contributed Rupees 5000 to the treasury.

It seems every Christian denomination at some time made a bid to
win this Hindu reformer into its fold. In the summer of 1820 or 1821,
Dr. Middleton, Bishop of Calcutta, tried to angle him into the Anglican
Church by using special bait. He expatiated on "the grand career
which would be open to him by a change of faith." "He would be honoured in life and lamented in death, honoured in England as well as in
India; his name would descend to posterity as that of the modern Apostle of India."[123]

For Ram Mohan, the incident was reminiscent of the devil taking Jesus to a very high mountain, and showing him all the kingdoms of the
world and their magnificence. "Everything will I give you," he said to
him, "if you will fall down and worship me." The reply of Jesus was, in
effect, the response of the Brahmin to the Bishop: "Thou shalt worship
the Lord thy God and him only shalt thou serve" (Matthew 4: 11).

## VII. The Brahmanical Magazine

Between the years 1821 and 1823, a second line of controversy developed between Ram Mohan and the Serampore Baptists. The feud was triggered by the 14 July, 1821 publication of a letter in the *Samachar Darpan*, a Bengali weekly published by the Baptists of Serampore. The writer of the letter adduced certain philosophical and ethical arguments against the Hindu *shastras* and invited responses through the columns of the paper.

Ram Mohan obliged with a rebuttal, but the editor refused to publish it. Not one to be easily discouraged, Ram Mohan thereupon launched the *Brahmanical Magazine* (with its Bengali version, *Brahmana Sevadhi* ) "for the purpose of answering the objections against the Hindoo religion."[124] The preface to the first edition questions the ethics of the missionary enterprise when it is aided and abetted by the rulers of the land. During the first thirty years of their occupation of Bengal, the British gave the impression—by word and conduct—that they would not interfere with the religion of their subjects. However, events of the following two decades witnessed a radical shift in policy with missionaries publicly endeavoring to convert Hindus and Muslims. They not only exalt their own religion, but debase that of others, and bribe the natives to believe.

Ram Mohan considers such proselytizing of a subject people a breach of ethics. He is not against proselytism *per se*, but against its indulgence by rulers who always have the upper hand. He explains that the rights of the people of Bengal have been encroached upon by the British whom they fear, in a manner which cannot be justified before God or man: "For wise and good men always feel disinclined to hurt those that are of much less strength than themselves, and if such weak creatures be dependent on them and subject to their authority, they can never attempt, even in thought, to mortify their feelings."[125]

The preface continues with Ram Mohan pointing out that India has been a prey to degradation by conquerors because her own civilization has been too humane to learn the art of warfare, and because her own ranks have been dangerously divided by caste. As a result, the present situation in India is no different than ancient times when the Greeks and Romans, who were immoral idolaters, scorned their Jewish subjects who professed belief in one God. The English rulers are intoxicated by the same vaunting pride, and it is therefore not surprising that they should act toward their hapless subjects with the same derision. The missionaries who belong to the same race as the rulers, inspire the same fear in the natives, and thereby exercise an unfair leverage over them.

Ram Mohan then appeals to another side of the English character—their pride in thinking of themselves as the guardians of justice in the eyes of the whole world. He reminds them that inasmuch as the British are celebrated for their humanity, fairness, and equity, "it would tend to destroy their acknowledged character if they follow the example of the former savage conquerors in disturbing the established religion of the country." It is contrary to reason and justice to propagate a religion by resorting to abuse, insult, and material inducement. If they can prove the superior truth of the Christian religion in a manner that is fair and just, "many would of course embrace their doctrines," but failing this, "they should not undergo such useless trouble, nor tease Hindoos any longer by their attempts at conversion."[126]

Moving from the preface, we come to Ram Mohan's reply to the letter in the *Samachar Darpan* which attempts to prove the follies of the Hindu *shastras*, and thereby discredit their authority. In the first number of the *Magazine*, four strictures advanced against the doctrines of the *Vedanta* are discussed. Throughout his discussion, Ram Mohan shows that to every belief there is a surface and a depth. The surface divides, but the depth unites. The Christians' problem is that they look at Hindu beliefs on the surface; if they were only to look into the depth dimension of things, they would discover beliefs that are not too dissimilar to their own, and in some respects, even superior. The failure to make this transition from surface to depth, places the Christians in embarrassing violation of the two precepts of Jesus: that you must first remove the beam from your own eye before you attempt to remove the speck of dust from your neighbor's eye; and that it is folly to strain at a gnat and swallow a camel. A few examples will suffice.

Replying to the criticism against the supremacy and eternity of *Maya*, Ram Mohan answers that "the followers of the *Vedanta* (in common with Christians and Musalmans who believe God to be eternal) profess also the eternity of all his attributes."[127] Since *Maya* is the creating power of God, the Vedanta calls it eternal. If it is improper to consider the attributes of God eternal, "then such impropriety applies universally to all religious systems, and the *Vedanta* cannot alone be accused of this impropriety."[128]

Again, the doctrines of the *Nyaya Shastra* are faulted because they declare that, though God is one and the souls are many, both are imperishable; that space, time, and atoms are eternal; that "the power of creation resides in God in a peculiarly united relation;" that God regulates the moral life of the soul; and that his will is immutable. On the basis of such doctrines, it is held, that God cannot be considered the true creator of the world because he creates with already existing matter, etc.

Ram Mohan replies that all theistic believers, whether followers of *Nyaya Shastra* or Christians, believe that God is eternal, and that the soul has no end. Both profess that the soul is subject to future rewards or punishments within the governance of God. "If any fault be found with these doctrines, then the system of the *Nyaya* and of Christianity both must be equally subject; for both systems maintain these doctrines."[129]

He is saying in effect, let us play fairly; here is a case of the pot calling the kettle black. The question of fairness is taken up in another instance which Ram Mohan exposes in the second number of the *Magazine.*

The *Samachar Darpan* anathematized the *Puranas* and the *Tantras* as absurd and unreasonable, pointing out that whereas some *shastras* speak of the unity, omnipresence and incomprehensibility of God, this literature represents deity as many, as localized, and as having relationships.

Ram Mohan draws attention to the fact that "there is no end" of the *Tantras* and *Puranas*. Some are authoritative; others are not. The difference between authoritative and non-authoritative literature is concurrence with the *Vedas*. As Manu declares: "All *smritis* which are contrary to the *Veda*, and all atheistical works, are not conducive to future happiness: they dwell in darkness." Yet, the missionaries, either ignoring or ignorant of this canonical principle, seize on the darkest and least authoritative portions of the *Tantras* and *Puranas* to exhibit Hinduism in the worst light.[130]

Having given this first lesson in Hindu exegesis, Ram Mohan proceeds to the charge of absurdity. In order to prove the errors of the *Puranas* and *Tantras*, critics say that the *Puranas* represent God as possessing various names and forms, being husband, father, subject to the senses, and dependent on the body. Ram Mohan humbly asks the Christian gentlemen "whether or not they call Jesus Christ, who is possessed of the human form, and also the Holy Ghost, who is possessed of the dove shape, the very God?"[131] He lists all the human features attributed to Jesus in the gospels and says to the missionaries: If you acknowledge all this, then you cannot fault the *Puranas*, charging that in them, names and forms are attributed to God, thus denying his omnipresence; that God is a sensate being; and that he is considered as having a wife and child. All the errors you point out, such as the plurality of gods, their sensual indulgence and their locality, are applicable to you in a complete degree. Should you reply that everything is possible with God, no matter how contrary to the laws of nature, this argument could be applied equally by the Hindus to their incarnations, as you do to yours. The venerable Vyasa has spoken truthfully in the *Mahabharata*:

> O king! a person sees the faults of another although they are like the grain of mustard seed, but although his own faults are big as the Bel fruit, looking at them he cannot perceive them.[132]

Actually, the Raja continues, the case of the Hindu scriptures against the Christian scriptures is not quite equal. Whereas Hinduism looks upon the anthropomorphism of the *Puranas* and the *Tantras* as pedagogically intended for those who are ignorant and lacking higher insight; Christianity elevates its anthropomorphism to the level of absolute truth.

In the course of his criticism, the editor of the *Darpan* expressed his joy at "perceiving that the natives have begun to arouse themselves from that state of morbid apathy and insensibility which is a certain symptom of moral death and of universal corruption of manners." Ram Mohan exposes the editor's smug righteousness in the concluding section of the third number of the *Magazine*. As to "morbid apathy," it is obvious that the editor is unaware of the literary endeavors of the natives of Bengal, producing "hundreds of works on different subjects."[133] On "moral death" ascribed to the Hindu, he says, a comparison might easily be drawn "between the domestic conduct of the natives and that of the inhabitants of Europe, to show where the grossest deficiency lies." And as the abusive terms made use of by the editor, calling the Hindu religion a child of the "father of lies," etc., Ram Mohan says, "common decency prevents me from making use of similar terms in return."[134]

Notwithstanding his humble request to refrain from offensive language in literary debate, Ram Mohan was surprised to find that the Baptist press had issued a tract charging the doctrines of the *Vedas* with atheism. This induced our indefatigable polemicist to publish the fourth number of the *Brahmanical Magazine* after a lapse of two years.

In a morally elevated style, he says in his preface that, in keeping with the liberal and universal spirit of tolerance which is "a fundamental principle of Hindooism," he is ill disposed to oppose any system of religion, much less Christianity. But when the missionaries do not scruple to wound Hindu feelings by making indiscreet assaults upon their revered *Vedas*, "should he submit to such wanton aggression without endeavouring to convince these gentlemen, that, in the language of their own Scriptures, they 'strain at a gnat and swallow a camel' (Matt. XXIII.24)?" Hence, the missionaries may possibly "learn *from experience* a lesson of *Charity*, which they are ready enough to inculcate upon others while overlooking, at the same time, the precept given by their God: 'Do unto others as you would wish to be done by;' in other words, if you wish others to treat your religion respectfully, you should not throw offensive reflections upon the religion of others."[135]

In Chapter Two, Ram Mohan faces the charge of atheism which, in the theological definition of the missionaries, meant denial of belief in the Trinity and atonement. He meticulously puts forth reasons why Hindus reject these doctrines of Christianity.

First, in respect to the doctrine of Trinity, he states that it is not only diametrically opposite to the senses, to experience, to the uniform course of nature, and to the first axioms of reason, but that the most celebrated writers of the church palpably contradict one another in offering explanations. He presents ten contrasting explanations and asks if these explanations of the Trinity, given by leading theologians, are not capable of puzzling any inquirer, if not driving him to atheism? Were a Hindu or Muslim prepared to become a Christian, "would he not sincerely repent of his rashness" upon discovering that the internal differences of this religion are as wide as the East is from the West? Would he not be amazed "that a nation who are so celebrated for their progress in the arts and sciences, for the enjoyment of political and civil liberty, and for their freedom of inquiry and discussion, should neglect their religious faith so much as to allow it still to stand upon the monstrously absurd basis of popery?"

Just as moral categories entered his critique of the doctrine of Trinity, they do so again in his critique of the doctrine of atonement. In fact, he questions this whole doctrine on moral grounds.

In the theology of the Baptists, the doctrine stated that human sin offended God's holiness and had to be punished. Divine justice had to prevail over divine mercy. To do justice to the holiness of God the Father, God the Son, in wondrous compassion, took the form of a man and offered his sinless life on the cross as a vicarious sacrifice for the sins of the world.

Ram Mohan finds these views untenable on four counts. First he questions the split between justice and mercy in the being of God. He asks:

> Is it not evident, that God the Father is more strict about the observance of Justice than God the Son? and that God the Father was less liable to the influence of Mercy than God the Son? and that God the Holy Ghost manifested neither Mercy nor Justice in the sacrificial atonement? Do not these circumstances completely overthrow the doctrine which these Gentlemen preach, viz., that God the Father, Son, and Holy Ghost are equally just and merciful?[136]

Second, the doctrine of atonement views divine justice according to the standard of human justice. That is, just as a human judge cannot allow his compassion to interfere in a capital crime, but must punish it with death, so also, God could do no other than ask for death. For the sake of argument, Ram Mohan accepts this view of divine justice, but questions whether it is compatible with the canons of justice "to release millions of men each guilty of sins unto death, after inflicting death upon another person (whether God or man), who never participated in their sins, even though that person had voluntarily proposed to embrace death? or whether it is not a great violation of justice, according to the human notion of it, to put an innocent person to a painful death for the transgressions of others."[137]

Third, in the case of sins against men, such as theft or injury, is it not a disregard of justice, by human standards, that sins perpetrated against one person should be absolved by another, without his concurrence in that pardon? Is it not an infringement of justice by the Savior to "wash away with his blood" the sins committed by one man against another with total disregard to that individual's sufferings? "But if Christians really imagine that true believers in the vicarious sacrifice of Christ have their past sins as well against God as against men, washed away by his blood, are they not extremely presumptuous and culpable in inflicting punishment upon their fellow Christians for any crime they may have committed, knowing that atonement has already been made for it by the blood of their God, which was shed on the cross?" Yet Christians daily exact punishment on one another, despite the vicarious sacrifice of their Lord.

Fourth, since faith is necessary for the acquisition of Christ's meritorious sacrifice, it seems forgiveness is not the result of mercy universally shown to all men, as is preached, but proceeds from a reciprocal consideration. This means that the majority of mankind, being isolated and unaware of the Christian means of salvation, must rely for their spiritual well-being on a virtuous life and sincere repentance for their sins. Yet, Christians inconsistently and umercifully condemn these poor souls for presuming to think that they can work out their own salvation by moral living. This makes the Christians who boast of their faith the ones more guilty of pride and self-sufficiency, since for this single merit of being born in a Christian land "they think themselves fully entitled to salvation; and at the same time they contemn and deprecate the merits of others, who nevertheless consider that both faith and good works proceed from the grace of God."[138]

These palpable flaws in the Christian doctrine of atonement pose the moral dilemma of how people can ascribe unreasonableness to one system of religion, on the thinnest of grounds, while closing their eyes to gross irrationality in their own system:

> For, is there any notion more unreasonable and conducive to immoral practices than the idea that God *has blood*, and that blood is offered *by God* to reconcile *to God* such men as, at any time during their lives, place faith in that *blood of God, however guilty* these men may be of offending God and injuring their fellow-creatures.[139]

It is clear that in the judgment of Ram Mohan, Hindus and Muslims should be mercifully delivered from such unreasonable and unethical beliefs as Trinity and atonement, or else their last state shall be worse than their first. Jesus had such "play actors" as the missionaries in mind when he said:

> Alas for you, you scribes and Pharisees, play actors that you are! You lock the doors of the kingdom of Heaven in men's faces; you will not go in yourselves neither will you allow those at the door to go inside.

> Alas for you, you scribes and pharisees, play actors! You scour sea and land to make a single convert, and then you make him twice as ripe for destruction as you are yourselves.[140]

Ram Mohan brings his defense against atheism to a close by stating his own "religious creed" in which, following the model of the *Gita*, ethics is defined as "divine homage." He declares:

> In conformity with the Precepts of our ancient religion, contained in the holy *Vedanta*, though disregarded by the generality of moderns, we look up to One Being as the animating and regulating principle of the whole collective body of the universe, and as the origin of all individual souls which in a manner somewhat similar, vivify and govern their particular bodies; and we reject Idolatry in every form and under whatever veil of sophistry it may be practised, either in adoration of an artificial, a natural, or an imaginary object. The divine homage which we offer, consists solely in the practice of *Daya* or benevolence towards each other, and not in a fanciful faith or in certain motions of the feet, legs, arms, head, tongue or other bodily organs, in pulpit or before a temple.[141]

## VIII. Ram Doss and Rivals

By the beginning of 1823, Ram Mohan was convinced that the Bible was too important to be left to the Christians. He therefore proposed starting a monthly magazine in the spring of 1823 to make a critical study of the Bible in the light of current doctrines. The offer for publication was immediately taken up by Dr. R. Tytler, a truculent trinitarian. Though an M.D., he nursed pretensions of being a doctor both of body *and soul*. When Ram Mohan refused publication of his article unless it was endorsed by a theologian—a device to keep amateurs out —the doctor's blood pressure rose and he vented a bilious attack, haranguing the Hindu "heretic" and denigrating his damnable deities. He wields his pen like a scalpel when Ram Mohan informs him that he is indifferent to his particular belief, whether he be a follower of Christ or a believer in the divinity of his "Holy *Thakoor Trata* Ram, or Munoo."[142]

Tytler is appalled that Ram Mohan should place his belief in the "holy Saviour" on par with "a Hindu's belief in his *Thakoor*!!!"[143]

The doctor obviously needed a good dose of his own medicine, and Ram Mohan decided to supply it generously. This episode brings out a humorous side to the Raja's personality which is too often overlooked by writers. They concentrate on the gifts of his mind; but humor was a gift of his heart. It reveals his measure of serenity and confidence in his grasp of life. Humor has been called "a peerless weapon of the British when dealing with foreign countries." With Ram Mohan, the shoe was on the other foot. In his writings we often hear him laugh at the British, but gravity is concealed behind the jest.[144]

Ram Mohan engages Tytler under the pseudonym of Ram Doss. Through private and public correspondence, he makes four challenges to this irate Englishman, first to solicit his cooperation in opposing the obnoxious Unitarian; and second, "to refute his insinuations against Hindooism and prove that it was based on the same sacred basis (the manifestation of God in the flesh) with Dr. Tytler's own Faith."[145] He points out striking resemblances between Christian stories of incarnation and Hindu stories. Ram was of royal lineage, as Christ was of the lineage of David. He too performed wonderful miracles, was tempted by the devil, ascended up to heaven, and is worshipped by millions.[146] There is a numerical difference between the Three Persons of the Christian Trinity and the Hindu belief in three hundred and thirty millions of Persons in the Godhead.

> But all such numerical objections are founded on the frail basis of human reason, which we well know is fallible, you must admit that the same omnipotence, which can make three ONE and one THREE, can equally reconcile the unity and Plurality of three hundred and thirty millions, both being supported by a sublime mystery which far transcends all human comprehension.[147]

In view of these common beliefs between Hindus and Christians, it is proper to cultivate "a good understanding and brotherhood among all who have correct notions of the manifestation of God in the flesh, that we may cordially join and go hand in hand opposing and, if possible, extirpating the abominable notion of a SINGLE GOD, which strikes equally at the root of Hindooism and Christianity."[148]

The editor of the *Bengal Hurkaru* refused to insert Ram Doss' letter claiming a common basis for Christianity and Hinduism on the plea that the claim is false. In his opinion there was a real difference between the doctrine of the divine incarnation in Christianity and the Hindu belief that God appears in the shape of material images.

Ram Doss retorts to this prejudiced journalism by asking if there is a single Hindu alive who thinks that "the divine Ram, the son of Dushuruth by Koushilya his mother according to the flesh, was composed either of wood, stone or metal?" Of course, Hindu temples are full of effigies of the holy Ram, but these are installed "for the pious purpose of attracting the attention of devotees to that Divine Incarnation—although many good Hindoos do not consider such representation as necessary, and worship Ram directly without the intervention of any sensible object." No more than the image of Jesus in churches is to be identified with his person, must the representations of the divine Ram in Hindu temples be identified with his sacred person.[149]

Once again Ram Mohan proved too clever a controversialist for his challengers. Deprived of arguments, Tytler could only return torrents of abuse and resort to evasive answers which proved he had lost the case. His embarrassed Lord might well have said to the good doctor: "Physician, heal thyself."

With Tytler in trouble, a friend, calling himself "A Christian," came forward to rescue him with a letter to the *Hurkaru*. With patronizing charity he finds it "gratifying to the lovers of science, to behold a few intelligent Hindoos emerging from the degraded ignorance and shameful superstition, in which their fathers for so many centuries have been buried." At the same time he finds it a case of "biting the hand that feeds you" when "these very individuals who are indebted to Christians for the civil liberty they enjoy, as well as for the rays of intelligence now beginning to dawn on them, should in the most ungenerous manner insult their benefactors by endeavouring to degrade their religion, for no other reason, than because they cannot comprehend its sublime Mysteries."[150]

Ram Doss is cited for making the offensive insinuation that Hinduism and Christianity are founded on the same basis. He then appeals to the Christian readers:

> Are you so far degraded by Asiatic effeminacy as to behold with indifference your holy and immaculate RELIGION thus degraded by having it placed on an equality with Hindooism—with rank idolatry—with disgraceful ignorance and shameful superstition?[151]

Ram Doss's reply is a hard-hitting statement defending Hindu culture and religion, its echoes being heard down the corridors of time. With the stout heart of a true nationalist, he tackles each of the aspersions that have been hurled against his people.

He is prepared to grant India's indebtedness to England if the "ray of intelligence" alluded to meant the introduction of mechanical arts; but not so in respect to science, literature, or religion. He says history can prove that "the world was indebted to *our ancestors* for the first dawn of knowledge which sprang up in the East, and thanks to the Goddess of Wisdom, we have still a philosophical and copious language of our own, which distinguishes us from other nations who cannot express scientific or abstract ideas without borrowing the language of foreigners."[152]

The slur against "Asiatic effeminacy," he says, overlooks the fact that Jesus and all of the Old Testament prophets were Asiatics, "so that if a Christian thinks it degrading to be born or to reside in Asia, he directly reflects upon them."[153]

Answering the Christian boast whether the coming of Ram to the earth was heralded, as was the coming of Christ, by prophecies reaching back 4,000 years, Ram Mohan replies affirmatively, but with this difference: the Hindu prophecies were made by inspired men "more than 4,000 years previous to the event in the most precise and intelligible language; not in those ambiguous and equivocal terms found in the *Old Testament*, respecting the Incarnation of Jesus Christ, an ambiguity which it is well known has afforded our common enemies, the Unitarians, a handle for raising a doubt of Jesus Christ being a real Manifestation of God in the flesh."[154]

Did Ram perform miracles to demonstrate his divinity? The answer is yes. "The divine Ram performed miracles more stupendous, not before multitudes of ignorant people only, but in the presence of Princes and of thousands of learned men, and of those who were inimical to Hindooism."[155]

In answer to the question whether human character has ever been elevated so highly by any religion as by "the sweet influence of Christianity," Ram Doss illustrates from history that there has been no religion which has been "the cause of so much war and blood-shed, cruelty and oppression, for so many hundred years as this whose 'sweet influence' the Christian celebrates."

If there be any of exemplary character among Christians, it is wholly due to the benefits of their superior education; "a proof of which is, that others of the same rank in society, although not believers in Christianity, are distinguished by equal propriety of conduct, which is not the case with the most firm believers, if destitute of Education or without the means of improvement by mixing in company with persons, better instructed than themselves."[156]

The "Christian" considers it unjust for the Hindus to quarrel with Christianity because they cannot comprehend its sublime mysteries. He is informed that the roles can be reversed for the identical reason, and "since both these mysteries equally transcend the human understanding, one cannot be preferred to the other."[157]

In closing, Ram Doss rallies to the main issue, namely, the incarnation of deity as the common basis of Hinduism and Christianity. He argues that "If the manifestation of God in the flesh is possible, such possibility cannot be reasonably confined to Judea or Ayodhya, for God has undoubtedly the power of manifesting himself in either country and of assuming any colour or name he pleases." If this is not possible, as the infamous Unitarians contend, "such impossibility must extend to all places and persons." He therefore hopes that "the *Christian* will reflect with great seriousness on this subject" and will let him know the result.[158]

No results were forthcoming, so the correspondence concluded here. This controversy of Ram Doss and the "Christian" began on May 3, and ended on May 23, 1823.

## IX. Humble Suggestions

This is a convenient juncture at which to examine and evaluate Ram Mohan's moral attitudes toward the different religious groups which he confronted. Our task is made easy by having the entire material collated in a tract which Ram Mohan published on March 15, 1823, under the pseudonym of Prosanna Koomar Thakur. It is entitled *Humble Suggestions* and is chiefly intended to counsel his countrymen against indulging in the same opprobrious abuse as is meted out to them by the Christians. We have just been treated to the fiery rhetoric of Dr. Tytler who called Ram Mohan a "runnagate," and charged that both Hinduism and Unitarianism "proceeded from the Devil." Ram Mohan had heard that song before, but instead of allowing it to embitter him, he reflects upon the special implications of his religious beliefs and comes forth with the following ethical guidelines which are his *Humble Suggestions* for coexistence in a religiously pluralistic society.

Those who subscribe to the Vedic belief in the unity of God and who are prepared to regulate their conduct according to the Golden Rule, should be cordial towards "such of their own countrymen as maintain the same faith and practice, even though they have not all studied the Vedas for themselves, but have professed a belief in God only through an acquaintance with their general design."[159] All the followers of Guru Nanak, Dadu, Kabir, etc., should be treated as brothers.

Among Europeans, one should feel no reluctance to cooperate with Unitarians "merely because they consider Jesus Christ as the Messenger of God and their Spiritual Teacher; for oneness in the object of worship and sameness of religious practice should produce attachment between worshippers."[160]

As for Protestant Trinitarians, we "should act towards them in the same manner as we act towards those of our countrymen who, without forming an external image, meditate upon Rama and other supposed incarnations, and believe in their unity."[161]

In respect to Trinitarian Roman Catholics, it becomes us to act towards them in the same manner as we act towards such as believe Rama, etc., to be incarnations of God, and form external images of them. "For the religious principle of the two last-mentioned sects are one and the same with those of the two similar sects among Hindoos, although they are clothed in a different garb."[162]

When Protestants and Roman Catholics try to convert us—believers in the one and true God—"even then we should feel no resentment towards them, but rather compassion, on account of their blindness to the errors into which they themselves have fallen: since it is almost impossible, as everyday's experience teaches us, for men, when possessed of wealth and power, to perceive their own defects."[163]

The *Calcutta Journal* immediately responded with a smile at Ram Mohan's comparisons of Christian and Hindu sects because of his ignorance of Christian scriptures, but felt this theological naiveté should not deny him "the praise of liberality." "The charitable disposition he inculcates towards persons of a different faith, and forbearance towards even those whose speculative notions are the most abhorrent to one's mind, deserve, abstractedly considered, our unqualified approbation."[164]

The *Calcutta Christian Observer* was less charitable. It grudgingly recognizes the writer's "goodwill," but denounces it for its "sceptical liberalism" and suggests that "it would afford a powerful inducement to the friends of Christianity to endeavour to fill up with the divine doctrines and the holy precepts of the Bible, the void that will be caused in the native mind in proportion as the increase of knowledge banishes the fictions of heathen superstition. We cordially rejoice at every increase of Hindoo knowledge and liberality; but the following "humble suggestion" is a proof how little of sound theology or intelligible morality is to be expected from Oriental Unitarianism."[165]

## X. Return to Roots

This brings to an end Ram Mohan's struggles with the trinitarian Christians. The narrative of events makes it plain that the intemperate attack of the *Friend of India* upon the publication of the *Precepts of Jesus*, and all of the onslaughts that followed, threw Ram Mohan back into the lap of Hindu culture and religion. Without this barrage from the Baptists it is conceivable that, in his enthusiasm to synthesize Christianity with Hinduism, his liberal spirit could have carried him beyond the bounds justified by his Vedantic faith. The label, "Christian," ascribed to him by several ecclesiastical sources was more than wishful thinking, as biographers often suggest. There are good reasons for deducing that Ram Mohan was a Christian.

The Christ that steps out of the pages of the *Second Appeal* presents us with a strange encounter of a third kind—as mystifying as some of the Hindu incarnations Ram Mohan relegates to the realm of mythology. Jesus is not God incarnate. He is a man. But what sort of a man? He is fantastic as in "fantasy"! He is Superman! He lived with God before the creation of the world,[166] and God loved him before the world's foundation.[167] Being perfectly subject and obedient to the Father, he was commissioned to come to the world as chosen Messiah.[168] He alone deserves to be called "the Son of God."[169] He is the first born of every creature, and is superior to the angels.[170] His entrance into the world was by virgin birth—"the miraculous influence of God came upon Mary, so that though a Virgin, she bore a child."[171] God has committed to him the final judgment of all who have lived since creation.[172] And he has been endowed for this incomprehensible task with the gift of supernatural wisdom.[173]

All this . . . and yet a man? Trinitarians saw Jesus as a sinless man and reasoned against the background of their doctrine of original sin that a sinless man must be God in the flesh, "for all [men] have sinned and fallen short of the glory of God." "There is none righteous, no not one." Ram Mohan suggests that we look for another explanation. He asks the trinitarians if a sinless man is a *perfect man*. But our question to

Ram Mohan is: How *perfect* can *a man* be without ceasing to be a *man*; for angelic perfection is hardly part of the human estate. This type of "perfection" is beyond the realm of ethics, for, as the *Gita* points out, morality is a field of battle where combatants rise and fall.

Ironically, this wholesale deference to Christian theology was drastically changed at the hands of Christians. We are not suggesting that he changed his views about Jesus or his precepts, but that his tilt in the Christian direction was stopped or slowed down.

The years 1820 to 1823 were most formative in the life of Ram Mohan. We see him return to his roots. Earlier, he had some depreciative statements to make in respect to the *Puranas* and *Tantras*, but when the Hindu *shastras* were attacked, he rallied to their support.[174] Earlier, he could only see the identification of deity and icon in the mind of the Hindu worshipper, but Ram Doss declares that there is not a single Hindu who identifies the divine Ram with a material image.[175] Earlier, he was appalled by the moral lassitude of his people, and the superiority of biblical religion to elevate the conduct of the foreigners, but Ram Doss skips all that and informs "the Christian" that his people's hands are red with the blood of immoral wars, and that if some of them demonstrate superior ethics, it is wholly due to superior education.[176]

It is a tribute to the large-heartedness of Ram Mohan that he gave the missionaries so much credit when first associating with them. He thought they would understand and appreciate his universal faith which laid so much store by the insights of Christianity. He expected them to respond in kind. But when they maligned everything Indian, he felt he had to stand up and be counted for his people. It was one thing for a native reformer to criticize members of his own household in order *to lift them up*; it was another thing for foreign snobs to deride them in order *to put them down*.

The prophet says, "there is a time for everything," and now was the time for Ram Mohan to speak positively for his people out of the same love from which he spoke out earlier against the errors of their ways.

It is, again, a great tribute to this man that though rebuffed by the missionaries, he retained his good spirits. Professor William Theodore De Bary sees it differently. He points out that though Ram Mohan "urged his countrymen to feel no resentment toward the missionaries," he was "less than compassionate in his reply to a public letter charging him with having insulted the Christian religion."[177] However, it seems this eminent scholar may be mistaking a spirited defense for bitterness. Ram Mohan never did anything half-heartedly, and the pride of his people was at stake; a pride without which the people could never become a nation. De Bary loses sight of the fact that simultaneously with the struggle against the Baptists, Ram Mohan maintained close ties with the Presbyterian missionaries though they, too, were trinitarians. There was no bitterness here; he helped them in their projects, as we have seen.

In brief, Ram Mohan did not let personality mar the weightier issues of religion and morality. And one reason he could do this was because he had detached Christianity from Christians, and the Bible from believers. He did not fight against the Christians; he fought for Christianity purified from institutional accretions. He did not attack believers; he defended the Bible agains their narrow Calvinism. This was why, after the rebuff, there was no need for Ram Mohan to crawl into a cultural cocoon and develop xenophobia. Christianity in its essence was hardly the white man's religion. Jesus himself was an Asiatic! So Christianity still meant much to Ram Mohan, but the rebuffs and insults cautioned him against going overboard.

## XI. *Chariprashna Uttar*

We have just said that missionary hostility forced Ram Mohan to take a closer look at his own roots; but his understanding of Hinduism versus the Hindus was the same as that of Christianity versus the Christians. This is amply demonstrated by another hassle in which Ram Mohan found himself, initiated by an orthodox Hindu. This self-styled "Establisher of Religion" published his *Four Questions* through the Bengali weekly, *Samachar Darpan* (April 6, 1822). Ram Mohan replied through his *Answer to Four Questions (Chariprashna Uttar)*. Without going into details, the ethical thrust of Ram Mohan's answers was that Hinduism was more than a system of external rules and rituals. If taken legally and literally, it makes hypocrites of all adherents. In essence, it is knowing God and performing "those practices most beneficial to man."[178] His biographer sums up the controversy, saying it was "analogous to that between the 'tithing of mint and anise and cumin,' and 'the weightier matters of the law.' Against the Rabbinism of the Hindu religion, Rammohan appealed to its Propheticism."[179]

## XII. The Unitarian Experiment

The essence of propheticism, both Jewish and Muslim, is two-fold: monotheism expressed through ethical living. For seven years, from 1821 when he severed ties with the missionaries, to 1828, when he established the *Brahmo Samaj*, Ram Mohan functioned as a prophet-at-large under the auspices of Christian Unitarianism.

What was the particular mystique which attracted Ram Mohan to Unitarianism?

Part of the answer we have already noticed in his *Humble Suggestions*, and in the tract, *Answer of a Hindoo to the question, Why do you frequent a*

*Unitarian place of worship, instead of the numerously attended established Churches?* In the first document he refers to Unitarians as "those Europeans who believe God to be in every sense One, and worship Him Alone in spirit, and who extend their benevolence to man as the highest service to God."[180] The fact that they consider Jesus Christ as the messenger of God poses no problem "for oneness in the object of worship and sameness of religious practice should produce attachment between the worshippers."[181] In the second document Ram Mohan gives his reason why he prefers to worship in a Unitarian church: "because Unitarians believe, profess, and inculcate the doctrine of the divine unity—a doctrine which I find firmly maintained both by the Christian Scriptures and by our most ancient writings commonly called the *Vedas*."[182]

So the first reason why he associated with Christian Unitarians was because they subscribed to the same theology which he had previously discovered in Vedic and Islamic religion.

This still does not fully explain his preoccupation with Unitarianism for seven years. If monotheism was equally found in the Hindu *shastras*, why did he not invest his time and energy building a Vedic institution for its propagation? The answer is found in three areas.

First is in the area of morality. Ram Mohan placed a premium on the *Precepts of Jesus* as a means for elevating his countrymen. The Unitarians regarded the practice of these precepts as the highest service to God. Second is in the area of education. Indian children needed to be enrolled in Western schools, and Ram Mohan felt most confident about Unitarian missionaries doing the job best because they had none of the usual doctrines to disseminate through public education. Third, all of the above values needed embodiment in a community of believers. *Vedic* religion could not supply this communal structure because its religious self-expression was historically individualistic. What Hinduism lacked, Unitarianism supplied.

And so it was that Ram Mohan experimented with Unitarianism as a means for drawing people into the fold. Inspired by belief in one God and one humanity, together they could work toward the enlightenment and happiness of all people.

The experiment was doomed from the beginning because it lacked one essential element of communication, though Ram Mohan was not unaware of this component, and even criticized the missionaries for overlooking it. It was the element of indigenization. In a traditional society, only what was native was natural. What was good for Boston and Birmingham was not good for Bengal. So by 1823 Ram Mohan's Unitarian church closed its doors for lack of public response, and Mr. Adam, the minister, returned home broken-hearted.

## XIII. *The Brahmo Samaj*

Like a phoenix, a new theistic movement was born out of the ashes of the Unitarian Church, and was called the *Brahmo Samaj* (Divine Society). There are two accounts of its inception.

According to the first account, Ram Mohan and some of his disciples were returning from a Unitarian service when Tarachand Chakravarti and Chandrasekhar Dev raised the question: "What need is there for us to go to the prayer-house of strangers to perform worship? We ought to erect a house of our own in which to worship one God." This proposal is regarded as "the first germ of the *Brahmo Samaj*."[183]

The narrative continues that Ram Mohan soon acted on the proposal by consulting key comrades who helped him organize a meeting in which the proposal was adopted. Until their own place of worship could be secured, a house was rented from Ram Kamal Bose at 48 Chitpore Road.

According to the second account, Mr. Adam is the progenitor of the *Brahmo Samaj*. Upon his instigation and with financial support, a Hindu Unitarian Association was formed. However, though he was disappointed that it based its authority on the *Vedas* rather than on the Christian scriptures; nonetheless, he encouraged its formation as "a step towards Christianity."[184]

The two accounts are not necessarily contradictory. Adam could well have mooted the proposal with Ram Mohan, who only gave it careful consideration when it was promoted by Dev and his followers.

Regardless of who originated the idea, Adam or Dev, both were disciples of Ram Mohan and drew their energy and inspiration from him. The disciple was the proximate cause but the master was the primary cause. It was he who first sowed the seed of a universal religion in his *Gift to Monotheists*. The seed of *Vedantic* knowledge was distributed at Rangpur through meetings with representatives of various sects. Through the foundation of the *Atmiya Sabha*, the seed was disseminated through open discussions on many subjects. It was scattered far and wide by his translations of the *Upanishads* bearing the pure germ of monotheism. With the publication of the *Precepts* some of the seed fell among thorns, some on rocky ground, and some fell on fertile soil. Out of the good soil sprang the Unitarian church. For a while it blossomed, but its stock was too exotic to grow in Indian clime. The finest flower of this seed of universal religion was the *swadeshi* (indigenous) specimen of the *Brahmo Samaj*. Thus, the *Brahmo Samaj* had a long lineage, germinating in the mind of the master in diverse forms until the time for its denouement arrived.

On August 20, 1828, at 48 Chitpore Road, Jorasanko, Calcutta, the *Brahmo Samaj* became a reality—"the first religious movement of Modern India."[185] Tarachand Chakravarty was its secretary. The inaugural preacher was Ramchandra Vidyavagis, younger brother of Hariharananda Tirthaswami, Ram Mohan's longstanding *sannyasin* (holy man) friend. His sermon was on the spiritual worship of God, based on these words of the Hindu *shastras*:

> God is only One without an equal, in Whom abide all worlds and their inhabitants. Thus he who mentally perceives the Supreme Spirit in all creatures, acquires perfect equanimity, and shall be absorbed into the highest essence, even into the Almighty.[186]

Ram Mohan later described the discourse as "exhibiting the simplicity, comprehensiveness and tolerance which distinguish the religious belief and worship formerly adopted by one of the most ancient nations on earth and still adhered to by the more enlightened portion of their posterity."[187]

Regular meetings of the *Samaj* were held first on Saturday evenings. Mr. Adam describes the order of worship:

> The service begins with two or three of the Pandits singing, or rather *chanting* in the cathedral style, some of the spiritual portions of the Ved, which are next explained in the vernacular dialect to the people by another Pandit. This is followed by a discourse in Bengali . . . and the whole is concluded by hymns both in Sanskrit and Bengali, sung with the voice and accompanied by instrumental music, which is also occasionally interposed between other parts of the service. The audience consists generally of from 50 to 60 individuals, several Pandits, a good many Brahmins and all decent and attentive in their demeanour.[188]

The description of the *Brahmo* service highlights some matters of ethical concern.

First, there is the importance Ram Mohan attached to worship. Unlike modern Western philosophers for whom philosophy is only a view of life, for Ram Mohan it was both a *view* and a *way*, and worship made the twain one. Through chanting, meditation, listening openly to the word, ideas and values were internalized and assimilated. This existential posture was perfectly in accord with the lifestyle of the early Greek philosophers who, like Socrates, lived and died by their beliefs.

Next, there is the distinctly Christian form of worship, not only in its order, but in its congregational structure. Ram Mohan had opted for this form because he recognized that the individualism of Hindu worship lacked the social combustibility that comes from worship in unison with others. Coals separated from one another tend to flicker and fail, but brought together in one heap, they burn more brightly than the sum of their parts. For a religion geared to ethical action, this kind of internal combustion was a necessity. Collective experience was important where new ground was being broken, and it made for mutual reinforcement.

Adam decries Ram Mohan's use of the *Veda* as the basis of worship, so the charge goes, inasmuch as he did not believe in its "divine authority." This allegation makes Ram Mohan sound somewhat hypocritical in his religious practice. But this kind of criticism follows logically from the mind of a scriptural dogmatist. For such a mind, "divine authority" is tantamount to scriptural infallibility. You either believe that the scriptures are fully and equally inspired and are unerring in every way, or you are not a true believer at all. There is no middle ground for the fundamentalist mind. Of course Ram Mohan did not believe in the infallibility of the *Vedas*, but this did not mitigate the profound reverence he had for these bearers of ancient wisdom. Adam says he suspected Ram Mohan was using the 'Ved' "solely as an instrument for overthrowing idolatry"; and furthermore, it had lately gained ground in his mind that he was employing "Unitarian Christianity in the same way, as an instrument for spreading pure and just notions of God, without believing in the divine authority of the Gospel."[189]

It may be granted that Ram Mohan's objective of *Brahmo* worship was the overthrow of idolatry by introducing ideas of pure monotheism, and that his employment of Unitarian Christianity was for the purpose of "spreading pure and just notions of God." It follows that he would have had to believe sufficiently in the *Vedas* to find the pure monotheism, and in the gospels to find just notions of God; but if, indeed, he had such beliefs, how could he be accused of being purely utilitarian towards either the *Vedas* or the gospels? The only dimension of belief that is missing is dogmatic infallibility, and Ram Mohan was better off without it. Armed with the irrational weaponry of Biblical infallibility, the controversy of the idolater with the Christian only amounted to a shouting match. The author of *Tuhfat* had seen through the pretensions of all claims to scriptural authority, but as his other writings attest, he was smart enough not to throw the baby out with the bath water. The *Vedas* and the gospels were still sacred to Ram Mohan, though neither was considered the work of divine dictation.

The next point which merits discussion from an ethical point of view is the ministry of the *Brahmo Samaj*. It was for *Brahmins* only. Some scholars argue that Ram Mohan and his associates compromised their egalitarian principles on the subject of the ministry by yielding to orthodox caste rules. *Brahmanical* Orthodoxy demanded that the Hindu scriptures which were read as the first part of the divine service be recited only by *Brahmins* for *Brahmins*. The founders of the *Samaj* did not contest this rule; instead, they got around the problem by segregating an enclosure for the recital of the *Vedas* by *Brahmin* priests for the benefit of the *Brahmins* in the congregation. Non-*Brahmins* who included Hindus of all castes, and even Muslims and Christians, were allowed to participate in the two other phases of *Brahmo* worship, namely, listening to discourses in Bengali and the singing of devotional songs.

Some critics dub this arrangement as cowardly compromise because whereas Ram Mohan preached a humanistic message, in practice he deferred to caste. Others charge that, at heart, Ram Mohan was a caste-ridden Hindu and that all his so-called humanism was only window-dressing to make him appear progressive.

Neither of the above conclusions fit in with so much of the evidence to the contrary which we have documented in this book. We must therefore approach the problem from another perspective. It seems to me that this step has best been taken by Professor Dilip Kumar Biswas. He supports the evidence we have presented in his statement that "Roy definitely did not believe in the caste system." This is especially true in respect to his public writings and his private letters. At the same time he had to make the above compromise "under a peculiar circumstance over which he had no control." We give below Professor Biswas's lucid explanation in its entirety:

The *Vedas* are divided into two parts: (1) the *Mantras* (consisting of the Samhitas); (2) the *Brahmanas* (consisting of the Brahmanas, Aranyakas and Upanishads). All these collectively composed the Brahmanical *shruti*. Now, it is a well-known fact that the Bengali Brahmana community was traditionally deficient in the *Mantra portion of the shruti*. The Bengali Brahmana, inspite of his mastery over *Nyaya, smriti and Tantra*, had been the object of taunts and gibes from the Brahmanas of upper India for his "ignorance of the Vedas," throughout the ancient and medieval periods. The situation remained the same in the early years of the 19th. century. The charge was not altogether without foundation. For this reason the recitation of Vedic *Mantras* in Calcutta was *the monopoly of a community of Tailanga (Andhra) Brahmana residents of the city*, there being no Bengali Brahmana competent for the job. Roy had thus no other alternative before him than to requisition the services of these South Indian Brahmanas for the task of reciting the Vedic *Mantras* in the service of his Samaj. These southerners were men of uncompromising orthodoxy and could not be persuaded to recite the *Mantras* before a mixed audience consisting of men of all castes and communities. So Roy had to accept the situation. That this did not indicate his acceptance of caste rules would be evident from an analysis of the second part of the service. This consisted of the exposition of the *Upanishads* in the shape of a discourse or sermon. The task was entrusted to Pandit Ramchandra Vidyavagis, a learned Bengali Brahmana and a disciple of Roy. We have fortunately seventeen of his discourses before us in the shape of a booklet. He is found to start on each occasion with the recitation of a few *Upanishad* passages and then to follow up with a detailed exposition in lucid Bengali. All these were unhesitatingly done before the general audience (including Shudras or non-Brahmanas) and none present raised any objection. The *Upanishads* like the *Mantras* also form part of the *shruti*, and from the orthodox standpoint, cannot be read before or heard by anybody other than a Brahmana. So recitation and exposition of the *Upanishads* before a public including non-Brahmanas was also a clear infringement of caste rules which Roy and his associates had not only permitted but had also encouraged. Ramchandra Vidyavagis soon acquired two new assistants in Pandit Utsavananda Vidyavagis and Pandit Ishvarchandra Nyayaratna who came to share the task of giving Upanishadic discourses. It appears therefore that the Bengali Brahmanas—at least those who had come under Roy's influence—were more liberal than their southern counterparts in contemporary Calcutta and had no objection to reading and expounding the *shruti* in public. Roy and his associates had to accept the compromise on the recitation of the Vedic *Mantras* simply because without such recital the Hindu character of the service would not be complete, and *no competent Bengali Brahmana was at the time available for the job.*

The situation had changed only fifteen years later when Debendranath Tagore, the second leader of the Brahmo Samaj, could persuade a body of southern Brahmanas in the city to recite the Vedas *publicly* in one of the functions of the Brahmo Samaj. The silent working of the spirit of Roy who was then dead, had softened the attitude of even the Andhra Brahmanas who now had no objection to chant the *Mantras* before Shudras.[190]

What were some of the public reactions to the establishment of the *Brahmo Samaj*?

The editor of the *India Gazette* says this "is at least curious, if not instructive, as exhibiting the tendency of educated natives, *to reject all the established forms of belief and worship*, under comprehensive tolerance of a universal Theophilanthropism!"

"A Christian," picking up on this announcement, writes to the *John Bull* that "if such are to be the fruits of educating the natives, it will become a question of the very highest moment, with every Christian and every well-wisher to his race, how far he is not lending his aid in promoting such education to introduce Atheism itself, and to undermine every foundation of happiness."[191] The writer then raises a political bogy: "that as they are such latitudinarians in religion, as to 'reject all the established forms of belief and worship,' so they are also staunch *liberals* in their politics."[192]

The editor of the *John Bull* has little hope for "this new fangled project." He says: "We will venture to foretell, judging from those who are said to be at its head, that the day of its existence will be but short lived."[193]

A rejoinder came from the pen of "Argus," appearing in the columns of the *Bengal Hurkaru* and *Chronicle* (January 12, 1830). The writer asks to compare the editorial remarks of the *John Bull* and the views of the "Christian" with the extract from the Trust Deed of the *Brahmo Samaj*, "and then impartially to judge whether the charge of 'Atheism' and the 'undermining every foundation of human happiness' brought against the projectors of the Institution, be not evidently malign and false; and whether the object of the 'Chitpore Road Association' be not eminently calculated to promote and extend the purest spirit of Philanthropy and Benevolence among men of every persuasion, creed and colour."[194]

The English press was not alone in ridiculing the *Brahmo Samaj*. A rival association was formed by leading Hindus of the Orthodox community called the *Dharma Sabha*. Pandit Bhowanicharan Banerji was the president, and Radhakanta Deb, the secretary. Through its organ, the *Samachar Chandrika*, it made daily attacks upon the theistic reformers. The latter defended themselves through the journalistic voice of the *Sambad Kaumudi*. Pandit Shivanath Shastri has left us an animated account of the feud that ensued. It seems the common people joined in the fray, having been excited by the tracts written by the reformers in the simplest Bengali which had as much appeal for them as for the intellectual classes. "In the bathing ghats at the river-side, in market places, in public squares, in the drawing-rooms of the influential citizens, everywhere the rivalry between the two associations, became the subject of talk. Lines of comical poetry, caricaturing the principles of the great reformer, were composed by the wags of the time and passed from mouth to mouth, till the streets rang with laughter and ridicule."[195] From Calcutta, the agitation spread inland, and "everywhere the question was discussed between the two parties."

Six days after the organization of the *Dharma Sabha*, a "brick-built messuage" located at 55 Chitpore Road, Jorasanko, was dedicated as the permanent place of worship for the *Brahmo Samaj*. Ram Mohan and three other friends put up the cash for the property. The Trust Deed of the property, dated January 8, 1830, plus an endowment of 6,080 Rupees was deposited with the Trustees.[196]

The Trust Deed specifies that the building and land is to be used for public meetings, open to "all sorts and descriptions of people, without distinction, as shall behave and conduct themselves in an orderly, sober, religious, and devout manner."[197]

"The Eternal, Unsearchable, and Immutable Being, who is the Author and Preserver of the Universe" is to be adored and worshipped, "but not under, or by any other name, designation, or title, peculiarly used for, and applied to, any particular Being, or Beings, by any man, or set of men, whatsoever."

No image, statue, painting, portrait "or the likeness of anything" is to be admitted within the building; and neither is any sacrifice permitted, or the killing of any creature, "either for religious purposes or for food."

Eating, drinking, feasting or rioting are all prohibited in or out of the buildings.

No object used in worship which is sacred to any religious group, "shall be reviled, or slightingly or contemptuously spoken of, or alluded to, either in preaching, praying, or in the hymns, or other mode of worship."

All elements of worship should be such as have "a tendency to the promotion of the contemplation of the Author and Preserver of the Universe, to the promotion of charity, morality, piety, benevolence, virtue, and the strengthening of the bonds of union between men of all religious persuasions and creeds."

And also, a person of religious and moral standing should be employed as a resident superintendent to oversee the worship; and such worship is to be performed "daily, or at least as often as once in seven days."

The text makes it clear that Ram Mohan did not intend the *Brahmo Samaj* to be considered a new religion. Rather, it was a spiritual fraternity open to people of all faiths—Hindus, Muslims, Jews, and Christians—for the worship of "the Author and Preserver of the Universe" who transcends all description. Thus, piety and spirituality are humanized by an openness to "men of all religious persuasions," and faith is authenticated by the promotion of benevolence and virtue.

Viewed purely from an ethical perspective, the Trust Deed confronts us with the fundamental truth of the unity of man. It was on this assumption that "mankind is one" that the great reformer went about his task of unifying his beloved land. This faith was more than a notion; it was a necessity in the face of the senseless divisions which rent race from race, caste from caste, sect from sect, leaving the land divided, destitute and degraded.

The importance, therefore, of the *Brahmo Samaj* should not be gauged by the number of its adherents, but by the central tenet of its Trust Deed: One God, one world, one humanity!

# CHAPTER 6

# Social Reform

Ram Mohan was the first Hindu born of a high and privileged caste to take up the cause of social reform in modern India. His social reform was the concretization of his religious reform. "In all countries, and especially in India, social reform consists chiefly in doing away with the disabilities of sufferings incident to difference of sex or the accident of birth."[1] For Ram Mohan, this entailed combating sexism, on the one hand, and caste, on the other.

## I. Caste

The subject of caste reform is dealt with episodically throughout this work. Here, at the risk of some repetition, we shall merely summarize Ram Mohan's ideas and activities and respond to recent criticisms of his handling of the caste issue.

Historian Sumit Sarkar makes the charge that Ram Mohan was a backslider on the caste question, both on the level of social practice and of intellectual argument. In earlier situations, says the author, he had adopted a militant stance on caste,

> But Ram Mohun in his published writings and public life paraded his outward conformity to most caste rules (even to the extent of taking a Brahman cook with him to England!), wore the sacred thread to the end of his days, limited his direct attack on caste to a single *Vajrasuchi* translation, and concentrating all his social reform energies on the single sati issue, possibly even added to a slight extent to Vidyasagar's difficulties by hunting up all the texts glorifying ascetic widowhood. Such deviousness was perhaps not even tactically very wise, since the contradiction between theory and practice soon became the commonest orthodox charge against Rammohun, and one to which the reformer could only make the not entirely satisfactory rejoinder that his critics were equally inconsistent.[2]

The difficulty with this type of criticism is not so much that it is inaccurate as it is misleading. All attention is placed upon the deed, but the drama is missed for the deed. A fairer understanding of the Raja will be better served if, instead of looking at what he did or failed to do, we get to the dynamics of the whole saga of caste in the early nineteenth century.

First, it is ironic that the Raja should be tagged for backsliding at a time when the explosive question of the caste system and the problem of scheduled castes and tribes threatens to shatter the unity and stability of India in the 1980s. So colossal is this social and economic problem that it will now take a thousand Ram Mohans to ameliorate the situation. It behooves us, therefore, to understand and evaluate the Raja's reforms with due appreciation of the monstrous grasp that caste has had over the land, and not expect from him what Gandhi and other activists have failed to achieve in more enlightened times. A case in point is the relation between caste and education. Riding on the wave of independence, untouchables and backward classes were provided full opportunities for primary education, and new concessions and incentives were made available to bring them into higher education. The Constitution itself ensured that they be given every opportunity both in school and in work. "But even then," says Chitra Ghosh, educator and political scientist,

> the relation between caste and education can be clearly seen even today and the disparity is high. While 73% of Harijans are still illiterate, the percentage in the higher castes is only 4 percent. 10 percent of this class goes in for higher education than degree standard; while for the Harijans the number is less than one-half percent.[3]

The monster of caste, hedged in by constitutional constraints *in this day* and age, was as free in Ram Mohan's days as the tigers in the forests of Bengal. Ram Mohan speaks ominously of the "dread" and "doom" of caste, stalking the minds of the Hindu people.

In a letter to Rev. Ware (February 2, 1824), Ram Mohan mentions the authoritarian and prejudicial character of prevailing Hinduism, and states that "these are strongly supported by the dread of the loss of caste, the consequence of apostasy, which separates a husband from his wife, a father from his son, and a mother from her daughter."[4]

Then, in his introduction to the *Isha Upanishad*, he points out how "self-interested guides, who, in defiance of the law as well as of common sense," have succeeded in hiding from people "the true substance of morality, and have infused in their simple hearts a weak attachment to its mere shadow." The "shadow" is the blight of caste with its irrational taboos, "the least aberration from which (even though the conduct of the offender may in other respects be pure and blameless) is not only visited with the severest censure, but actually punished by exclusion from the society of his family and friends. In a word, he is doomed to undergo what is commonly called the loss of caste."[5]

How does one man dare to fight this "dread" and "doom"?

First, as the tigers of the *Sundarbans* (beautiful forests) could not be fought in the streets of Calcutta, but only in the *Sundarbans*, so the system of caste, in the absence of some central, constitutional restraints, could not be fought from the outside, but *only* from the inside by insiders. As only an insider could get inside such a closed system, Roy found it ethically expedient to maintain his caste standing within the community for which he labored. In addition, his *Brahmanic* status made it legally possible for him to bequeath his property for posterity. The servants he took with him to England could testify that even in that foreign land he observed the conduct of a Hindu, thereby ensuring the safety and perpetuity of his private estate.

As to the extent and manner to which he complied with caste rules, Mr. Adam has left the following record:

> All the rules in the present state of Hindu society he finds it necessary to observe, relate to eating and drinking. He must not eat the food forbidden to Brahmins nor with persons of different religion from the Hindu or of different caste to which he still adheres, and even this remnant I have reason to know he frequently but secretly disregards. . . . Both in the marriages and the deaths that happen within his domestic circle he rigidly abstains in his own person from every approach to the idolatrous rites usually practised on such occasions, although he does not prohibit the other members of his family from engaging in them if they think proper.[6]

The record makes it clear that his adoption of caste rules was selective and done openly, though in company with Europeans he felt discreetly free to relax some of the regulations pertaining to inter-dining.

Sarkar brands such compliance as devious and tactically unwise, since the Orthodox charged Ram Mohan with hypocrisy, and the best retort that Ram Mohan could come up with was *tu quoque*. The conclusion seems premature to us.

Ram Mohan elevated the issue of caste from the personal and social levels to the national level. Having placed it in its most strategic perspective, he argues on the principle, as did Gandhi after him, that caste is made for men, not men for caste. The founding impulse of the *Varna* system was humanistic. The later system of caste enshrined in the *Smritis* or *Brahmanical* codes are a blight upon the people, not only causing personal misery, but the chief cause behind national disunity and political imprisonment.[7] A true Hindu is one who finds his spirituality, not in these codes which lack the support of common sense and are perpetuated by pious predators, but in the rational religion of the *Upanishads*.

In the *Chariprashna Uttar (Answers to Four Questions)*, Ram Mohan refuses his rite-observing opponent the refuge of double-standards. He points out that the ritualistic rules had become so picayune and pervasive that the present situation was one of, "Let him who is without blame cast the first stone." Under these circumstances, one who tried to remove the speck of dust from his neighbor's eye had to be bluntly reminded of the boulder in his own eye.

In the second answer Ram Mohan justifies the wearing of the sacred thread while disregarding certain native manners and customs on the grounds that *sanatana dharma* (eternal law) consists in "the knowledge of God and the performance of those practices most beneficial to man." Again, Hinduism was humanistic.

In the third answer he reminds his opponent that the fish upon his plate is not exactly a vegetable, and that exclusive vegetarianism is not enjoined by the earliest *shastras*. His position was historical; his opponents' practice was hypocritical. For Sarkar to accept as valid the testimony of the latter and to call Ram Mohan devious, is to reverse their roles. It would have been fairer for the historian to concede that were a Jesus Christ in the *chapals* (sandals) of Ram Mohan, the Orthodox would have accused him of hypocrisy even though, while fighting Pharisaic legalism, he was trying to set his Jewish house in order. As a member of the Hindu household, symbolized by the sacred thread which said he still cared, Ram Mohan was not destroying *dharma* but was fulfilling it. He was subsituting the ancient spirit of the law for the later letter of the law, and if that made Ram Mohan devious, he was in good company!

All reformers in the great religions of the world were essentially interpreters. While setting their sights on the future, they aligned the future with the past so that the need for stability would be supported by a sense of continuity. "Every reformation is bound to involve an endorsement of the essential principle of conservatism, viz., the preservation of all that is valuable in the old order; and Rammohun's programme of reform was no exception to this general rule."[8]

Even so, as with all the great reformers, Ram Mohan was misunderstood, largely by those who had vested interests. This was as inevitable as his crusade was necessary, for the Buddha reminds us that no matter how good-intentioned a man may be, he is never above criticism *(natthi loke anindito—Dhammapada).*

Despite criticism, Ram Mohan never lost his zeal nor backslid from the position taken by the *Atmiya Sabha* (1819) which criticized "the absurdity of the prevailing rules respecting the intercourse of the several castes with each other."[9]

In order to discount the charge that Ram Mohan poured all his reforming energies into the single cause of *sati* and that he "pussy-footed" on the question of caste, we shall mention some of the steps he actually took to combat caste.

In 1819 he published translations of the *Mundaka* and *Katha Upanishads*, followed by the *Kena Upanishad* in 1823. In the introduction to the last volume he states his purpose thus:

> This work will, I trust, by explaining to my countrymen the real spirit of the Hindoo Scriptures, which is but the declaration of the unity of God, tend in a great degree to correct the erroneous conceptions, which have prevailed with regards to the doctrines they inculate. It will also, I hope, tend to discriminate those parts of the Vēdas which are to be interpreted in an allegorical sense, and consequently to correct those exceptionable practices, which not only deprive Hindoos in general of the common comforts of society, but also lead them frequently to self-destruction, or to sacrifice of the lives of their friends and relations.[10]

The deprivation of "common comforts" to which he alludes is amplified in the following note:

> A Hindoo of caste can only eat once between sunrise and sunset cannot eat dressed victuals in a boat or a ship—nor in a tavern—nor any food that has been touched by a person of a different caste—nor, if interrupted while eating, can he resume his meal.[11]

In all of the above readings Ram Mohan attacks the evil of prejudice which is co-terminus with caste. He concurs with the Buddha that prejudice is *miccha ditthi* which is "the one-sided, partial, prejudiced view of things, of facts, and of truths." Obstinacy and exclusiveness are the prevailing attitudes of prejudice, characteristically expressed as "*Idameva saccam, mogham annam,*" which is to say, "What I think or believe, say or do is the only correct form of truth . . . and every other form is incorrect."[12]

As we have discussed, in 1820 Ram Mohan published his *Precepts of Jesus* followed by a *Second Appeal* (1821) and *Third Appeal* (1823) in which he reiterates the theme of the brotherhood of man under the fatherhood of God. This theme, first introduced in the *Tuhfat*, is maintained two decades later with the same "militant rationalism" which Sarkar find missing in works subsequent to the *Tuhfat*. Sounding no uncertain trumpet, Ram Mohan says of the *Precepts*:

> This simple code of religion and morality is so admirably calculated to elevate men's ideas to high and liberal notions of God, who has equally subjected all living creatures, *without distinction of caste*, rank or wealth, to change, disappointment, pain and death, has equally admitted all to be partakers of the bountiful mercies which he has lavished over nature. . . . (italics supplied).[13]

In 1822 Ram Mohan published *Answers to Four Questions* in which he debunks *Brahmanic* legalism in which caste was the core.

In 1827 he published with a Bengali translation, a portion of the *Vajra-Suchi* by Mrityunjayacharya. The work is a polemic against caste. It alone is cited by our critic as a single blow against this social evil.

Overlooked also is an item in the *Sambad Kaumudi* (No. VIII) from a "Philanthropist," probably Ram Mohan himself, who,

> observing the misery and intolerable distress under which a great major-
> ity of Hindoos labour from prejudices of caste, which have so far infa-
> tuated them as to believe that were they to follow any useful branch of
> mechanics, it would bring disgrace upon the dignity of their caste,
> strongly impresses upon them the folly and perniciousness of such delu-
> sive notions, and recommend them to make themselves familiar with such
> Arts as would tend to their comfort, happiness, and independence; and
> not to pass their lives solely in drudgery and servitude.[14]

Aside from these many publications, Ram Mohan's educational reforms substantiate his firm stand on the caste issue. In 1827 he supported the Presbyterian missionaries in their efforts towards native
education, just as he had earlier supported the Baptists. This education
was open to all members of the community. His own Anglo-Hindu
School, recognized for its academic excellence, also kept an open admission policy.

Ram Mohan also promoted inter-caste marriage as a means for tran-
scending social barriers. He urged that the *Shaiva* form of marriage be
as recognized as *Vaidik* marriages. The former is inculcated in the following *shloka* of the *Mahanirvana Tantra*:

> There is no discrimination of age and caste or race in the Saiva marriage.
> As enjoined by Siva, one should marry a woman who has no husband and
> who is not 'sapinda,' that is, who is not within the prohibited degrees of
> marriage.[15]

The editor of the *Modern Review* comments: "Had his views prevailed, widow-marriage, inter-caste and inter-racial marriage, and post-
puberty marriage would all have been considered valid according to
Hindu usage."[16]

By 1828 Ram Mohan was so adamant that the evils of caste were a
national liability that he felt Hinduism had to undergo some internal
overhauling in order to improve the lot of the people. He regrets that
the previous system was "not well calculated to promote their political
interest." Caste loyalties deprived them entirely of patriotic feeling,
and "the multitude of religious rites and ceremonies and the laws of
purification have totally disqualified them from undertaking any difficult enterprise." He therefore thought it "necessary that some change
should take place in their religion, at least for the sake of their political
advantage and social comfort."[17]

The change he wanted to inject was that insight of the Mahabharata which Hinduism had lost and needed to regain:

This whole world was originally of one caste,
O Yudhisthira; on account of different vocations,
the four-fold-caste was established.

His crowning effort toward the revitilization of the spiritual life of people and their emancipation from caste was the founding of the *Brahmo Samaj* in 1828. The inaugural preacher articulated what was on the mind and in the heart of the founder—salvation as the perception of the "Supreme Spirit *in all creatures*" (italics supplied).

Some doubt hangs over Ram Mohan's decision to confine the ministry of the *Samaj* to *Brahmins*. As stated in the previous chapter, while the *spirit* of the *Brahmo* worship was universal and inclusive, its *form* was Hindu, and to that degree, bearing the limitations of that tradition. The form required the reading of the *Mantras*. Since the Bengali *Brahmins* who were eligible for the reading of the *Samhitas* had no real mastery over this particular portion of the *Vedas*, Ram Mohan had to enlist the services of *Andhra Brahmins* living in Calcutta. But, as is well-known, these southerners were ultra-conservative, and would not brook the reading of the sacred scriptures before the sort of mixed audience which frequented the *Samaj*. To satisfy their religious taboos, Ram Mohan had to aquiesce in setting apart an enclosure for the recitation of the *Vedas*. This was not *a compromise*, but *a concession* to a "peculiar circumstance," as Professor Dilip Kumar Biswas has explained.

However, in keeping with the universal spirit of the *Brahmo* worship, though Ram Mohan was impeded with respect to clergy, he was uninhibited with respect to congregation. Public meetings of the *Samaj* were thrown open to "all sorts and descriptions of people without distinction." The desegregation of the laity was more important, anyhow, than the desegregation of the clergy. Even *Shudras* and *Mlecchas*, debarred from hearing the *Vedas* for centuries, were now free to join in the services. Ram Mohan addressed them all as "brothers."

Caste was cognate to rank, and Ram Mohan's attitude toward the one showed how he felt about the other. We see him constantly championing the cause of the underdog. He fought on behalf of the rack-rented *ryot* (peasant) before the Select Committee of the House of Commons. He also took up the cudgel for the "miserable molungees"—thousands of native laborers who were kept in economic slavery by their capitalistic masters.

In a happier vein, Dr. T. Boot, an eminent American physican practicing in London, says this of the Raja's egalitarianism. "While he paid just deference to rank in obedience to the conventional etiquette of society, he honoured above all men the poor gardener whom he met

within some rich establishment in India, who had, uninfluenced by th
authority of his superiors, examined the scriptures, and adopted th
faith of the unity of God. He went to the garden every day to walk wit
him; he often said to us, 'I could have taken him in my arms as
brother.' "[18]

Finally, as the first *Brahmin* in the public limelight to cross the forbic
den waters, Ram Mohan showed he could rise above the unreasonz
bleness of caste restrictions which impeded intercourse with othe
members of the human family.

The mere listing of the above points, developed elsewhere in th
text, should leave the reader somewhat skeptical when he reads thz
Ram Mohan "limited his direct attack on caste to a *single Vajra-suci*
translation," and concentrated "all his social reform energies on th
single sati issue." Theoretically, more could have been done, but, ui
like *sati*, the abolition of caste was not an idea whose time had com
The British class system lent aid and comfort to the Hindu caste sy
tem. Even in the *Samaj* it took another fifty years and the vigoroi
leadership of Keshub Chunder Sen to eliminate the vestiges of caste.[19]

Today, constitutional democracy has rendered caste illegal in tl
public domain, but the problem is not any less diminished than in Ra
Mohan's time. As a matter of fact, caste is presently being politicize
The solution to the problem includes, but transcends legal power ar
even moral power. What is needed is a religious solution backed up l
legal, moral, and social supports. And herein lies the real contributic
of the Raja. The value of his reform lies not so much in what he di
for no matter how much he accomplished it would have been nugato
considering the enormity of the problem, as we are discovering evi
today. Roy's contribution lies in his showing Hindus that they have
religious task. They need spiritual freedom. The *Shudras* of Hindust;
must lose their chains, but so must the *Brahmins*, and all of the oth
castes! Inhumanity must die in order that humanity may be rebor
The rebirth of humanity is through the discovery of divinity.

> Turn inward, mind!
> Why such confusion?
> *The object of your search*
> *is the Quintessence in all beings.*
> Manifest as the heat in the sun
> and the chill in the moon
> are His ways.
> Expressed as Atman in you
> is the Universal (Italics supplied).[20]

## 2. Sati

We now turn to that aspect of social reform for which Ram Mohan is remembered best—his fight against *sati*.

*Sati* (anglicized as suttee) is a feminine noun made from the verbal root *sat*, meaning truth. A *sati* was therefore a widow who was considered true and virtuous because she allowed herself to be burnt upon the funeral pile of her husband (rarely, she took poison or was buried alive). A change in the above meaning of the virtuous wife came about when Christian missionaries incorrectly referred to the act of self-immolation itself as *sati*.

*Vedic* literature suggests that during its times *sati* was a "mimetic ceremony."[21] The *Atharva Veda* declares: "Get up, O Woman, to the world of the living; thou liest by this one who is deceased; come! to him who grasps thy hand, thy second spouse, thou hast now entered into the relation of wife to husband."[22] Both here and in the *Rig Veda*,[23] the widow ascends the funeral pyre of her dead husband as part of her "ancient duty," but although she lies by the corpse of her dead husband, she is told to rise and go forth with her new spouse to a life of "progeny and property." Once she departs, the pyre is set ablaze. Thus, the Vedic Indians ceremonialized an earlier custom enjoining widows to cremate themselves along with their dead husbands.

By about the sixth century, the ancient custom was revived in areas where *Brahmanic* influence was dominant—along the Ganges, Bengal, Oudh, and Rajputana.[24] In the opinion of R. W. Frazer, the custom was revived under the pressure of priests "anxious to obtain command over the property of the widow. In order to give the custom a religious sanction, a passage in the *Rigveda* which directed the widow to rise from her husband's funeral pyre and go forth in front (*agre*) was altered into to go into the fire (*agneh*)."[25]

Though sanctified by age and priestly self-interest, *sati* was never universally practiced. It was rare in parts of Panjab, and was prohibited in most sections of the South.[26]

During the Moghul period, the custom was "frowned upon,"[27] but it was never completely prohibited for fear of alienating the Hindu subjects. As Muslim power declined, the practice was revived. "In areas exposed to Western influence, such as Bengal proper, or otherwise exposed to a high degree of social flux, such as the Banaras region under the newly risen Rajas of Banaras, sati became a popular custom."[28] In the Madras Presidency, during the second decade of the nineteenth century, the practice was only known in the Telegu area and in parts of Tanjore. In the Bombay Presidency, the rite was limited to the Konkan district. Only in the Bengal Presidency was the popularity of the custom truly felt, particularly in Calcutta and the neighboring districts of Burdwan, Hooghly, Nadia, and the twenty-four *Parganas*. Almost sixty percent of all *satis* in the Presidency between the years 1815 to 1826 came from these localities.

At first it might seem strange that *sati* was most popular in areas most directly affected by the British impact. The fact is that the British establishment provided new opportunities for upward social mobility. These opportunities were seized by urbanites who became rich by the system; but in the midst of doing *puja* (homage) to Mammon, they lost a good deal of their traditional virtues and social standing. *Sati* provided these *nouveaux riches* with a means of demonstrating their allegiance to the older norms from which life in the city had seduced them. This explains "why even when the family of the suicide was prosecuted, there was no loss of caste, infamy or disgrace; they in fact gained in social stature and were 'backed with applause and honour.' Duress exerted on the prospective sati was therefore a demonstration of the piety of the family. No wonder the practitioners of the rite were most ruthless with the widow who after making the fatal decision to commit sati later wavered."[29]

Other factors which helped popularize *sati* at this time were the economic motive which was brought home to Ram Mohan by the immolation of his sister-in-law, once the family suffered economic reversals; and allied to this was the manipulation of family property. Property rules gave wives and mothers a certain stake in the distribution of property. In competitive times "where there was a high chance that a widow would inherit property or use it for bargaining purposes," these privileges were deemed dangerous.[30] The safest and most sanctimonious way of avoiding this danger was to persuade surviving wives to blaze a path of virtue! Ram Mohan clearly saw this proprietary greed behind the high incidence of *sati* and drew the attention of the governor-general to it in his *Appeal*.

In the face of the popularization of this rite, the British found themselves in a touchy situation where they had to respect the religious and social liberties of their subjects, or else they would be courting unrest and rebellion.

The great service of Ram Mohan was to show the rulers how this dilemma which had baffled them for upwards of a quarter of a century could be resolved. In order to appreciate both the wisdom and courage of this service, we must set it in its historical context.

Warren Hastings authorized the preparation of a manual of Hindu law for magistrates in order to avoid any infringement of the declared policy of religious liberty. The *Brahmin* pandits who had a free hand in composing this document made sure that the custom of *sati* was given full veneration and thereby assured its protection by government. The government accepted the custom on the terms of these authorities, but the ensuing policy of non-interference brought the administration into a collision course with the Evangelicals, both at home and abroad. Often eagerness to give Ram Mohan all the credit for ending *sati* makes historians overlook the daring and dedicated efforts of the Christian missionaries. William Carey of Serampore deserves special recognition for his courageous efforts to stop *sati*.

Despite the hands-off policy of the government, Britishers acting in individual capacities took it upon themselves to follow their conscience. There is the case of Captain Tomeyn who, in 1772, rescued a widow from burning and thereby stirred up a riot. In 1789 M. H. Brooke, a Collector of Shahabad, refused permission for concremation, defending his position before Lord Cornwallis in the following words:

> The rites and superstitions of the Hindu religion should be allowed with the most unqualified tolerance, but a practice at which human nature shudders, I cannot permit within the limits of my jurisdiction without particular instructions.[31]

The instructions Collector Brooke received from the governor-general were to refrain from any show of force in preventing future *satis* inasmuch as "the public prohibition of a ceremony, authorized by the tenets of the religion of the Hindus, and from the observance of which they have never been restricted by the ruling power, would in all probability tend rather to increase than diminish their veneration for it, and consequently prove the means of rendering it more prevalent than it is at present."[32]

The government could not maintain its neutrality very long. There were atrocious incidents where young widows were drugged into performing *sati*, or were the gullible victims of greedy relatives and priests. The government therefore decided to bring the custom under strict supervision without violating the principle of non-interference.

In a letter dated February 5, 1805, Lord Wellesley requested the *Sadar Nizamat Adalat* (chief judicial authority in India) to verify "by means of reference to the Pundits," the extent to which the institution of *sati* was "founded upon the religious opinion of the Hindoos."[33] The Chief Pandit, Ghanashyam Sharma, professed that every woman of the four castes is allowed concremation,

> provided she has not infant children, nor is pregnant, nor is in a state of uncleanliness, nor under the age of puberty; in every one of such cases she is not allowed to burn herself with her husband's body.
>
> But a woman who has infant children, and can procure another person to undertake the charge of bringing them up, is permitted to burn. It is contrary to law, as well as to the usage of the country, to cause any woman to burn herself against her wish, by administering drugs to stupefy or intoxicate her.[34]

Pandit Sharma went on to eulogize *sati*, quoting Sanskrit scriptures, and added that a woman who loses nerve at the critical moment can "recover her purity by undergoing a severe penance."[35]

The Nizamat submitted its suggestions to the government, but the administration did not draw up any rules at that time. Seven years later, on April 17, 1813, the rules were formulated based on the principle that *sati* be permitted whenever it is countenanced by Hindu religion and law; and that it be prevented when prohibited by the same authorities. The prohibitions included cases in which the widow was: (1) unwilling; (2) under sixteen years of age; (3) pregnant; (4) drugged or intoxicated; or (5) mother of a child under three years of age, unless legal guardianship were secured on behalf of the child and a "Form of Engagement" duly signed.[36] The last provision was added in 1815.

Further clarification of the legal disabilities preventing a widow from ending her life involved the practice of widow burying by the *jogi* sect of East Bengal. The Hindu law officers of the Provincial Court of Appeal for Dacca gave the opinion that in conformity with the customs of the *jogis* (though not founded on scriptures), it was lawful for a widow to be buried alive with her dead husband.[37]

On the issue of tying the widow to the funeral pile, or pressing her down with green bamboos to avoid escape, the pandits of the *Sadar Diwani Adalat* opined that "no authority permits any restraints be used."[38] In case the woman extricated herself, the pandits stated that she could be restored to society "by undergoing a penance."[39]

In 1817 the *Nizamat Adalat* collated all of the regulations in a minutely worked out form which was then to be released for publication, but the administration changed its mind upon discovering that co-terminus with its efforts to control *sati*, incidents jumped significantly, especially in the Calcutta Division. Statistics of *satis* for the years 1815 to 1818 showed an ominous trend, soaring from a total of 378 to 2,365 in three years. Calcutta led with a hike from 253 to 1,528.[40]

Reasons given by the British law officers for the upswing in the Calcutta area were: (1) the influence of the worship of Kali—"the idol of the drunkard and thief"; (2) the masochistic enjoyment of pyromaniacs; and (3) the lending of respectability to the custom by government supervision. Local officials considered the last factor embarrassing to the British humanitarianism, for it amounted to " granting the authority of the Government for burning widows," and therefore culpability in its increase.[41]

British policy did not change throughout the ruling terms of Hastings and Amherst, but during this time foundations were being laid on which Bentinck could later take his stand.

First, there was Mrityunjay Vidyalankar, Chief Pandit of the Supreme Court, ranking Hindu scholar, and formidable advocate of Hindu orthodoxy. Commissioned by the Chief Judge of the *Sadar Diwani Adalat* to determine the precise measure in which *sati* is supported by the *shastras*, this colossus of Hindu *dharma* produced some surprising findings. He stated that scriptural injunctions apply only to those who feel the pain of disease or separation; who act voluntarily; and that the "act of dying is not enjoined; but merely the mode of it." If you are bent on suicide, say the scriptures, "put an end to yourself by such and such means. . . ."[42]

For his part, Vidyalankar recommended "a life of abstinence and chastity" as more "highly excellent" than the woman burning herself.[43]

The second great figure at this time was Ram Mohan Roy. He was certainly reinforced in his own thinking by the opinions of Vidyalankar.

The Raja's anti-*sati* campaign began in 1811–1812 while he was stationed in Rangpur. The fiery death of his sister-in-law (1812) forged in him a determination to save all the sisters of his land from this unworthy rite. Among his early efforts he used to frequent the cremation grounds in the Calcutta area in order to dissuade women who were about to sacrifice their lives. The *Asiatic Journal* reports that on one occasion he got the priests to light the fire prior to the woman ascending the pile, hoping that the flames would intimidate her. He insisted that this procedure was directed by the scriptures. Contrary to his expectations, one of the wives courageously walked into the flames and was followed by the second. As she stood before the flames, she addressed the bystanders with great animation: "You have just seen my husband's first wife perform the duty incumbent on her, and will now see me follow her example. Henceforward, I pray, do not attempt to prevent Hindu women from burning, otherwise our curse will be upon you."[44]

The reformer was not deterred. Such incidents only spurred his zeal to have the practice banned. He probably had a hand in drawing up a document signed by a great number of reputable Hindus in Calcutta. This was a counter-petition to the one presented by the Orthodox community asking the government to repeal all regulations as infringements upon their religious liberties. Ram Mohan's faction charged that,

cases have frequently occurred, where women have been induced by the persuasions of their next heirs, interested in their destruction, to burn themselves on the funeral piles of their husbands; that others, who have been induced by fear to retract a resolution, rashly expressed in the first moments of grief, of burning with their deceased husbands, have been forced upon the funeral pile, and there bound down with ropes, and pressed by green bamboos until consumed by the flames; that some, after flying from the flames, have been carried back by their relations and burnt to death. All these instances, your petitioners humbly submit, are murders, according to every shastur, as well as to the common sense of all nations.[45]

Aware of the government's concern for religious liberty, the petitioners further point out that *sati* has little basis in scripture. To the contrary, "in the opinion of many of the most learned Brahmins, founded on their shasturs, all kinds of voluntary death are prohibited."[46] *Manu*, the *Vedanta*, the *Gita*, and the *Smritis* are cited in support. In addition, the humanitarian legislations of the British government are both cited and invoked. Just as the law banned such inhumane practices as female infanticide, the hope is expressed that the government will intervene to bring the evils of *sati* to a speedy end.

In 1818 Ram Mohun published a Bengali tract entitled, *A Conference between an Advocate for, and an Opponent of the Practice of Burning Widows Alive*. An English translation was also made in the hopes that its arguments "might tend to alter the notions that some European gentlemen entertain on this subject."[47] The reference here is to the protection of religious rights in a situation where religious claims are erroneously accepted. The whole argument of this tract is conducted on a moral plane.

First, the "Advocate" of concremation and postcremation (*anumaran*) of widows lists several sacred lawgivers—*Angira, Vyasa, Harita, Vishnu,* and *Gotama*—enjoining *sati*.

The "Opponent" accepts these injunctions but points out that whereas the scriptures are written on different levels to cater to the moral development of diverse individuals, we must finally evaluate the lesser moral injunctions by the higher ones. Manu is the most unimpeachable witness of moral law. Therefore, the commands of *Angira* and the like must be judged in the light of *Manu*. And on the authority of the great lawgiver, widows are enjoined to pass their days cheerfully by living a life of simplicity and virtue.

Furthermore, every act is qualified by its motivation. The driving force behind concremation is always some form of sensual gratification. Such virtue has its own reward; but being the product of selfish desire, it sooner or later is dissipated. Rites, dutifully performed, may bring one to the celestial abode of the gods, but when merit is exhausted, one is again subjected to birth, disease, and death. Therefore, instead of seeking the pleasures of transient heaven, one should have faith in the Supreme Being which leads to absorption, and from which there is no returning to this life of suffering. Such is the testimony of the Upanishads.

Having been routed on the grounds of scripture, the "Advocate" takes shelter in tradition. The "Opponent" dislodges him here, too, first by showing that the custom is relatively recent; and secondly by demonstrating that because a vice has become a custom there is no good reason to believe that its guilt is mitigated. If time hallowed guilt, "the inhabitants of the forests and mountains who have been in the habit of plunder, must be considered as guiltless of sin, and it would be improper to endeavour to restrain their habits. The *shastras*, and the reasonings connected with them, enable us to discriminate right and wrong. In those *shastras* such female murder is altogether forbidden. And reason also declares, that to bind down a woman for her destruction, holding out to her the inducement of heavenly rewards, is a most sinful act.[48]

Displaced from scripture and tradition, the "Advocate" assumes the role of a moral pragmatist. If women are allowed to survive their husbands, these weak creatures may go astray and bring disgrace to their husbands. The "Opponent" questions such false pragmatism:

> What can be done, if, merely to avoid the possible danger of disgrace, you are unmercifully resolved to commit the sin of female murder. But is there not also a danger of a woman's going astray during the life-time of her husband, particularly when he resides for a long time in a distant country? What remedy then have you got against this cause of alarm?[49]

The "Advocate" objects to the assertion that female destruction is promoted through want of feeling. The root of all his good deeds are deep feelings such as mercy and kindness. The "Opponent" acknowledges his charitable dispositions in other cases, but explains to him that because he has grown up with the practice of *sati*, habit has desensitized him to the pain women undergo as they writhe under the "torture of the flames."

The "Advocate" is impressed and says he shall "carefully consider." The "Opponent" is greatly satisfied. "By forsaking prejudice and reflecting on the Sastra, what is really conformable to its precepts may be perceived, and the evils and disgrace brought on this country by the crime of female murder will cease."[50]

This storybook ending could only belong to fiction. In real life, the advocates of *sati* were now ready to place this Hindu heretic on a pile and do away with him. Despite this danger, Ram Mohan was prepared to venture all the risks that his campaign entailed. He was practical enough to hire protection, but at no time did he allow threat of harm to adjust conviction to circumstance. Earlier, he had written to an American Unitarian that he was prepared to stick by the precepts of Jesus "even at the risk of my own life." Now he was proving it.

On the brighter side, reactions of the English press were supportive of his campaign. The news media welcomed the above tract "from the pen of the virtuous Reformer of India," and gave it all possible publicity.[51] Said the *Calcutta Gazette* (December 24, 1818):

> The Sanskrit authorities which are said to enjoin the sacrifice of widows on the funeral pile of their deceased husbands, have lately undergone a free examination by a learned and philosophical Hindoo. The question of itself is of the highest importance, and the true interpretation of the religious law which has stained the domestic history of India for so many ages with blood, will no doubt diminish, if not extinguish the desire for self-immolation. The safest way of coming to a right understanding on a point so interesting to humanity, is a rigid investigation of the rules of conduct laid down in the books which are considered sacred by the Hindoos. This appears to have been done with great assiduity, anxiety, and care, and the consequence has been a decision hostile to the ancient custom.[52]

Fourteen months later, Ram Mohan produced a *Second Conference* (February 20, 1820) three time the length of the first. It is dedicated to the marchioness of Hastings, from which we gather that he had the full backing of the governor-general. The fact is that Hastings and his successors were hoping that the impasse in which they found themselves in respect to *sati* would be lifted by the labors of Ram Mohan and other natives whose enlightened thinking on the subject would finally place the custom in a state of desuetude.

The tack of the First Conference is followed in the *Second*, but with a plethora of scriptural quotations reinforced by moral arguments. Of particular interest to us is his defense of Hindu women in Section IX.

With his fictional "Opponent" demolished by the use of Sanskrit sources, he brings up the buried question of women's rights. He argues that the real reason why men are anxious to have widows burn themselves to death on the funeral pyres of their husbands is the low opinion men have of the opposite sex. They are considered mentally and morally inferior, irresolute, and untrustworthy. Should they survive their husbands, they are apt to disgrace their families, as might be expected from their flaws in character. To restrain them from folly the scriptures prescribe an impossible regimen of ascetic observances. Life becomes so burdensome that these unfortunate widows find death preferable to existing. Besides, there is the dangled inducement of rewards in heaven. The cumulative effect of all these fears and hopes trick women into volunteering to perish with their husbands. The male members of the family are happy and eager to oblige. To make sure the death wish of their dear ones is fulfilled, they remove every possibility of escape by tying them down to the pile.

The "Opponent" questions the premise on which *sati* is practiced, namely, that women are constitutionally weaker than men. If this can be proven wrong, *sati* as a precaution against woman's folly must be considered a gross crime. To prove that this condescending view of female nature is erroneous, the "Opponent" points out the basic "injustice of its thinking." Women are considered morally and mentally inferior, and on the level of performance this might well be correct. But the inferiority is not a fault of nature but of nurture. If women were given educational opportunities and yet fell short of expectations, the mean assessment of womanhood might be justified. But since women are generally kept void of education and social acquirements, it is unjust to call them inferior.

Secondly, women cannot be charged with want of resolution. Males shudder at the thought of death whereas women resolutely lie beside the corpses of their husbands and allow themselves to be consumed by flames.

Thirdly, as to trustworthiness, the number of women deceived by men is ten times greater than that of men betrayed by women.

Fourthly, with respect to women's subjection to passion; husbands revel in polygamy, while the wife is married to but one husband, and at his death, desires either to follow him to death, or to live a life of harsh austerity.

Fifthly, the accusation that women are in want of virtuous knowledge is unjust. Without virtue, it would be impossible for them to endure the slights, indignities, and cruelties which men maliciously inflict on their daily lives. "At marriage the wife is recognized as half of her husband, but in after conduct they are treated worse than inferior animals."[53] If the husband is rich, "he indulges in criminal amours to her perfect knowledge," and if the husband is poor, she suffers the most trouble in the family. Her infinite capacity for forgiveness and understanding enables her to survive, but should she try to escape, the law returns her to her husband like lost chattel, and she reaps revenge. "These are facts occurring every day, and not to be denied. What I lament is, that seeing the women thus dependent and exposed to every misery, you feel for them no compassion, that might exempt them from being tied down and burnt to death."[54]

The stir created by these publications was phenomenal. "They served to arouse public interest in the question of *sati* on a scale hitherto unthinkable. Public discussion of the subject was taken up by the vernacular newspapers which had begun to appear after 1818."[55] The *Samachar Darpan* and the *Sambad Kaumudi* were active campaigners, often clashing with the *Samachar Chandrika* which was pro-*sati*. The liberal voice of the English press could be heard through the columns of the *Friend of India*, the *India Gazette*, the *Bengal Hurkaru*, and the *Calcutta Journal*.

Ram Mohan's treatment of *sati* in his literary works and newspaper publications is quite characteristic of him. He condemned *sati* on moral grounds and on the basis of those very scriptures which were held sacred by his opponents. Thus, taking the position that true Hinduism is both moral and rational, he was able to move with the winds of liberalism which were blowing from the West.

Lord Wellesley felt a stirring of these winds and responded by suppressing infanticide on Saugor island in 1803, but skirted the issue of *sati* for fear of Hindu reprisal. For the next twenty-five years, the winds lay low, with each governor-general hoping that with the spread of education and the "unostentatious exertions" of local officers, the problem would die a natural death.[56] Metcalfe, in Delhi, was the only exception. The quarter century concluded with the caution of W. B. Bayley against trying to dig up "inveterate religious prejudices" so deeply rooted in antiquity.[57] A year later, the restless winds of liberalism began to blow again. In 1828 Lord William Bentinck, a protege of Jeremy Bentham, was appointed governor-general. "In 1829 Bentinck acted where others had called for reports and suppressed suttee by Regulation XVII of 1829."[58]

Bentinck moved fast, but he was no bull in a china shop. He first gathered useful data from key persons. In July of 1829, he contacted Ram Mohan. The *Calcutta Monthly Journal* reports: "An eminent native philanthropist, who has long taken the lead of his countrymen on this great question of humanity and civilized government, has been encouraged to submit his views of it in a written form, and has been subsequently honoured with an audience by the governor-general."[59]

Ram Mohan helped Bentinck in forming a decision by breaking the moral deadlock which had stymied earlier administrators—the deadlock between the principle of *life* and the principle of *liberty*.

Ram Mohan convincingly demonstrated to the Governor-General that the custom they had pledged themselves to protect in the name of religious liberty was "nowhere enjoined as a duty; and that a life of piety and self-abnegation was considered more virtuous."[60]

On the practical side he also gave convincing testimony that the motives behind the proponents of *sati* were often less inspired by creed than by greed. The poor, defenseless creature upon the funeral pyre might have been prayed for, but, in truth, she was preyed upon.

Thus, on the grounds of scripture and morality Ram Mohan showed the governor-general that the elimination of *sati* could not amount to an infringement of religious freedom. The only remaining issue was the right to life. Both of these considerations are reflected in Bentinck's Preamble to the *sati* Regulation of December 4, 1829.

> The practice of suttee, of burning or burying alive the widows of Hindoos, is revolting to the feelings of human nature; it is nowhere enjoined by the religion of the Hindoos as an imperative duty; on the contrary, a life of purity and retirement, on the part of the widow is more especially and preferably inculcated, and by a vast majority of that people throughout India the practice is not kept up nor observed: in some extensive districts it does not exist; in those in which it has been most frequent, it is notorious that, in many instances, acts of atrocity have been perpetrated which have been shocking to the Hindoos themselves, and in their eyes unlawful and wicked. The measures hitherto adopted to discourage and prevent such acts have failed of success, and the Governor-General in Council is deeply impressed with the conviction that the abuses in question cannot be effectually put to an end without abolishing the practice altogether. Actuated by these considerations, the Governor-General in Council, without intending to depart from one of the first and most important principles of the system of British government in India, that all classes of the people be secure in the observance of their religious usages, so long as that system can be adhered to without violation of the paramont dictates of justice and humanity, has deemed it right to establish the following rules, which are hereby enacted to be in force from the time of their promulgation throughout the territories immediately subject to the presidency of Fort William.[61]

Let us now take a brief look at Bentinck's Minute on *sati* dated November 8, 1829. Our purpose is to show how the governor-general differed from Ram Mohan in the execution of their common goals.

Of all the people whose advice he sought toward the abolition of *sati*, Bentinck refers to Mr. Horace Wilson, the Orientalist, and to Ram Mohan Roy. He reports Wilson as saying that abolition will incur "extensive dissatisfaction" and that its "success will only be partial." Bentinck agrees with the first, but doubts the latter. He acknowledges that "a similar opinion as to the probable excitation of a deep distrust of our future intentions, was mentioned to me in a conversation by that enlightened native, Ram Mohun Roy, a warm advocate for the abolition of suttees, and of all other superstitions and corruptions, engrafted on the Hindoo Religion, which he considers originally to have been a pure Deism."[62]

Ram Mohan had recommended that the practice be suppressed by the quiet and unobtrusive enforcement of regulations, with the law officers standing chiefly in the background. "He apprehended that any public enactment would give rise to general apprehension that the reasoning would be, 'While the English were contending for power, they deemed it politic to allow universal toleration, and to respect our religion, but having obtained the supremacy their first act is a violation of their professions, and the next will probably be, like the Mahommedan conquerors, to force upon us their own Religion'. "[63]

Bentinck admits that "much truth is contained in these remarks" but strongly dissents. He then inquires into the evil, and the extent of danger which may practically result from abolition. He concludes that "from the native population, nothing of extensive combination or even partial opposition may be expected from the abolition."[64]

Ram Mohan was correct in his apprehensions. Historians Biswas and Ganguli point out that "the abrupt abolition of the evil custom of Sati came to be regarded by the masses of conservative Hindus and even by Muslims exactly in the same light as he feared. This sentiment among others served as a powerful motive force behind the Mutiny of 1857."[65]

It is a credit to Ram Mohan that once Bentick had cut "the Gordian knot," he fully aligned himself with government policy. He helped mobilize favorable public opinion and closely briefed the government on community developments.

The Orthodox community reacted with stunned dismay, but there was no resort to violence. Their activities were limited to closing ranks, publicising the injustice they felt perpetrated upon them, and preparing petitions to countervail the new Regulation.

On January 14, 1830 the Orthodox community of Calcutta presented the governor-general with a Petition against the *sati* Regulation. Attached was a paper of "Authorities" signed by one hundred and twenty pandits. Twenty-eight pandits appended their signatures to an additional paper of legal authorities presented by a deputation from the interior.

The petitioners charged that their religion had been betrayed by apostates who had been instrumental in shaping governmental policy. In fact, "under the sanction of immemorial usage as well as precept, Hindoo widows perform, of their own accord and pleasure, and for the benefit of their husbands' souls and for their own, the sacrifice of self-immolation called suttee, which is not merely a sacred *duty* but a high privilge to her who sincerely believes in the doctrines of their religion."[66]

The *sati* Regulation is therefore tantamount to interference in matters of religion and "an unjust and intolerant dictation in matters of conscience," which is bound to fail.[67]

Instead of relying on the "assertion of men who have neither any faith nor care for the memory of their ancestors or their religion," his Lordship is asked to consult "none but pundits and brahmins, and teachers of holy lives, and known learning and authority."[68]

The Petition was signed by Maharaj Sree Grischunder Bahadur, and eight hundred others.

Subsequent to a conference on the subject of the Petition, Bentinck delivered the following reply:

> The governor-general has read with attention the petition which has been presented to him; and has some satisfaction in observing that the opinions of the pundits, consulted by the petitioners, confirm the supposition that widows are not, by the religious writings of the Hindoos, commanded to destroy themselves; but that, upon the death of their husbands, the choice of a life of a strict and severe morality is everywhere expressly offered; that in the books usually considered of the highest authority, it is commanded above every other course, and is stated to be adapted to a better state of society; such as, by the Hindoos, is believed to have subsisted in former times.
>
> Thus none of the Hindoos are placed in the distressing situation of having to disobey either the ordinances of the government, or those of their religion.[69]

The voice of Ram Mohan can very clearly be heard in Bentinck's argument. He concludes that the abolition of *sati* is "an urgent duty of the British government," and therefore denies the prayer. The Petitioners are assured that they have further legal recourse by appealing to the King in Council.

Two days later, January 16, 1830, the governor-general was presented with congratulatory addresses—one from the Christians of Calcutta bearing eight hundred signatures, and one from three hundred native gentlemen. The latter was presented by Ram Mohan. The opening paragraph expresses thanks for the invaluable protection which his lordship's government has afforded to the lives of the Hindu females, and for his humane and successful exertions in rescuing the Indians "from the gross stigma hitherto attached to our character, as wilful murderers of females and zealous promoters of the practice of suicide."[70]

"Excessive jealousy" is cited as the progenitor of this custom with Hindu princes as the culprits. Under the cloak of religion, they used their arbitrary power to sanction widow burning so as to prevent their wives from "forming subsequent attachments." The system, "being admirably suited to the selfish and servile disposition of the populace, has been eagerly followed by them, in defiance of the most sacred authorities."[71]

The Hindu Address and Bentinck's reply bring to light a concern with international opinion that motivated Ram Mohan and his supporters. There is also the recognition which Ram Mohan perceived very early in his career as a reformer, that the Hindus were blessed by a moral character that was capable of giving a much better account of itself. In the words of the governor-general:

> Those who present this Address are right in supposing that, by every nation in the world, except the Hindoos themselves, this part of their custom has always been made a reproach against them, and nothing so strongly contrasted with the better features of their own national character, so inconsistent with the affections which unite families, so destructive of the moral principles on which society is founded, has ever subsisted amongst a people, in other respects so civilized.[72]

In the meantime the Orthodox Hindus became fully aware that a long, hard fight lay ahead of them, and they would have to form an organization to protect their religion. Accordingly, in January of 1830, the *Dharma Sabha* was formed as a "means for protecting our religion and our excellent customs and usages."[73] The *Dharma Sabha*'s relationship to the government was ambiguous. On the one hand it stood as the orthodox watch-dog of governmental encroachments; on the other, it made good use of government patronage. One of the first items of business of the fledgling organization was to look into the matter of making an appeal to the King of England relative to the regulations forbidding *satis*.

In the same year, Ram Mohan published a tract: *Abstract of the Arguments Regarding the Burning of Widows Considered as a Religious Rite.* Though *sati* was now officially outlawed, nevertheless it seemed desirable to Ram Mohan that "the substance of those publications should be condensed in a concise but comprehensive manner, so that enquirers may with little difficulty, be able to form a just conclusion, as to the true light in which this practice is viewed in the religion of the Hindus."[74]

First, *sati* is at best optional, not obligatory. *Manu* plainly enjoins widows to "*continue till death* forgiving all injuries, performing austere duties, avoiding every sensual pleasure, and cheerfully practising the incomparable rules of virtue which have been followed by such women as were devoted to only one husband." Further, should the concremation be made into an obligatory duty, it "would necessarily bring a stigma upon the character of the living widows, who have preferred a virtuous life to concremation, as charging them with a violation of the duty said to be indispensable."[75]

Secondly, the practice of *sati* is not of equal merit as the living of a virtuous life. The Vedas decisively state: "From a desire, during life, of future fruition, life ought not to be destroyed."[76] Support for concremation is found in Angira, Vyasa, Harita, and others, but these authors recommend concremation "to obtain future carnal fruition." The Bhagavad Gita condemns such rites performed for fruition. The Gita's position is supported by *Manu, Yajnavalkya,* and by Smartta Raghunandana, a modern expounder of law in Bengal.

The third point touches on the mode of concremation. Where the rite is prescribed in scripture, the ascent of the widow onto the funeral pile of her husband is always a voluntary act, allowing her ample scope for the last minute retraction which can later be absolved by offering penance.

We can feel the lifting of a tremendous moral burden as Ram Mohan concludes his tract with his thanks to heaven for protecting women from "cruel murder, under the cloak of religion, and our character, as a people, from the contempt and pity with which it has been regarded, on account of this custom, by all civilized nations on the surface of the globe."[77]

In June 1832 the Orthodox Hindus petitioned the Privy Council in England against the *sati* Regulation, but their prayer was not granted. Reactions to the dismissal of the case did not explode into hostility, but became occasions for expressing disenchantment with the government. Bitter feelings were also expressed against Ram Mohan, the devil in the pile.

Looking back upon this long campaign, the man who stands out as a Goliath among the governors is William Bentinck. Whereas his peers wrote Minutes, Bentinck made history. As a humanitarian and Utilitarian, he was of the firm conviction that the inhuman rite of *sati* had no place in the moral order of society.

This is the point at which the great moral reformer, Ram Mohan Roy, enters the picture. Without his consultation, the government's solution to the problem could at best have been coercive—a military action. Ram Mohan helped make it persuasive—a moral action. The Hindu scholar showed convincingly that the moral action he appealed for was rooted in the authoritative scriptures of the Hindus. The sting was thus taken out of the charge that the British were militarily meddling in the religious affairs of the people. To the contrary, Ram Mohan so elevated the British intervention that the arm of the law now looked like the arm of the Lord!

On November 10, 1832, a meeting of the *Brahmo Samaj* of Calcutta was held at which time it was decided to send an address of congratulation to His Majesty, King of England, because the aboliton of *sati* by the Indian government had been confirmed by the Privy Council in England. As a gesture of honor, it was voted that Ram Mohan be entrusted with the task of presenting the address to the King. It was also moved "that as the Raja had devoted much labour to this matter, thanks were likewise due to him. The motion was seconded . . . and agreed to by all with great satisfaction."[78]

Today there is less unanimity as to who was finally responsible for the defeat of *sati*—Roy or Raj? The above discussion demonstrates the futility of this question. "The fact remains that Roy was an embodiment of the anti-*sati* movement both to the anti-*sati* and pro-*sati* groups as well as to the British rulers. And, it was only he who provided a consistent explanation of the practice and a theory of reform which could be understood by all these groups."[79]

# CHAPTER 7

# Educational Reform

The spread of Western education was the most potent catalyst in stimulating the Indian mind and in shaping new attitudes towards all aspects of life—aesthetic, social, moral, and religious.[1]

India was no stranger to learning, for the love of learning had deep roots going back to antiquity. There is hardly a country in the world where wisdom has been so prized and venerated as the home of the *Veda* (literally, knowledge). *Saraswati*, tutelary deity of writers and poets, has long been worshipped with offerings of flowers, fruits, and incense. Writing on *The History and Prospects of British Education in India*, F. W. Thomas stated in 1891: "From the simple poets of the Vedic age to the Bengali philosophers of the present day, there has been an uninterrupted succession of teachers and scholars. The immense literature which this long period has produced is thoroughly penetrated with the scholastic spirit: and the same spirit has left a deep impression on the social conditions of the people among whom that literature was produced."[2]

But times change, sometimes causing radical shifts in educational needs. Traditional education, both Hindu and Muslim, was oriented to exploring the spiritual world. The phenomenal world was looked upon as belonging to a lower order, and hence, less attention was paid to it.

This is not to say that Indians were unaware of astronomy, logic, law, mathematics, medicine, and science, but "experimental studies and empirical sciences were not adequately cultivated."[3]

Thus, while Europe, following the Renaissance, took giant steps into the modern era, India had little knowledge of the scientific age and even less interest. "In matters of education and intellectual progress India was passing through a period analogous to the Middle Ages of Europe."[4]

Raja Ram Mohan Roy was the first Indian to realize that in order for India to be delivered from medieval darkness, and to take her place among the enlightened nations of the world, she needed the same knowledge that made Europe great.

117

Let us now examine Ram Mohan's innovative activities in promoting the new education in Bengal within the context of other agencies involved in the same enterprise. These agencies have been categorized as: (1) missionary; (2) non-official; and (3) government.

The Protestant missionary activity received a fresh impetus when, in 1757, Bengal came under British rule. Schools were started by Kiernander, of the Danish mission, and by chaplains of the Company—David Brown, Henry Martyn, and Daniel Corrie. Back in England the cause of missionary education was championed by such notables as Charles Grant and William Wilberforce.

The most illustrious name in this galaxy of educational pioneers was William Carey. From the very beginning Carey recognized the importance of education. While an indigo planter in Mudnabatty (1794), he "founded the first school for native Indian children established in Northern India under European supervision, with Sanskrit for Hindus, Persian for Muhammadans, and with various branches of useful knowledge, and the doctrines and duties of Christianity for all."[5] This school was the precursor of the entire Indian Elementary School System later run by the government.

When he moved to Serampore in 1799, Carey and his colleagues established a vernacular school (1800) for Indian boys which rapidly enrolled forty pupils. By 1817 forty-five schools educating two thousand children dotted the vicinity of Serampore. The labors of Carey, Marshman, and Ward were growing by leaps and bounds. The crown of these endeavors was the foundation of Serampore College in 1818. The prospectus described it as "a College for the instruction of Asiatic Christians and other youth in Eastern Literature and European Science." Though the end of education was religious, Hindu and Muslim students were allowed the free exercise of their consciences. English was the medium of instruction for advanced levels, but the vernacular was emphasized for primary and secondary levels. The governor-general, the Marquis of Hastings, served as the first patron of the college, and Colonel Jacob Krefting of Denmark, served as the first Governor of the College. In 1827 Dr. Marshman secured a Royal Charter from the King of Denmark vesting the College with power to confer degrees in all faculties—"Serampore was the first College in India to possess such power."[6] Today, with few alterations, "the whole Ionic pile" still stands. The massive gates, a gift of the King of Denmark, overlook the picturesque Hooghly river. Often must these gates have opened for Ram Mohan who frequented this impressive center of learning.

Carey's educational work earned him the high esteem of successive governors. Commenting on Carey's recognition of his work and character, Lord Wellesley said: "I esteem such a testimony from such a man greater honour than the applause of Courts and Parliaments."[7]

Thus, by their educational and literary endeavors, the Serampore missionaries "laid the foundations of English education and Bengali prose literature. It is along lines laid down by them that intellectual development has taken place in subsequent times."[8]

In addition to the Baptists of Serampore, other missionary groups entered the field of education. These were: the Church Missionary Society, the London Missionary Society, and the Society for the Promotion of Christian Knowledge. In the footsteps of Carey, they generally reached out to the masses, educating them in Western ideas by means of the vernacular. What these dedicated souls failed to see was that the commercial and social opportunities of the time had clearly whetted the taste of the Bengali middle class for English education, so that though the vernacular schools flourished at the beginning, later, several had to close their doors. Only the institutions of higher learning continued. Serampore College still stands and is held in high repute both at home and abroad.

For his part, Ram Mohan welcomed the missionaries as agents of the new learning. His educational philosophy was sympathetic to the missionary position in that he opposed a purely secular education. He believed that both religious and moral instruction should be part of a school's curriculum.

Soon after his arrival in Calcutta, Ram Mohan paid a visit to the Baptists at Serampore. He must have been greatly impressed by their educational schemes because, soon thereafter, the Reverend William Yates, in a letter dated August 1816, says that Roy "offered Eustace a piece of ground for a school."[9]

Ram Mohan lent similar support to the Unitarians when, in 1822, at his own expense, he opened the Anglo-Indian School "for imparting a free education in English to Hindu boys."[10] He suggested to the Unitarians of America that they send a few teachers, "well qualified to teach English literature and science, and noted for their moral conduct," to help educate the children of the poorer classes.[11]

The Presbyterian missionaries seemed to have impressed him the most by their talents in education, and therefore received his enthusiastic support. The most outstanding educator of this group was Alexander Duff (1806–1878). He inaugurated a new phase of missionary work in India. In his bid to reach the influential classes, and members of the upper castes, he promoted Western education communicated through the English language. In his judgment the English language "is the lever which, as the instrument of conveying the entire range of knowledge, is destined to move all Hindustan."[12]

Ram Mohan was instrumental in getting the Presbyterian Board to send Duff to India, and met him upon his arrival. As historian Tara Chand sees it, the meeting of these two great minds was fraught with exciting possibilities:

The representative of the West, zealous for the conversion of the pagans of India through English education, met the outstanding Indian of the time, the harbinger of a new age, who believed with equal ardour that the spread of modern knowledge was necessary to restore the vanished greatness of his motherland. Although the purpose of the two were poles apart—the first stood for the destruction of the values India had cherished during thousands of years, and the other desired to purify and perpetuate the ancient faith by removing the dust and corruption of the ages, the two agreed to co-operate for their immediate objective, namely, the advancement of Western learning.[13]

The second agency promoting the new education in Bengal was the non-official group, comprising "public spirited Bengalees, aided by some broad-minded English philanthropists and reformers."[14]

With British dominance in Bengal there arose a bourgeois social revolution and the emergence of a new middle class, largely out of the ranks of the Hindu community. Their keen utilitarian sense made it plain that in order to climb to the top of the social heap they needed to know the thought and language of the rulers. The key business opportunities and prime civic appointments lay in an English education. Some of the more public-spirited utilized their new-found knowledge to open elementary schools for Bengali boys eager for this type of education. Some schools were commercially inspired, but their standards were low. Functionally oriented, and without suitable text-books, these commercial schools went little beyond meeting basic clerical and administrative skills.

Philanthropic Englishmen also opened up schools geared to the new education. One of the more successful ones was the Dhuramtollah Academy established by David Drummond in 1810. He introduced his students to Western classics and tried to develop their rational capability. Henry Derozio, the Anglo-Indian scholar, was a prize graduate of the institution.

The Calcutta School society, established in 1819 for the purpose of advancing elementary education and teacher training was also an important agent in furthering the cause of English education.

The most prestigious and permanent product of non-official enterprises was the establishment of the *Vidyalaya* or Hindu College (later called Presidency College) in 1817. This institution was the brain-child of David Hare, a professional watch-maker and jeweler, but whose first love was promoting education and liberal social reform. It was Hare's ambition to establish a college in which English literature and European science would be taught through the medium of the English language. He succeeded in winning the support of several eminent Hindu gentlemen who, under the leadership of Sir Edward Hyde East, Chief Justice of the Calcutta Supreme Court, organized a committee to raise funds for the college. A ranking *Brahmin* objected to Ram Mohan's par-

ticipation in the committee because of his criticism of idolatry, whereupon Ram Mohan graciously bowed out. This self-effacing act of Ram
Mohan in a cause he dearly espoused is a tribute to the magnanimity of
the man. "There was no difficulty," writes Peary Chand Mitra, "in getting Rammohun Roy to renounce his connection, as he valued the education of his countrymen more than the empty flourish of his name as a
committee-man."[15]

Roy not only cooperated with other agencies in promoting Western
education in Bengal; he started his own schools.

In 1816–1817 he built a school at Suripara, Calcutta. Admission was
free for the two-hundred students enrolled. A class for intellectually
gifted children was held at his garden-house in Maniktala. English, Sanskrit, and geography were taught to the pupils who numbered fifty by
1818.

In 1822 under the auspices of the Calcutta Unitarian Committee,
Ram Mohan started the Anglo-Hindu School in the proximity of Cornwallis Square, Calcutta. Its purpose was the same as the *Maha Vidyalaya*.
Its managers were William Adams and David Hare. The *Bengal Chronicle* (January 10, 1828) gives a glimpse of the school:

> This institution is . . . principally supported at the expense of Rammohun
> Roy with the aid of a few philanthropic individuals, both among his own
> countrymen and Europeans, who are friendly to the communication of
> liberal education to the Natives of this country; and it must have afforded
> a very high degree of pleasure to that distinguished individual as well as
> to those who have aided him in his benevolent exertions, to observe the
> progress which several of the pupils have made in their studies. To the
> intelligent observer it must also have been an additional source of gratifi-
> cation to notice among the scholars several of the children of the native
> gentlemen who contribute to the support of the school, in no respect dis-
> tinguished from those who receive their education gratuitously.[16]

In a similar vein the *Calcutta Gazette* (February 28, 1829) praises Ram
Mohan's liberality and his efforts to ameliorate the intellectual condition of his countrymen, and then adds: "As the founder of the Institution, he takes an active interest in its proceedings; and we know that he
is not more desirous of anything than of its success, as a means of ef-
fecting the moral and intellectual regeneration of the Hindus . . . it
must always be to him a pleasing prospect, that when millions yet unborn shall hail the return of knowledge to his country, they will associate that circumstance with the name of Rammohun Roy."[17]

Ram Mohan did not have to wait for the "millions yet unborn" to
witness the success of his benevolent endeavors. A grass-roots movement for intellectual excellence spread among the top students of the
Hindu College, the School Society's English Schools, and Ram Mohan's
school. By 1830 some seven societies were formed, seventeen to fifty

members belonging to each group. They met once a week for "discussing questions in literature and science; and sometimes in politics."[18] The medium of discussion was the English language.

The precedent set by the English speaking scholars was soon emulated by those in Bengali literature. A literary society, under the designation of *Surbututtwa-deepeeka Subha* (Society for the Diffusion of all Branches of Knowledge), was started at the Anglo-Hindu School. One of its proponents voiced its principle objective thus: "As no Society has been formed in Calcutta for the cultivation of the Bengalee language, we have proposed to establish one for that purpose; and we believe that the country will be greatly benefited by its influence."[19]

We now turn to the third context within which Ram Mohan carried out his educational reforms—his relationship with the government.

In the early stages the British government did nothing to aid education. An erroneous notion has long prevailed that the British introduced English in order to raise a cadre of clerks to keep the state machinery running. But "nothing can be further from the truth. The English education was introduced in this country, not by the British Government, but in spite of them."[20]

The first official to advance the notion of a system of English education was Charles Grant, a civil servant of the Company. Like Ram Mohan, he was strongly convinced that the moral and social decadence of the people stemmed from their "dense and widespread ignorance," and that these evils were eradicable through an English education.

The pitch Grant and other officials made on behalf of English was based on the supposition that English would be the best means for assimilating the Indian subjects, on the one hand, and giving them direct access to high officials, on the other. Further, Western literature and science would not only free the people's minds from medieval superstition, but enable them to think and act productively in all practical matters of their life. Against the fears that the enlightenment of the natives in Western ideas and values might be politically disadvantageous to the rulers, Grant argued that, to the contrary, the Indians would be grateful for this new knowledge, and that it would spur greater trade.

The Court of Directors and members of the House of Commons demurred. Political stability was their chief concern. As to morals, they held that "the Hindus had as good a system of faith and of morals as most people and that it would be madness to attempt their conversion or to give them any more learning or any other description of learning than what they already possessed."[21] Basically, they were of the opinion that it was premature for the government to sponsor a system of education in India at a time when no such system existed in England.

Nevertheless, with the assumption of ruling powers, the Company did feel a certain obligation to continue the Muslim practice of educational patronage. This led to the opening of the Calcutta *Madrassa* (1780) by Warren Hastings. His purpose was to pacify the Calcutta

Muslims by qualifying their sons for "responsible and lucrative offices in the State, even at that date largely monopolised by the Hindus, and to produce competent officers for the Courts of Justice."[22]

Similarly, to conciliate the Hindus a Sanskrit College was establish in Benares (1791) by the Resident, Jonathan Duncan.

In 1801 Lord Wellesley opened the Fort William College which became a prominent center for developing Indian prose literature.

Notwithstanding these token efforts, Lord Minto was dismayed by British apathy toward Indian education and its failure to keep alive the literature of the Hindus. In his Minute of 1811, he ascribed the slow death of Indian science "to the want of that encouragement which was formerly afforded to it by princes, chieftains, and opulent individuals under the native governments."[23]

Government apathy could not ignore indefinitely the rise of the new spirit in education. The work of the missionaries and the non-official agencies finally had an impact. In 1813 the Company's Charter was renewed with a directive from Parliament to the Company to take steps for the "introduction of useful knowledge and religious and moral improvements," and moreover that "a sum of not less than a lac of rupees should be set apart each year, and applied to the revival and improvement of literature and the encouragement of the learned natives of India, and for the introduction and promotion of a knowledge of the sciences among the inhabitants of the British Territories in India."[24]

For a decade the above clause lay dormant in the records. There was not a single year in between 1813 and 1823 that the sum of money allocated for education was fully spent. Only in 1823 was a Committee of Public Instruction formed in Bengal, and plans were drafted for a Sanskrit College in Calcutta. On August 21, 1821 it was resolved that the upper class of Hindu society be instructed in the literature and science of the West through the medium of Sanskrit. As a first step the committee thought it pedagogically sound to start with an Oriental curriculum and gradually ease into the Western area. Initial studies were therefore to be confined to the sacred literature of the Hindus taught in the Sanskrit language.

In the opinion of Ram Mohan, this decision of the Committee was a retrograde step. They were marching backward into the future. A power-play was going on between the Orientalists and the Anglicists. The former were now in command, but Ram Mohan's sympathies lay with the latter. Ram Mohan not only stood for English as the medium of instruction in higher learning, but he wanted India's new educational system to boast a modern curriculum offering courses in science and technology. On December 11, 1823 he dispatched a letter to Lord Amherst making known his objections to the establishment of the Calcutta Sanskrit College.

First, he grateftuly acknowledges that the establishment of the new Sanskrit College in Calcutta "evinces the laudable desire of the Government to improve the Natives of India by Education."[25]

When Parliament ordered that a considerable sum of money be devoted annually to the instruction of the people, the hope was that a seminary would be founded employing European teachers to instruct in "Mathematics, Natural Philosophy, Chemistry, Anatomy, and other useful sciences, which the Nations of Europe have carried to a degree of perfection that has raised them above the inhabitants of other parts of the world."[26]

It now transpires that plans are being laid for a Sanskrit school under the Hindu pandits to "impart such knowledge as is already current in India." The character of such an institution would be similar to those which existed in Europe prior to Lord Bacon. It could only succeed in loading the minds of youth with "grammatical niceties and metaphysical distinctions" which have no practical bearing for the benefit of society.

Sanskrit, the proposed medium of instruction, requires a lifetime for mastering, and "the learning concealed under this almost impervious veil is far from sufficient to reward the labour of acquiring it."[27]

Since the money allocated by the government was ear-marked for the improvement of the Indian subjects, the above considerations demonstrate that the objective will be defeated. "No improvement can be expected from inducing young men to consume a dozen years of the most valuable period of their lives in acquiring the niceties of the Byakurun or Sangscrit Grammar." Neither can any improvement be expected "from such speculations as the following which are the themes suggested by the Vedant: In what manner is the soul absorbed into the deity? . . . . Nor will youths be fitted to be better members of society by the Vendantic doctrines, which teach them to believe that all visible things have no real existence; that as father, brother, etc., have no actual entirety, they consequently deserve no real affection, and therefore the sooner we escape from them and leave the world the better."[28]

Similar disqualifications are applied to the study of all forms of scholastic knowledge—the *mimamsa, nyaya shastra*, etc.

To appreciate the uselessness of encouraging such imaginary learning as characterized above, Lord Amherst is asked "to compare the state of science and literature in Europe before the time of Lord Bacon, with the progress of knowledge made since he wrote."

In closing he says that if it had been a conspiracy to keep Britain in ignorance of real knowledge, Baconian philosophy would not have been allowed to displace scholastic learning which perpetuated that ignorance. Similarly, the Sanskrit system of education "would be best calculated to keep this country in darkness," if such had been the intention of Parliament. But as the declared policy of the British legislature is the improvement of the native population, "it will consequently promote a more liberal and enlightened system of instruction, embracing mathematics, natural philosophy, chemistry and anatomy, with other useful sciences which may be accomplished with the sum

proposed by employing a few gentlemen of talents and learning educated in Europe, and providing a college furnished with the necessary
books, instruments and apparatus."[29]

Pandit Sivanath Sastri is moved by the foresight displayed by Ram
Mohan in this letter to Lord Amherst. He says: "When we reflect that
these lines were penned by a native of Bengal at a time when the current ideas of education were low and old-fashioned, our wonder knows
no bounds, and we feel them to be characteristic of the great man
whom Providence had designed to be the maker of the new India."[30]
And Bishop Heber, Metropolitan of India, who delivered this letter
(December 11, 1823) to his Lord Amherst, wrote that: "For its good
English, good sense and forcible arguments [it] is a real curiosity, as
coming from an Asiatic."[31] Though patronizing in tone, the letter
clearly establishes this "Asiatic" as a man of unusual insight. The principles he has enunciated are relevant today as guidelines for a national
policy of progressive education.

In case there is misunderstanding, in his strong remarks on the Vendanta and Sanskrit language, Ram Mohan was not downgrading these
subjects. We have seen in his controversies with the Christian missionaries how spiritedly he defended the Sanskrit language and India's ancient wisdom enshrined in the Vedas.[32] Later, in 1826, he founded the
*Vedantic* College for the "propagation and defence of *Hindu* Unitarianism," with instruction in *"Bengali and Sanskrit"* (italics supplied).[33] The
point he was emphasizing was that at this particular juncture India
could only move forward by adopting the same education which had
thrust Europe into the modern age.

In his articulation of these sentiments, Ram Mohan was acting as a
spokesman of the people not only the upper and middle class Hindus
residing in Calcutta, but common folk in the hinterland; all of whom
recognized that English was the golden key to prosperity. It is this solid
consensus which explains why no members of the Hindu orthodoxy
opposed Ram Mohan's plea for a Western-oriented college in place of
the government's Sanskrit College.

More surprising is the fact that the government failed to appreciate
the representative character of Ram Mohan's arguments. In its forwarding letter (January 2, 1824) to the General Committee of Public
Instruction, the government stated:

> In furnishing your committee with a copy of the above paper, His Lord
> ship in Council, abstain remarking that it is obviously written under an
> imperfect, and erroneous conception of the plan of education and course
> of study which it is proposed to introduce into the new college that the
> defects and demerits of Sanscrit Literature and philosophy are therein
> represented in an exaggerated light; and that arguments in favour of en
> couraging native learning as well as the positive obligation to promote its
> revival and improvements imposed on the Government by the terms of

the Act of Parliament directing the appropriation of certain funds to the object of public education have been wholly overlooked by the writer.[34]

On these grounds the government considered it inappropriate to honor the letter of Ram Mohan with a reply.

To show how correct Ram Mohan was in his assessment of what the people wanted, one can point to the fact that whereas the Sanskrit, Arabic and Persian publications of the Committee of Public Instruction gathered dust in warehouses, the English publications of the School Book Society sold upwards of 31,000 books over a two year period.[35]

It was not long before the Committee of Public Instruction developed its own Anglicist faction which lobbied for liberal, Western education imparted through the English language. They supported the well-known "filtration theory" which calculated that though Western education could only reach a limited number of students, this elite would serve as the core through whom education would seep down to the masses through the medium of vernacular literature.

The triumph of the Anglicists was assured when Alexander Duff, the Scottish missionary, was appointed to the committee. We have already seen the part Ram Mohan played in requesting the Presbyterian Church to send missionary teachers. Soon after his arrival, the young Scotsman paid a visit to the "Erasmus of India." They both concurred in their educational goals. Ram Mohan emphasized that all true education "ought to be religious, since the object was not merely to give information, but to develop and regulate all powers of the mind, the emotions, and the workings of the conscience."[36] Duff expressed the need for premises for his school, and Ram Mohan promptly obliged.

Inspired by his Brahmin benefactor, Duff threw his considerable weight with the English party in the Committee of Public Instruction. The Party's hands were strengthened also by the forward-thinking mind of William Bentinck. He gave the principle of promoting education embodied in the Charter Act of 1813 "a new force and direction," stipulating "the content of the learning should be western knowledge and the medium of instruction English." He regarded "the British language, the key to all improvements," and general education as a "panacea for the regeneration of India."[37]

The governor-general's stand on the new education was fortified by Thomas Babington Macaulay who joined the Committee as the new Law Member in 1834. His famous Education Minute of 1835 was the most vociferous indictment of Oriental education. Half of the members of the Committee still advocated Sanskrit or Arabic as the medium of Indian education, but this fiery statesman would brook no opposition. Scorning Oriental studies, he declares that he has never found one among the Orientalists who could deny "that a single shelf of a good European library was worth the whole native literature of India and Arabia." The choice is therefore clear for the policy-makers. It is a question:

Whether, when it is in our power to teach this language [English], we shall teach languages in which by universal confession there are no books on any subject which deserves to be compared with our own; whether when we can teach European science, we shall teach systems which by universal confession whenever they differ from those of Europe differ for the worse; and whether, when we patronise sound philosophy and true history, we shall countenance at the public expense medical doctrines which would disgrace an English farrier, astronomy which would move laughter in girls at an English boarding-school, history abounding with kings thirty feet high and reigns 30,000 years long, and geography made up of seas of treacle and seas of butter.[38]

Under such a heavy barrage the Orientalist party was roundly discomfited. Macaulay won the full support of Bentinck, and on March 7, 1835, the Committee decided to earmark all funds for English education. The Sanskrit College and the *Madrassa* would continue, but they would not be eligible for new financial increments.

Many years later, the Report of the Education Commission appointed by Lord Ripon in 1882 observed that "It took twelve years of controversy, the advocacy of Macaulay, and the decisive action of a new Governor-General, before the Committee could, as a body, acquiesce in the policy," urged by Ram Mohan Roy.[39] The Report is a tribute to Ram Mohan, vindicating his advocacy of Western education.

## CHAPTER 8

# Political Reform

Abraham Lincoln once remarked that the world has never had a good definition of the word liberty. The problem is, to define liberty is to limit it, and in limiting it you destroy it. But while liberty cannot be defined, it can be demonstrated, and one of the finest demonstrations of liberty is the life and labors of Raja Ram Mohan Roy. Like Lincoln, he had an intense and unquenchable passion for liberty which was the key to his whole life. One can see him pursue it in all areas of his life—religious, moral, social, and intellectual. But our main task here is liberty in politics which is the highest political end.[1]

Ram Mohan Roy was a pioneer of Indian freedom. Historians call him "the prophet of the new age." He drew a blueprint for political agitation along constitutional lines which, fifty years later, helped to bring to birth the Indian National Congress. His political views have a modern ring and "in essential features represent the high-water mark of Indian political thought of the nineteenth century."[2]

Ram Mohan would have agreed with Aristotle that "the good of man must be the end of the science of politics." "Man" for him was not merely "Indian man" but "International man." But politics, like charity, begins at home, so we shall start with his activities on the national front.

His English biographer, Miss Sophia Dobson Collet, hails him as the "tribune and prophet of New India." The prospect of an India educated and "approximating to European standards of culture, seems to have never been long absent from Rammohan's mind; and he did, however vaguely, claim in advance for his countrymen the political rights which progress in civilization inevitably involves."[3]

The Raja's political ideas were rooted in his religious view of man as "eternally free." This insight of the Upanishads was at odds with the caste ridden beliefs and practices of the prevailing religion of India. Political reform therefore went hand in hand with religious reform. The intimate connection between religion and politics is clear from the following extract of one of his letters. He regrets to say:

The present system of religion adhered to by the Hindus is not well calculated to promote their political interest. The distinction of castes, introducing innumerable divisions and sub-divisions among them, has entirely deprived them of patriotic feeling, and the multitude of religious rites and ceremonies and the laws of purification have totally disqualified them from undertaking any different enterprise .... It is, I think, necessary that some change should take place in their religion, at least for the sake of their political advantage and social comfort.[4]

Further, some of the very virtues of Hinduism, he thought, had become its political vices. Hindu civilization had produced an ethos of refinement and sociability which, carried to extremes, had proven politically emasculating. The metaphysical manners of his people had rendered them too meek and mild to withstand their many conquerors. He says, "We have been subjected to such insults for about nine centuries, and the cause of such degradation has been our excess in civilization and abstinence from the slaughter even of animals."[5]

In spite of the degrading effects of centuries, Ram Mohan was a firm believer in the power of the people to rise again. In terms of their native capabilities, the Indians were not one whit inferior to the Europeans. He met racism head-on, regarding no man his superior. He debunked the myth of "Asiatic effeminacy" and pointed out that almost all of the great personalities of antiquity were Asians. The world was indebted to the ancient Indians for the first dawn of knowledge, and if, they seemed backward compared with the Europeans, it was only in respect to technological advancement and democratic institutions.[6]

To help bridge this gap, he welcomed the British presence. He believed that England had a cultural and humanitarian mission to perform in India. The alliance, in his view, would introduce Indians to modern world-culture, set up institutions of democratic government, and bring the nation into the family of other free and enlightened peoples of the world. He conceived this British mission in India in almost messianic terms as is evident by the eulogy with which he concludes his *Final Appeal to the Christian Public*:

I now conclude my Essay by offering up thanks to the Supreme Disposer of the events of the universe for having unexpectedly delivered this country from the long-continued tyranny of its former Rulers, and placed it under the government of the English, a nation who not only are blessed with the enjoyment of civil and political liberty, but also interest themselves in promoting liberty and social happiness, as well as free inquiry into literary and religious subjects, among those nations to which their influence extends.[7]

This statement should be taken as a mixture of hope and fact. So far as the facts were concerned, he did not feel himself to be in the best position to assess the quality of British rule in India, but left that judgment to posterity. He states, "At present the whole empire (with the exception of a few provinces) has been placed under British power, and some advantages have already been derived from the prudent management of its rulers, from whose general character a hope of future quiet and happiness is justly entertained. The succeeding generation will, however, be more adequate to pronounce on the real advantages of the government."[8]

While the future was open, he could look down the road and see certain possibilities. His remarks on the settlement of Europeans in India reflect his vision. Dated July 24, 1832, these remarks constitute his "mature considerations," and therefore must be given precedence over earlier fragments of data on the subject.

He first lists "Advantages" of the settlement of Europeans in India. They are reckoned as: (1) the introduction by Westerners of modern systems of agriculture, commerce, and mechanical arts; (2) removal of superstitions and prejudices by the spread of communication; (3) improvement of laws and the whole judicial system; (4) protection against the abuses of power; (5) diffusion of European arts and sciences, and the cultivation of the English language through schools and seminaries; (6) multiplying channels of communication to enable managers of public affairs to collect authentic information about the country; and (7) military security against foreign invasion.

We give the eighth and ninth items in full because they clearly tell us how Ram Mohan felt about India's connection with Britain:

Eighthly—The same cause would operate to continue the connexion between Great Britain and India on a solid and permanent footing; provided only the latter country be governed in a liberal manner, by means of Parliamentary superintendence, and other such legislative checks in this country as may be devised and established. India may thus, for an unlimited period, enjoy union with England, and the advantage of her enlightened Government; and in return contribute to support to the greatness of this country.

Ninthly—If, however, events should occur to effect a separation between the two countries, then still the existence of a large body of respectable settlers (consisting of Europeans and their descendants, professing Christianity, and speaking the English language in common with the bulk of the people, as well as possessed of superior knowledge, scientific, mechanical, and political) would bring that vast empire in the East to a level with other large Christian countries in Europe, and by means of its immense riches and extensive population, and by the help which may be reasonably expected from Europe, they (the settlers and their descendants) may succeed sooner or later in enlightening and civilizing the surrounding nations of Asia.[9]

Next, the Raja lists some of the principle "Disadvantages" that the settlement of Europeans might bring, along with the remedies calculated to prevent them from occurring. Mapping the future, he says: (1) Because of the common bonds between settlers and the ruling class, there is the possibility that Europeans may dominate the Indians and discriminate against them on the grounds of religion, colours, and habits. The potential problem can be obviated by only allowing, for the first twenty years, the immigration of "educated persons of character and capital," and by the enactment of trial by jury; and (2) Europeans could have the upper hand over the populace by having readier access to persons in authority. This should be remedied by placing Indian and European attorneys on the same footing before the judges.

The fourth point is of special interest. Ram Mohan argues that in certain quarters there is apprehension that "if events should occur to effect a separation (which may rise from many accidental causes, about which it is vain to speculate or make predictions), still a friendship and highly advantageous commercial intercourse may be kept up between the two free and Christian countries, united as they then will be by resemblance of language, religion, and manners."[10]

This remarkable document gives us Ram Mohan's vision of the new India in a clear and concise way. He sees India as a country governed in a liberal manner, with parliamentary superintendence, and all necessary legislative checks and balances. People of all classes and stations in life would have the same civil rights with jury trials—the juries being composed impartially of Europeans as well as Indians.

The first European settlers, he envisaged, would be of superior caliber, acting from motives of benevolence, public spirit, and fellowship. Their presence would certainly serve as a social leaven, not only by raising European standards, but also by emancipating Indians from ignorance and superstition, thereby securing their affection and loyalty.

It would be an India, enlightened by European education, with schools dotting the whole country, and the English language spoken far and wide.

Economically, India would be strong, geared to the advanced technology and agricultural methods of the West.

Politically, India would be safe from foreign invasion, protected by British power.

Should the political ties between the two countries be severed, the European inhabitants of India would continue to raise the country's standards until it reached the level of the countries of Europe, and through India's influence surrounding Asian countries would similarly be modernized.

The above discussion makes it abundantly clear that while Ram Mohan believed that India needed to undergo a period of political tutelage, he also believed that India would one day come of age and become an independent nation in its own right. The settlement of British colonialists in India was only a means toward an end, namely, a free India in a foreseeable future.

We cite the following evidence in support of Ram Mohan's vision of a free and unbound India. In a letter to J. Crawford, dated August 18, 1828, he speculates:

Supposing that some 100 years hence the Native character becomes elevated from constant intercourse with Europeans and the acquirements of general and political knowledge as well as of modern arts and sciences, is it possible that they will not have the spirit as well as the inclination to resist effectually any unjust and oppressive measures serving to degrade them in the scale of society? *It should not be lost sight of that the position of India is very different from that of Ireland, to any quarter of which an English fleet may suddenly convey a body of troops that may force its way in the requisite direction and succeed in suppressing every effort of a refractory spirit. Were India to share one fourth of the knowledge and energy of that country she would prove from her remote situation, her riches and her vast population, either useful and profitable as a willing province, an ally of the British Empire or troublesome and annoying as a determined enemy* (italics supplied).[11]

The second piece of evidence is taken from a statement of Ram Mohan to M. Victor Jacquemont, a French naturalist and traveller. He declares, "India requires many more years of English domination so that she might not have to lose many things while she is *reclaiming her political independence*" (italics supplied).[12]

Thirdly, Stanford Arnot testifies that while Ram Mohan anticipated India's political freedom, he always contended for "the necessity of continuing British rule for at least forty or fifty years to come for the good of the people themselves . . ."[13]

Fourthly, the most explicit testimony supporting Ram Mohan's vision of a free India comes from none other than his co-worker, the Reverend William Adam:

He saw—*a man of his acute mind and local knowledge could not but see—the selfish, cruel and almost insane errors of the English in governing India, but he also saw that their system of Government and policy had redeeming qualities not to be found in the native governments.* Without seeking to destroy, therefore, his object was to reform and improve the system of foreign government to which his native country had become subject; and without stimulating his countrymen to discontent or disaffection, his endeavour was by teaching them a pure religion and promoting among them an enlightened education to qualify them for the enjoyment of the more extensive civil and political franchise than they yet possessed . . . *he joined with some noble-minded, far-seeing Englishmen who have expressed the opinion that the wisest and most honourable course, the justest and most humane, which England can pursue towards India is by education and by a gradual development of the principle of civil and political liberty in the public institutions she establishes and sanctions, to prepare natives ultimately to take the government of their own country into their own hands. To co-operate in bringing about such a result was one of Ram Mohun's unceasing aims . . .* (italics supplied).[14]

In the meantime, Ram Mohan stood as watch-dog over the British political establishment. He clearly understood both the light and dark sides of the British character and worked for the triumph of the one over the other. In the words of Professor Rajani Kanta Guha, "The Government of India was in his day a benevolent despotism. Rammohun wanted that it should retain its trait of benevolence, but outgrow its irresponsible character, and steadily move towards a representative form calculated to fulfill the noblest political aspirations of the Indian people."[15]

To acomplish this goal, Ram Mohan was quick to seize upon the power of the press. Through the printed page he could not only keep his countrymen informed with useful knowledge, but also supply the rulers with *authentic information* about the facts of Indian life. He seems to have been guided by the Socratic principle that "knowledge is virtue"—that an enlightened government would somehow act more benevolently than one that was out of touch with the people.

It followed from this that the indispensable prerequisite of good government was a free press. But insistence on freedom of the press made him irritate the Achilles heel of the British statesmanship which was "the unwavering faith of the Olympians at home in the infallibility of the man on the spot."[16] The Raja, however, was sceptical of all forms of infallibility—religious, rational, and most of all, the political infallibility of petty bureaucrats. "*He held that every good ruler must be conscious of the great liability to error in managing the affairs of a vast empire*, and therefore he should be anxious to afford every individual the readiest means of bringing to his notice whatever may require his interference. This object can be secured only by the *unrestrained liberty of publication*. Endowed with unusual physical and moral courage, he confronted the hauteur of the ruling caste with unruffled dignity" (italics supplied).[17]

Ram Mohan entered the field of journalism soon after the government of Lord Hastings abolished press censorship in August 1818. From the time of the publication of Hicky's *Bengal Gazette* in 1780, the English press had been in hot water with the government because of its outspoken criticism of governmental mismanagement. When criticism went too far, the government of Lord Wellesley clamped down with certain restrictive regulations issued in May of 1799. Editors held in violation of these regulations were to be deported to Europe.

Obviously, the above punishment could not be meted out to Indian editors also held in contempt. Therefore, in the name of fairness to European editors, and also because of his more liberal views, when Lord Hastings took the reigns of government, he restored free discussion in the press and only held the press responsible to the laws of sedition and libel.

The Court of Directors in London were furious at the government's action and drafted a dispatch (April 7, 1820) reprimanding Lord Hastings. But this dispatch was not transmitted to the government of India inasmuch as the Board of Control failed to respond to the Court of Directors; and hence, the censorship of the press was abolished.

Indians hailed the lifting of restrictions with jubilation. The tenor of excitement is expressed in the following statements by leading citizens of Madras. They observed: "while contemplating this important subject it must have occurred that to the attainment of truth, freedom of enquiry was essentially necessary; that public opinion was the strongest support of just Government; and that liberty of discussion served but to strengthen the hands of the Executive . . . . Such freedom of discussion was the gift of a liberal and enlightened mind, an invaluable and unequivocal expression of those sentiments evinced by the whole tenor of your Lordship's administration."[18]

After the Regulation of 1818, two towering figures made their appearance upon the stage of Indian journalism—J. S. Buckingham, the liberal voice of the *Calcutta Journal*, and Ram Mohan Roy, though not the founder of native journalism, unequivocally its chief architect. He started the *Sambad Kaumudi (The Moon of Intelligence)*; the *Brahmana Sevadhi (Brahmanical Magazine)*; the *Jam-i-Jahan Numa (The Mirror that Reflects the World)*; and the *Mirat-ul-Akhbar (Mirror of Intelligence)*.

The *Brahmanical Magazine* was the organ through which he defended Hinduism against the attacks of the Christian missionaries. The *Sambad Kaumudi* and the *Mirat-ul-Akhbar* dealt not only with social and religious issues, but were also politically oriented. The prospectus of the Persian newspaper reads in part:

> In taking upon myself to edit this Paper, my only object is, that I may lay before the Public such articles of Intelligence as may increase their experience, and tend to their social improvement; and that to the extent of my abilities, I may communicate to the Rulers a knowledge of the real situation of their subjects, and make the subjects acquainted with the established laws and customs of their Rulers: that the Rulers may the more readily find an opportunity of granting relief to the people: and the people may be put in possession of the means of obtaining protection and redress from their Rulers.[19]

The voice of the liberal press, both Indian and European, proved too strident and dangerous for the British administrators whose policies came constantly under fire. Adam and Bailey, both members of the Council in India, wrote strong notes on the question of the freedom of the press.

Bailey expressed official fear that an unleashed press could very easily foment insubordination, discontent, and infidelity among the native troops, which would seriously affect the stability of the British empire.

In point of fact, Bailey's true apprehension was that the Indians, though apathetic for the present, might be roused in the near future by the liberal press and begin making demands for political rights and privileges. As a staunch Christian, Bailey was also offended by the manner in which Christian missionaries were publicly censured in the *Brahmanical Magazine* without regard for their position as members of the ruling class.

The theory which guided Bailey's policy was that laws must be suited to the level of society. He explains his viewpoint with the following logic:

> It is a primary and almost humane part of our policy to adapt our laws to the state of society, and not prematurely introduce the institution of a highly civilized society among a less enlightened people. In England the laws regarding the press have kept pace with the progress of public opinion and with other institutions of a free people; the minds of men have been gradually prepared for the exaggeration and misrepresentation which must ever attend freedom of publication.[20]

The Anglo-Indian press expressed similar misgivings about the Regulation of 1818, as did the Council. The *Asiatic Journal* warned about the perilous responsibility taken upon themselves by those who removed the censorship of the Indian press, and anticipated evil times ahead unless the resident authorities acted with "resolution, constancy, union, and vigour." Among the papers blacklisted by the *Asiatic Journal*, the *Sambad Kaumudi* was preeminently maligned as:

> A Journal published in the language of the natives, conducted by natives, designed for the perusal of native Indians, and of them most exclusively, is set on foot, for the purpose of fomenting their accidental discontents, of opening their eyes to the defects of their rulers, of encouraging and giving utterance, not only to their complaints, but to their remonstrances.[21]

The Council had by now made up its mind on the need to remove the dangers posed by the Regulation of 1818. The liberal press tried to argue that the free vernacular press was rendering yeoman's service to the government by acquainting it with the "real situation and sentiments of the whole population."[22] The *Calcutta Journal* (April 5, 1823) raises the point that if "a spark of discontent" is kindled anywhere is it not best that it be immediately discovered by the free press, instead of being smothered in silence, "until it secretly extend far and wide, and then suddenly burst into an unquenchable flame?"[23] But none of these arguments of the liberal press allayed the fears and suspicions of the Council.

The opportunity to act upon their trepidations was seized by Adam himself who officiated as acting governor-general upon the departure of Lord Hastings. The *Mirat* describes the despotic tactics of Adam to curb freedom:

> The eminently learned Dr. Bryce, the head minister of the new Scotch Church, having accepted the situation of Clerk of the Stationery belonging to the Honourable Company, Mr. Buckingham the editor of the Calcutta Journal observed directly as well as indirectly that it was unbecoming of the character of the minister to accept a situation like this; upon which the Governor-General, in consideration of his disrespectful expression, passed an order that Mr. Buckingham should leave India for England within the period of two months from the date of the receipt of this order, and that after the expiration of that period he is not allowed to remain a single day in India.[24]

The expulsion of Buckingham was followed by the capricious promulgation of a Rule and Ordinance, dated March 14, 1823, "enacting that a daily or any periodical paper should not be published in this city [Calcutta] without an Affidavit being made by its Proprietor in the Police Office, and without a Licence being procured for such a publication for the Chief Secretary to Government; and that after such licence being obtained, it is optional with the Governor-General to recall the same, whenever His Excellency is dissatistifed with any part of that paper."[25]

Ram Mohan was most indignant. He raised a strong protest against Adam's Ordinance, and, in company with five other Indian sympathizers, submitted a memorial to the Supreme Court. His English biographer says of this document: "It may be regarded as the *Areopagitica of Indian history*. Alike in diction and in argument, it forms a noble landmark in the progress of English culture in the East."[26]

We shall paraphrase and quote the highlights of the Memorial because of its singular importance.

Roy begins by furnishing "proofs" of Indian loyalty to the British government because the preamble to the Rule and Ordinance had implied certain political apprehensions.

First, there is the fact that the natives of Calcutta have invested major capital with the government. Secondly, landholders have improved their estates and increased their productivity because of their faith in promises made by the government at the time of the Permanent Settlement in 1793. Thirdly, Indians have come to the assistance of the British during the last wars fought by them against neighbouring powers. Fourthly, the Hindu community of Bengal is outspoken about the continual literary and political improvements that have enriched their lives under the present system of government.

These unequivocal proofs of loyalty and attachment are tributes to the wisdom and liberality of the British government in the means they have adopted for the gradual improvement of social and domestic conditions, and for the establishment of institutions of learning and justice.

The vernacular and English press have contributed to the good of society by diffusing useful and political knowledge, and have in no way been socially and politically irresponsible. Yet, the government has seen fit to promulgate a Rule and Ordinance imposing severe restraints on the press through requirements of oaths and licenses.

The situation is serious because Hindus have an "invincible prejudice against making a voluntary affidavit, or undergoing the solemnities of an oath," and therefore they will prefer to leave the publishing field. If this happens, the present circulation of information which has significantly improved the general intelligence of the people will cease.

A shut down press will preclude Indians from keeping the government informed about the conduct of its executive officers; and by the same token, it will prevent them from communicating frankly with the King and his Council on the way the government is running British interests in India. Given the vastness of the area which must be combed for information, both King and local government stand to lose should the vernacular press go out of business.

The moment the precious right of free speech, to which they have been accustomed since the establishment of British rule, is withdrawn, the citizens of Calcutta will no longer be justified in making boast that Providence has placed them under the protection of the British nation, and "that they are secured in the enjoyment of the same civil and religious privileges that every Briton is entitled to in England."[27]

The Memorialists express confidence that the British government will not follow the political policy of Asiatic potentates who imagine rulers are best off when they keep their subjects in the dark about what is going on. History teaches the opposite: "For we find that as often as an ignorant people, when an opportunity offered, have revolted against their Rulers, all sorts of barbarous excesses and cruelties have been the consequence; whereas a people naturally disposed to peace and ease, when placed under a good Government from which they experience just and liberal treatment, must become the more attached to it, in proportion as they become enlightened and the great body of the people are taught to appreciate the value of the blessings they enjoy under its Rule."[28]

The high ethical tenor of the Memorial is repeated in its concluding statement. Every good ruler who is aware of human fallibility and has reverence for the moral order, must know that serious errors can be incurred in the operation of so vast an empire. He will, therefore, "be anxious to afford every individual the readiest means of bringing to his notice whatever may require his interference." To achieve this end, "the unrestrained Liberty of Publication, is the only effectual means that can be employed."[29]

The presiding judge, Sir Francis Macnaghten, "paid no regard whatever to the Memorial," having made up his mind before the hearing that he would rule in favor of the government.

Ram Mohan then appealed to the King in Council. The Appeal has been justly described as "one of the noblest pieces of English" composed by Ram Mohan. "Its stately periods and not less stately thought recall the eloquence of the great orators of a century ago. In a language and style for ever associated with the glorious vindication of liberty, it invokes against the arbitrary exercise of British power the principles and traditions which are distinctive of British history."[30]

To preserve the original argument and eloquence of the Appeal, we shall quote select paragraphs:

15th. The . . . Restrictions . . . will in fact afford the Government and all its Functionaries from the highest to the lowest, complete immunity from censure or exposure respecting anything done by them in their official capacity, however desirable it might be for the interest of the Country, and also that of this Honourable Company, that the public conduct of such public men should not be allowed to pass unnoticed. It can scarcely be doubted that the real object of these Restrictions is, to afford all the Functionaries of Government complete security against their conduct being made the subject of observation, though it is associated with a number of other restraints totally uncalled for, but well calculated to soothe the supreme authorities in England and win their assent to the main object of the Rule—*the suppression of public remark on the conduct of the public officers of Government in India* . . .

24th. Your Majesty's faithful subjects will not offer any more particular remarks on the superfluous Restrictions introduced to accompany those more important ones which are the principal object of Government, and will conclude with this general observation, that they are unnecessary, either because the offenses prohibited are imaginary and improbable, or because they are already provided for by the Laws of the land and either the Government does not intend to put them in force at all, or it is anxious to interrupt the regular course of justice, abolish the right of Trial by Jury and, *by taking the Law into its own hands, to combine the Legislative and Judicial power, which is destructive of all Civil Liberty* . . .

30th. A Government conscious of rectitude of intention, cannot be afraid of public scrutiny by means of the Press, since this instrument can be equally well employed as a weapon of defence, and a Government possessed of immense patronage, is more especially secure, since a greater part of the learning and talent in the country being already enlisted in the service, its actions, if they have any shadow of Justice, are sure of being ably and successfully defended.

31st. Men in power hostile to the Liberty of the Press, which is a disagreeable check upon their conduct, when unable to discover any real evil arising from its existence, have attempted to make the world imagine, that it might, in some possible contingency, afford the means of combination against the Government, but not to mention that extraordinary emergencies would warrant measures which in ordinary times are totally unjustifiable, *Your Majesty is well aware, that a Free Press has never yet caused a revolution in any part of the world because, while men can easily represent the grievances arising from the conduct of the local authorities to the supreme Government, and thus get them redressed, the grounds of discontent that excite revolution are removed; whereas, where no freedom of the Press existed, and grievances consequently remained unrepresented and unredressed innumerable revolutions have taken place in all parts of the globe, or if prevented by the armed forces of the Government, the people continued ready for insurrection* . . .

**34th.** *The British nation has never yet descended to avow a principle so foreign to their character,* and if they could for a moment entertain the idea of preserving their power by keeping their colonies in ignorance, the prohibition of periodical publications is not enough, but printing of all kinds, education, and every other means of diffusing knowledge should be equally discouraged and put down. For it must be the distant consequences of the diffusion of knowledge that are dreaded by those (if there be any such) who are really apprehensive for the stability of Government, *since it is well known to all in the least acquainted with this country, that although every effort were made by periodical as well as other publication, a great number of years must elapse before any considerable change can be made in the existing habits and opinions of the Natives of India, so firmly are they wedded to established custom. Should apprehensions so unworthy of the English prevail, then unlike the ancient Romans who extended their knowledge and civilization with their conquests, ignorance and degradation must mark the extent of British Power.* Yet surely even this affords no hope of perpetual rule, since notwithstanding the tyranny and oppression of a Ghengis Khan and Timurlan, their empire was not so lasting as that of the Romans, who to the proud title of conquerors, added the more glorious one of Enlighteners of the World. And of the two most renowned and powerful monarchs among the Moghuls, Akbar was celebrated for his clemency, for his encouragement of learning, and for granting civil and religious liberty to his subjects, and Aurungzebe, for his cruelty and intolerance, yet the former reigned happy, extended his power and his dominion, and his memory is still adored, whereas the other, though endowed with equal abilities and possessed of equal power and enterprize, met with many reverses and misfortunes during his lifetime, and his name is now held in abhorrence.

**36th.** *It is well known that despotic Governments naturally desire the suppression of any freedom of expression which might tend to expose their acts to the obloquy which ever attends the exercise of tyranny or oppression, and the argument they constantly resort to, is, that the spread of knowledge is dangerous to the existence of all legitimate authority,* since, as a people become enlightened, they will discover that by a unity of effort, the many may easily shake off the yoke of the few, and thus become emancipated from the restraints of power altogether, forgetting the lesson derived from history, that *in countries which have made the smallest advance in civilization, anarchy and revolution are most prevalent—while on the other hand, in nations the most enlightened, any revolt against governments which have guarded inviolate the rights of the governed,* *is most rare, and that the resistance of a people advanced in knowledge, has ever been—not against the existence,—but against the abuses of the Governing power . . . . It may be fearlessly averred, that the more enlightened a people become, the less likely are they to revolt against the governing power, as long as it is exercised with justice tempered with mercy, and the rights and the privileges of the governed are held sacred from any invasion . . . .*

43rd. *The abolition of this most precious of their privileges, is the more appalling to your Majesty's faithful subjects because it is a violent infringement of their civil and religious rights, which under the British Government, they hoped would be always secure.* Your Majesty is aware, that *under their former Muhammadan Rulers, the natives of this country enjoyed every political privilege in common with the Mussulmans . . . .* Although under the British Rule, the natives of India, have entirely lost this political consequence, your Majesty's faithful subjects were consoled by the more secure enjoyment of those civil and religious rights which had often been violated by the rapacity and intolerance of the Mussulmans; and notwithstanding the loss of political rank and power, they considered themselves much happier in the enjoyment of civil and religious liberty than were their ancestors; *but if these rights that remain are allowed to be unceremoniously invaded, the most valuable of them being placed at the mercy of one or two individuals, the basis on which they have founded their hopes of comfort and happiness under the British Power will be destroyed . . .*

54th. In conclusion, *your Majesty's faithful subjects humbly beseech your Majesty, first, to cause the Rule and Ordinance and Regulation before mentioned,* which has been registered by the Judge of Your Majesty's Court, *to be rescinded; and prohibit any authority in this country, from assuming the legislative power, or prerogatives of your Majesty and the high Council of the Realm, to narrow the privileges and destroy the rights of your Majesty's faithful subjects . . . .* Secondly, your Majesty's faithful subjects humbly pray, that *your Majesty will be pleased to confirm them the privilege, they have so long enjoyed, of expressing their sentiments through the medium of the Press, subject to such legal restraints as may be thought necessary . . . appoint a commission of intelligent and independent Gentlemen, to inquire into the real condition of the millions Providence has placed under your protection* (italics supplied).[31]

For all its moral and historical reasoning, the Appeal met with a similar fate as the Memorial. The Privy Council declined to intervene in the matter. Even so, it was not without public acclaim in certain European circles, as we gather from the following lines of a letter written by Colonel Leicester Stanhope, dated London, June 9, 1825:

Your memorial to the King of England, demonstrating the usefulness and safety of a free press in British India, and praying for its restoration, I forwarded with a letter, to the Secretary of the Board of Control. He honoured me with a courteous reply, stating that it had been graciously received by His Majesty.

The Memorial, considering it as the production of a foreigner and a Hindoo of this age, displays so much sense, knowledge, argument, and even eloquence, *that the friends of liberty have dwelt upon it with wonder* . . . (italics supplied).[32]

Soon after the passage of the Ordinance, Ram Mohan ceased publication of the *Mirat-ul-Akhbar*. The closing notice should be read as a protest against the press Regulation. He states the difficulties which made him relinquish publication of his paper. The difficulties, he enumerated, are as follows:

First: Although the Rule and Ordinance imposes no hardship on Europeans who use their friendship with the chief secretary to government, to obtain a license; Indians must bribe porters, and push and shove their way around in order to achieve the same. It is of little worth to undergo such turmoil and engage in the practice of chicanery for the purpose of obtaining what is, in fact, one's own option. As it is written: "The respect which is purchased with a hundred drops of heart's blood, do not thou, in the hope of a favour, commit to the mercy of a porter."[33]

Second: "To make an Affidavit voluntarily in an open Court, in the presence of respectable Magistrates, is looked upon as very mean and censurable by those who watch the conduct of their neighbours." Moreover, publishing a newspaper is not for everyone, for "He must resort to the evasion of establishing fictitious Proprietors, which is contrary to Law, and repugnant to Conscience."

Third: In addition to bringing upon oneself the disrepute of solicitation and the dishonor of making Affidavit, there is the constant worry that in the process of candid journalism, some turn of phrase may prove offensive to the government. Notwithstanding such innocent fallibility, one's license is revoked and doomed to disgrace. In such a tense enviroment, silence is preferable to speaking out. It is said: Thou O Hafiz, art a poor retired man, be silent: Princes know the secrets of their own Policy.

But silence is sometimes more eloquent than speech. The principles Ram Mohan laid down continued to speak for themselves. Though they soon prevailed, Ram Mohan's voice was silenced.

On September 15, 1835, Sir Charles Metcalfe rescinded the Regulation by passing Act XI. but Metcalfe's Minute on Act XI was virtually a restatement of Ram Mohan's petition of 1823. Therefore the triumph of Metcalfe should ever be associated with the triumph of Ram Mohan Roy in obtaining yet another freedom for his people.

Freedom was an ideal Ram Mohan deeply cherished, not only for Indians but for all the people of the world. He loved India, but was not a narrow patriot. He was a "nationalist-internationalist." His cosmopolitan sympathies made him look upon citizens of all nations as brothers. He sorrowed with those who were unjustly oppressed, and rejoiced when the bell of liberty was rung over any land. His politics were, therefore, the politics of internationalism. His global interests appear in different parts of the world.

We start with the nations of the East. We have already witnessed his vision of an independent India carrying the torch of freedom and enlightenment to all countries of Asia.

When he received the news of the overthrow of the Spanish tyranny by its South American colonies, he became so joyful that he threw a dinner party in his Calcutta home for European friends. The *Edinburgh Magazine* comments:

> The lively interest he took in the progress of South American emancipation, eminently marks the greatness and benevolence of his mind, and was created, he said, by the perusal of the detestable barbarities inflicted by Spain to subjugate and afterwards continued by the Inquisition to retain in bondage that unhappy country. 'What!' replied he, (upon being asked why he had celebrated by illuminations, by an elegant dinner to about sixty Europeans and by a speech composed and delivered by himself, at his home in Calcutta, the arrival of important news of the success of the Spanish Patriots), '*What! ought I to be insensible to the sufferings of my fellow-creatures wherever they are, or howsoever unconnected by interests, religion and language*' (italics supplied).[34]

Turning north, he was most impressed by the freedoms enjoyed by the United States which, in some regards, he thought, were even greater than those of England. He had hoped to travel there so as to witness democracy in action, but, unfortunately, the dream was never fulfilled.

Roy knew the history of Europe intimately and followed the rise and fall of freedom as if it were taking place in his own land. He was deeply anguished when he heard the Neapolitans, after forcing a constitution from their despotic king, were thrown back into servitude by the intervention of Austrian troops. So grieved was he that he cancelled a social engagement with a friend. On the other hand, he was thrilled by the news of the establishment of constitutional government in Spain and gave a public dinner party in the town hall to celebrate the occasion.

He was similarly pleased to hear of the victory of the liberal party in the Portugese Civil War. He wrote to Woodforde, August 22, 1833, "The news from Portugal is highly gratifying though another struggle is still expected."[35]

In connection with the French Revolution, when he received the report in Calcutta of the famous "Three Days" (July 27–29, 1830), we are informed that "so great was his enthusiasm that he could think and talk of nothing else!" According to the testimony of James Sutherland who accompanied Ram Mohan on his voyage to England, the Raja had severely injured his leg at the Cape, but the physical pain could not dampen his emotional excitement when he caught sight of two French frigates lying in the Bay, their revolutionary flags unfurled. He came aboard. "His reception was, of course, worthy of the French character and of him. He was conducted over the vessels and endeavoured to convey by the aid of interpreters how much he was delighted to be under the banner that waved over their decks,—an evidence of the glorious triumph of right over might; and as he left the vessels he repeated emphatically 'Glory, glory, glory to France!' "[36]

An outspoken advocate of Catholic emancipation through the pages of the *Mirat-ul-Akhbar*, Ram Mohan publicly criticized the British for their autocratic treatment of the Irish Catholics.[37]

Most of all, Ram Mohan was utterly engrossed by British politics. Sutherland has left a graphic account of his ardent interest in the Reform agitation which was taking place in England at the time of his arrival:

> As we approached England, his anxiety to know what was passing there became most urgent, and he implored the captain to lose no opportunity of speaking to any vessel outward-bound. At length near the Equator . . . . we fell in with a vessel which supplied us with papers announcing the changes of Ministry and his exultation at the intelligence may easily be conceived. We talked of nothing else for days . . . . It was in its probable beneficial effect on the fate of India that he regarded the event as a subject of triumph. When we got within a few days' sail of the Channel we fell in with a vessel only four days out, that brought us intelligence of the extraordinary circumstance of the second reading of the Reform Bill being carried in the House in which the Tories had so long commanded majorities, by a single vote! . . . Rammohun Roy was again elated with the prospect . . . . A few days afterwards, at that eventful crisis in our history . . . . Rammohun first landed in Great Britain.
>
> The effect of this contagious enthusiasm of a whole people in favour of a grand political change upon such a mind as his was of course electrifying, and he caught up the tone of the new society in which he found himself with so much ardour that at one time I had fears that this fever of excitement . . . would prove too much for him.[38]

The foregoing discussion clearly attests to the claim that Raja Ram Mohan Roy was "the first great modern International Ambassador."[39] In the schemes of lesser men, politics always divides, but with this world statesman, politics was a unifying force. He dreamed of a world united. In a letter to the Minister of Foreign Affairs of France, he reveals his plans for a congress of all nations in which to settle international disputes. For Ram Mohan Roy to conceive a "League of Nations" a whole century before the League of Nations became a reality, he had to be "a man of universal sympathies, profound interest in human destiny and far sighted vision."[40] But at the root of it all was his deep commitment to liberty—liberty of social intercourse, of movement, of belief, of expression—and he was an undaunted champion of that liberty for his own land as well as those of Europe and the New World.

The question scholars are raising today is: How could a man with such sympathies for liberal and nationalist movements abroad reconcile these feelings with the political domination of his own homeland? It seems Ram Mohan had retreated from his earlier political ideas.[41] The reference here is to the Autobiographical Letter in which it is stated that the young Ram Mohan undertook a long journey to the North animated by a "feeling of great aversion to the establishment of the British power in India."[42] There is also some speculation that Ram Mohan had once collaborated with anti-British zamindars, and even with bands of peasants while in Rangpur.[43] This early outrage is a far cry from his rationalization of British power as somehow the work of Providence. The shift in position is attributed to the economic ties Ram Mohan had later established with British free-trader liberals which led him to moderate his former political ideals.

Several difficulties stand in the way of this thesis. While Ram Mohan did not have the opportunity to choose his political circumstances, he did make every effort to liberalize those circumstances. His critics admit that within the colonial framework, Ram Mohan "did blaze the trail . . . for several generations of moderate constitutionalist agitation, focusing on demands like Indianization of services, the trial by jury, separation of powers, freedom of the press, and consultation with Indian landlords, merchants, and officials on legislative matters. His critique of the zamindari system and plea for an absolute ban on 'any further increase of rent on any pretence whatsoever' strikes a sympathetic chord in progressive hearts even today."[44]

To call this level of agitation "moderate" lacks historical appreciation which can only be felt when Ram Mohan is judged in the light of his peers. For instance, the leaders of the *Dharma Sabha* found no cause for distress under the government, even when the government was reacting negatively towards its appeal in behalf of the practice of *sati*. The *Samachar Chandrika* is on record saying:

> None of our countrymen feel a pleasure in hearing anything to the disadvantage of the Honourable Company; they always pray for the welfare of the Government . . . *We have been subject to no distress under the government of the Company*; it is only the abolition of Suttees which has given us disquietude" (italics supplied).[45]

By contrast, Ram Mohan was never quiet or willing to be quietened. He made so much political noise through his newspapers that he was branded a fomentor of public unrest. He not only agitated for good government, but was also inspired to undertake his political reforms in the hope of the ultimate substitution of good government by *self-government*. Remove this hope and you extinguish the spark that blazed the trail of progress. But it was more than hope—it was faith based on fact. The fact was that in Ram Mohan's day, "British rule was unsure of itself and uncertain about the future. The Western system of education was an instrument by which an *elite*, allied to the British rulers, could be created, but there was a danger that the heady wine of Western thought might also produce social revolutionaries of one kind or another, who would end up as political radicals. That explains the initial opposition of the British rulers to Western education, particularly because a small but self-conscious intellectual elite keenly desired it."[46] When the cause of Western education was won, Ram Mohan seems to have concluded "that the British rulers had opted for India's modernisation as a matter of enlightened self-interest."[47] The testimony we have presented leaves little doubt that Ram Mohan anticipated that within a matter of two generations, under a benevolent and enlightened leadership, the historical forces nurtured by education would ripen and India would stand on its own political feet.

This hope for independence was first religious and then political. The failure to read Ram Mohan's political ideas in their religious context makes it possible to assess him as a political moderate. But Ram Mohan was not a moderate. He was a modernizer because his *Vedantic* philosophy saw man as possessed of the same "natural rights" as were being published abroad in Europe under the impact of the French Revolution. "Thus he came to the conclusion that man *qua* man has certain inalienable rights which cannot be taken away on the pretext of maintaining the stability of a social or religious order or satisfying the pragmatic requirements of an economic or political system."[48]

From the standpoint of hindsight, Ram Mohan's hopes for independence were misplaced. His admiration of the British and his reliance upon the system was so great that he failed to perceive the essentially acquisitive character of the colonial mind. Perhaps this was inevitable within the context of his time and place. But whereas it took India *two hundred years* to win her independence, Ram Mohan was only prepared to wait for *forty or fifty years*. What would he have recommended at the end of this period had freedom not been forthcoming? His answer is clear: *An India come of age* should have "the spirit as well as the inclination to resist effectually." India has assets to be reckoned with—great power and a great people. She can prove "an ally of the British Empire or troublesome and annoying as a determined enemy."[49]

 *CHAPTER 9*

# Judicial Reform

In an article on "Trial by Jury in India," dated December 11, 1821, the Raja states:

> Among all the meritorious Institutions of the British Constitution, that of adjudication of Criminal cases by Twelve disinterested, honest and intelligent men, or in other words "Trial by Jury," is a source of infinite satisfaction to those who have the good fortune to reside in the Metropolis of India.[1]

Things were different under the previous regime. "During the Mussulman Government in this Country, the Natives were much afflicted, in consequence of the acts of injustice, cruelty, and oppression of these rulers, which is well known to everybody. . . . It is therefore, better for subjects to prefer death to being placed under the control of such unjust and despotic Government."[2]

The new judicial system was especially welcome because it was a modernized version of a much earlier system which had evolved within the culture of his own people, namely, the *Panchayat* system. However, Ram Mohan's "infinite satisfaction" did not prevent him from mounting an attack because he felt the British system was discriminatory in its judicial administration. As we shall presently see, it undermined the rights and interests of the Indian people. Ram Mohan therefore fought the system with such a show of legal maneuvering as would have done any jurist proud.

With the establishment of the Supreme Court in 1774, the jurors were selected from among "British subjects," a term whose ambiguity led to agitation by the Indo-Britons who felt unjustly excluded. From 1816 to 1822 they received no satisfactory response to their many appeals. This was about the time when Ram Mohan began his own campaign through the pages of *Sambad Kaumudi*.

While this agitation was in progress, an experiment was being conducted in Ceylon by Sir Alexander Johnston to test the advisability of
opening the jury system to the natives. In a letter dated May 26, 1825,
Sir Alexander writes that the best way to remedy the evils of administering justice are:

> . . . first to give the natives a direct interest in that system, by imparting to
> them a considerable share in its administration; secondly, to give them a
> proper value for a character for veracity, by making such a character the
> condition upon which they were to look for respect from their country-
> men, and that from which they were to hope for promotion in the service
> of their government; thirdly, to make the natives themselves, who, from
> their knowledge of their countrymen, can decide at once on the degree
> of credit which ought to be given to native testimony, judges of fact, and
> thereby shorten the duration of trials, relieve witnesses from protracted
> attendance on the courts, and materially diminish the expense of the gov-
> ernment. The introduction of trial by jury into Ceylon, and the extension
> of the right of sitting upon juries to every native of the island, under cer-
> tain modifications, seemed to me the most advisable method of attaining
> these objects."[3]

The thrust of this experiment, which was carried on for some sixteen
years, was that the experience in Ceylon was valid for India, inasmuch
as the former was a microcosm of the latter. If the experiment proved
productive for the security of the government and for the good of the
people in Ceylon, it was supposed that the same consequence could reasonably be expected in India as well.

The weight of the above evidence, along with pressure from the
Indo-Britons and other natives, forced the government to produce an
East India Jury Bill. Charles W. Wynne, President of the Board of Control, was sympathetic toward native feelings and was convinced that all
of them should be involved in the administration of justice. However,
he was equally pressured by Britishers who insisted that it would be
both incongruous for "placing the conquered in situations of judges of
the conquerors," and also injudicious because of "the little respect paid
by natives to veracity and sanction of an oath."

Bowing to the above pressure, Wynne inserted Clause III into the
Bill which reads: "That the Grand Juries in all Cases, and all Juries for
the Trial of Persons professing the Christian Religion, shall consist
wholly of Persons professing the Christian Religion.[4] The Jury Bill was
passed by Parliament on May 5, 1826.

The Hindu communities of Bombay, Madras and Bengal were
shocked by the prejudicial distinctions written into this legislative Act.
Ram Mohan himself considered it insulting and degrading to the natives of Bengal. Clause III of the Bill was not only contrary to the spirit
of British jurisprudence, it violated the principles of abstract justice. In
the *Sambad Kaumudi*, he clearly states the letter of the new law, and
then proceeds to analyze its unethical implications.

He begins by stating the purpose of the observations which appeared in the *Bengal Chronicle* (December 5) relative to Clause III of the Jury Act.

1. All classes of Natives, namely, Hindoos, Mussulmans, Christians, etc. will have the privilege of being chosen jurors, to judge in cases of murder, theft, and such other criminal suits; but it is left to the Judges of the Supreme Court to determine and make regulations respecting the qualifications of such persons as to their knowledge of the English language, and judgment in secular affairs; that is, the Judges will permit those only to act as jurors whom they shall think qualified for the task.

2. The Grand Jury is to be composed exclusively of Christians.

3. All classes, indiscriminately, will be eligible to the Petit Jury, which has the power of determining whether a person is guilty or not guilty; with this exception, that when either of the parties is a Hindoo, or a Musselman, or of any other class, Christians shall have the privilege of judging; that is, all the twelve persons, or any number of the jury, may be Christians.[5]

The Raja then proceeds to unravel some of the consequences of this new Act. In all cases of criminal offense, Hindus and Muslims will have to submit to the verdict of Christians, whether they be British or native. Whereas Christians will have the privilege of sitting in judgment on non-Christians, the latter, "although living in the same country, or even in the same hamlet with them, and partaking in their virtues and vices, shall have no power judging respecting them."

Ram Mohan observes that while the missionaries have been unsuccessful over the past thirty years in producing a single true Christian, the doors are now opened, and many persons, no longer able patiently to bear the reproach brought upon them by this Parliamentary Act," will espouse Christianity. "When the rulers of a country use force or art to win over their subjects to their own faith from that of their ancestors, who shall have the power to oppose?"

Ram Mohan thinks that the provision of the Act would have been more reasonable, fair, and ethical had it ordered that both Christians and non-Christians be tried by juries made up of members of their own constituency, or that members of the two groups had mutual responsibilities for sitting on each other's cases. Instead, the Act has laid all non-Christians, "without any regard to rank or respectability, prostrate at the feet of Christians, whether of this or of any other place."

The article concludes by informing all readers that a memorial on the subject has been sent to the proper authorities in England.[6]

The *Bengal Chronicle* praises the article for its "perspicuous analysis of the spirit and principles of Mr. Wynne's Bill." On the memorial, it says: "The prompt adoption of this legitimate mode of obtaining redress for a supposed grievance, originating not with the local authorities but with Parliament at home, must, we believe, be as gratifying to the Government here, as we are satisfied it will be to the public in general.[7]

Let us now examine briefly the contents of the memorial sent to England. Basically it is a petition of remonstrance initiated by Ram Mohan and signed by a large number of Hindu and Muslim gentlemen. It is addressed "To the Honourable the Commons of the United Kingdom of Great Britain and Ireland in Parliament assembled."[8]

The petitioners first express gratitude for the Jury Act which has partially admitted them to exercise one of the most valuable privileges of English law. At the same time, they consider it a sacred duty to themselves and posterity to protest the statute because it betokens a distrust in the petitioners; brands them with a stamp of inferiority; and establishes distinctions that are "not only useless but odious and impolitic.[9]

Adverting to Clause III of the Act, the petitioners argue that this clause subjects them to "heavy disabilities for adhering to the religious opinions of their forefathers, in the full enjoyment of which they are secured by repeated acts of the legislature and repeated assurances of the local Government, and which opinions therefore they conceive can never be made a ground of civil disqualifications, without a breach of the compact which has been made with them."[10]

Furthermore, the distinctions are wholly unnecessary. Fifty years prior, the government had deemed the native population fit to sit on juries without any restrictions; the only problem being that the recommendations were not written into law. The years that have lapsed have only served to make the populace more qualified for the same task by virtue of rapid acculturation.

The petitioners gently warn that the Act is unpopular among the respectable natives of Calcutta, and they would be averse to serving the courts in any future capacity under the prevailing system.

Four conceivable reasons are advanced as supportive of the unjust distinctions of Clause III.

The first is conversion to Christianity. A statute which holds out to non-Christians "the alluring hope of an equality of privileges with their rulers as the price of desertion of the faith of their ancestors," would be an open infraction of the solemn and repeated pledges to protect the laws, customs, and religion of the land. The religious opinions which the Indian people profess exercise as much influence upon their daily lives as the religious faith of any other people. Their religion is no abstract system, "but is interwoven with the laws, the manners, the daily necessities, and daily actions of every condition of human life. In such religions the faith and the fervour of their supporters are nourished and confirmed by the incessant demands which are thus created upon their time and attention."[11] Therefore, any interference with their religion would be particularly difficult to bear.

The second reason for excluding the petitioners might be the fear that Hindu and Muslim jurors would "greatly outnumber those of the Christian persuasion." This situation could be obviated by forming juries "half of Christians and half of Hindoos and Mohamedans."

The third possible reason for exclusion may be the supposition that "there were no individuals professing the Hindoo or Mohamedan Religions who moved in the rank of society from which the Grand Jurors are selected." This would fly in the face both of observable facts evidenced by several native merchants who are as wealthy and intelligent as their European counterparts, and it would also go against the project of the British Government to cultivate a landed aristocracy.

The fourth reason which may have been urged in favor of the restrictions is that the duties of the Grand Jury demand greater intellectual acumen than the duties of the Petty Jury, and that the Hindus and Muslims are not possessed of the necessary intelligence. In fact, the reverse is true. The duties of the Petty Jury, though less honorable, are more difficult than those of the Grand Jury. And though the natives may be less astute in their knowledge of English law than Europeans, "yet they are in fact from their superior acquaintance with the very peculiar habits, manners and prejudices of their own Countrymen much better qualified to judge of the value of their testimony and must prove most useful auxiliaries in the administration of Justice which never can be perfectly administered in any country without the aid of the people themselves."[12]

Having dismissed the possible grounds for discrimination, the petitioners pronounce the new Act injurious and degrading:

> It is injurious not only because it exposes them without defence to the operation of prejudices arising from religious feelings among the strongest which actuate the human mind if once awakened, but because the Indian born Christian being much more numerous than the Europeans, and the intercourse between them and Hindoos and Mohamedans much more frequent and familiar, feelings of rivalry and animosity are more likely to exist between them than your Petitioners and Europeans with whom their intercourse though increasing is necessarily more limited. It is degrading because your Petitioners now see those whom they certainly never regarded in any point of view as their superiors, and who were never so regarded by the European residents, elevated above them by the sole circumstance of their religious profession.[13]

The petitioners conclude with the entreaty that the invidious legal distinction made between them and their fellow subjects be completely abolished, either "by permitting half the Jurors to be chosen from those persuasions in all cases in which a Hindoo or Mohamedan may be arraigned at the bar of Justice," or by repealing Clause III and leaving the formation of jury lists to his Majesty's Judges who are pledged impartially to protect the natives.[14]

The arguments put forth in the above Petition are strikingly similar in thought, language and style to those propounded by Ram Mohan, especially in the *Sambad Kaumudi*. There is therefore good reason to believe that Ram Mohan either drafted the document himself, or had had a considerable part in its composition. Among the signatories were one hundred and sixteen Muslims and one hundred and twenty-eight Hindus. Even Charles W. Wynne admitted in the House of Commons that "the general style of it is highly creditable to the ability of those from whom it proceeds, and is demonstrative of the general progress of intelligence and education."[15]

The Petition was dispatched to J. Crawford, agent of the inhabitants of Calcutta. Ram Mohan supplied a covering letter. He states, in part, that in his Jury Bill Wynne "has by introducing religious distinctions into the judicial system of this country, not only afforded just grounds for dissatisfaction among the Natives in general, but has excited much alarm in the breast of everyone conversant with political principles. . . . In common with those who seem partial to the British rule from the expectation of future benefits arising out of the connection, I necessarily feel extremely grieved in often witnessing Acts and Regulations passed by Government without consulting or seeming to understand the feelings of its Indian subjects and without considering that this people have had for more than a half century the advantage of being ruled by and associated with an enlightened nation, advocates of liberty and promoters of knowledge."[16]

A similar petition from the natives of Bombay against certain provisions of the new Jury Act also reached the House of Commons by 1831.

Charles Grant, President of the Board of Control, took up the cause of the petitioners by sending a letter to the Chairman of the East India Company in which he enclosed a copy of a bill he proposed to submit to Parliament, relative to the appointment of justices of peace and juries in the East Indies.[17]

The chairman and deputy chairman shared little of Grant's enthusiasm. They reasoned: "Whilst the Court are most anxious to promote the advancement of the Natives of India to offices of trust and responsibility, they very strongly feel the necessity of exercising much caution in the adoption of measures for that purpose. To proceed too rapidly in such a case, would ultimately retard, instead of promoting the object sought to be attained."[18]

On the office of the justice of the peace, the writers indicate their support of employing "natives in the administration of Indian Law." But it was a horse of a different color to entrust them with "the administration of British Law, involving a power to take cognizance of charges against European functionaries."

On the Jury Act Robert Cambell and John Ravenshaw agree the "Juries for the trial of Christians, must consist wholly of Christians." They consider this legislation necessary for "guarding against the possibility of Christians, Europeans or Native, being tried upon questions involving life or death by Hindoos and Mussulmen."[19]

Grant's response (October 15, 1831) to the above communication clearly stated that the reasons why he was desirous to see his proposals adopted were "chiefly those which apply in every country that has reached an adequate degree of civilization."[20]

The court would not budge. On December 8, 1831, it issued a communication itemizing the points on which it chose to reject Grant's proposed bill.

Fortunately, by this time Ram Mohan was in England and was able to supply Grant with strong rebuttals to all of the objections raised by the court. Below are some of his answers:

*Objection:* It is not to be expected that the natives will voluntarily take the trouble to study English law and legislation to equip themselves for the office.

*Answer:* The bill only aims at rendering natives "eligible," "not to make acceptance of office compulsory on them. Persons who choose to qualify themselves by acquiring a competent knowledge of British law, and are willing to incur the responsibility, may be appointed by Government."[21]

*Objection:* It is not to be expected that the natives would voluntarily "undertake the duties of the office of unpaid magistrates when they found that they would thereby become liable to prosecution in the Supreme Court for any error or neglect of duty."

*Answer:* The Court itself has declared that it does not question the intellectual capabilities of the natives. They have every intelligence to acquire the requisite legal knowledge. And though it can be demonstrated that many current holders of the office are not sufficiently knowledgeable in English law and legislation, they must be saved the embarrassment. It is, however, a matter of keen irony that "the Court of Directors are the last persons who should expect an 'adequate knowledge of the English law books and acts of Parliament' from those whom they wish to be appointed as judges and justices of the peace over the millions of their fellow subjects."[22]

*Objection:* The natives are "defective in many qualities, particularly firmness of character, which are so necessary to inspire confidence, and so essential to enable them to discharge the duties of a justice of the peace with usefulness and credit."[23]

*Answer:* This vague charge of unfitness is inconsistent with an earlier declaration of the court to the effect that "the natives are invested with a considerable degree of authority in the ordinary functions of administering justice, collecting the revenue, and conducting the police and magisterial duties." The question arises: "How is it that persons deficient in 'so many qualities,' 'especially in firmness of character,' have been entrusted with such important functions, judicial, fiscal, and even magisterial? And what is the wide distinction between the latter and those of the justices of peace that makes persons who are fit for the one unfit for the other?"

*Objection:* The bill would give natives a candid view of Europeans and this would probably have the deleterious effect of "lowering the estimation of the European character."

*Answer:* The natives already have a direct cognizance of European conduct and character. Common police are empowered to arrest Europeans who violate the law, and do so regularly. "Has this coercion, at the very seat of the British Indian Empire, lowered the estimation of the European character, or impaired the British power in India?"[24]

*Objection:* Based on the principle that there must be some community of feeling between the jurors and the person judged, it is intolerable that an Englishman and a Christian should be tried by Hindus and Muslims.

*Answer:* "If the Hindoos and Mussulmans are to be excluded from acting as jurors on the trial of Christians on account of their want of community of feeling with them, the same objection applies to Christians acting as jurors on the trial of Hindoos and Mussulmans. The principle is the same in both cases, and justice knows no respect of persons."[25]

Armed with these rebuttals furnished by the reformer, Charles Grant finally introduced the Jury Bill at the House of Commons. On the occasion of its third reading (June 18, 1832), Grant declared:

> The object of this Bill is simply to repeal that prohibitory Act, and to entrust a discretionary power to the local Government. The two functions which the natives are, at present, prohibited from discharging are those of grand jurors and justices of the peace. Now, if the local authorities are fit to be entrusted with the powers of Government, they are, I think, the safest depositories of that discretion which this Bill is intended to create. This is not a matter of slight interest to the natives of India.
>
> My Right Honourable Friend says that the principle I have asserted is, that you should apply improvement where civilization is sufficiently advanced. I assert that the principle is this, that as far as possible, and as soon as possible, the natives of India are to be made partakers and sharers of the rights and liberties of English subjects, and of the advantages of the British Constitution; and that it is our duty, by every possible method, to advance the natives of India in every species of improvement.[26]

Despite fierce opposition from all but two members of the Court of Directors, the amended Indian Jury Act was passed on June 18, 1832, and became law on August 16, 1832.

The new bill made it lawful for the government in Bengal, Bombay, and Madras to appoint all properly qualified persons as justices of the peace. It also repealed the odious enactment that stated that "the Grand Juries in all cases, and all Juries for the Trial of Persons professing the Christian Religion, shall consist wholly of Persons professing the Christian Religion.''[27]

The response of the Anglo-Indian press to the Act was of keen acrimonious disappointment. Grant was maligned as an idealistic, political green-horn who must have been "mystified by Rammohun Roy." The *Asiatic Journal* opined:

> It is not often that we have occasion to speak favourably of the political measures of the Court of Directors or to use harsh language towards the enlightened Ex-Brahmin Rammohun Roy; and in the present instance, however, we have good reason to break our rule in either case . . . nor can anything be more impolitic than the *arguments evidently supplied by the Hindu patriot* who has sacrificed truth and honesty in order to pander to his passion for theory and assured Mr. Grant that all India regretted the non-appearance of native Grand Jurors while he must have known that such a statement was hardly true when predicted of even the enlightened population of the single city of Calcutta.[28]

The comments of Amiya Kumar Sen are apropos: "The fulminations of the Anglo-Indian Editor throw a flood of light on the influence of Ram Mohun over the mind of Mr. Grant and the decisive part he played in the removal of these grievances."[29]

By happy contrast with the *Journal*, the *Samachar Darpan* (September 15, 1832) eulogized Ram Mohan's role in the passage of the new Jury Act, and defended him against the attacks of the Hindu paper, *Samachar Chandrika*. The editor admits to the charge that he is partial towards Ram Mohan, and specifies the benevolent provisions of the above Regulation as contributing to this partiality. In his words:

> If we say that it was the remarks of Ram Mohun Roy which suggested these enactments to the Governor-General, then we cannot conceive a greater honour for him; if it be said that these useful regulations occurred simultaneously to both, without any mutual communication, we must regard this fact as a test of the just views, and the benevolent intentions of the Raja. In either case the Chundrika will see that his dislike of Ram Mohun Roy is misplaced; that our partiality to him is founded on reason.[30]

Ram Mohan himself was jubilant on the passing of Grant's Jury Bill. In a letter dated January 22, 1833, he praises the excellent exertions of Charles Grant against the imbecility of the Court of Directors. He thinks this just and liberal measure should have the effect of raising the Indian people morally and politically. Hindus and Muslims now have equal rights with Christians to assume the office of justice of the peace and to sit on Grand and Petty Juries. "No longer can a spirit of religious rancour find its way into India." He congratulates the change in nature and character of the English government and Parliament and praises its liberal politics. He confesses that India is far behind Britain in its knowledge of politics and observes that "moderation and prudence should not be lost sight of by our countrymen. We should not be too hasty and too sanguine in raising our condition, since gradual improvements are most durable."[31]

The Chief Justices of the three presidencies had mixed responses to the Act. Justice E. Ryan of the Calcutta Supreme Court welcomed the removal of the discriminatory provision based on religion. Sir W. Compton, Chief Justice of the Bombay Supreme Court, was glad for the legislation even though he thought it somewhat premature. The negative response came from Justice Sir Ralph Palmer of the Madras Supreme Court.[32]

As for the responses of the Indian people, there was no doubt how they felt upon being installed as jurors of the Supreme Court and justices of the peace. Professor Majumdar reflects: "It is not perhaps difficult to visualise even at this distant time what a day of jubilation it must have been to our countrymen when one of their highest ambitions came to be fulfilled and they were raised in their status and respectability by equalizing themselves with the rulers of the country in regard not only to civil but to criminal jurisprudence as well."[33]

The above narrative underlines the fact that *although Ram Mohan was a gradualist* in the reform movement, pacing every step of the people according to their increased capacities; *he was never intimidated by the rulers*, but utilized his uncanny insight into their psyche to confront the British conscience with such a formidable array of facts, that justice invariably prevailed.

# CHAPTER 10

# Administrative Reform

Closely related to Ram Mohan's judicial reform are his proposals for administrative reforms. When the question of the East India Company's Charter renewal came up before the House of Commons in 1831, a Select Committee was appointed to discuss the matter and make recommendations. Expert witnesses were invited to appear before the Committee to render their evidence as to conditions prevailing in India. There is some doubt whether Ram Mohan actually appeared before the Committee, the likelihood being that he presented his testimony through a series of "Communications" to the Board of Control.[1]

The full testimony is to be found in the Appendix to the "Report from the Select Committee of the House of Commons on the Affairs of the East India Company," published 1831–1833. The greater part of the evidence was published under the title, *Exposition of the Practical Operation of the Judicial and Revenue System in India, and of the General Character and Condition of Native Inhabitants, as submitted in evidence to the Authorities in England.*[2]

In the following section we shall consider his testimony in regards to the Revenue System of India. Here, we shall examine his proposals for reform in the judicial administration.

The text under study is significant for two reasons. First, "it is a succinct, admirable and trustworthy contemporary record written by one who is at home with his subject, so that every sentence conveys a sense of assurance and commendable breadth of vision."[3] Secondly, Ram Mohan's answers to the seventy-eight questions on the judicial system reveal something profound about the man himself. The profile is of a reformer whose outlook is rational and modern, and whose concern for justice makes him a formidable critic of the evils which beset the administration of the land.

Before we discuss all the events which took place in England, we must first find out how Ram Mohan's trip to England came about. In his own words:

From occasionally directing my studies to the subjects and events peculiarly connected with Europe, and from an attentive though partial, practical observation in regard to some of them, I felt impressed with the
idea, that in Europe literature was zealously encouraged and knowledge
widely diffused; that mechanics were almost in a state of perfection, and
politics in daily progress; that moral duties were, on the whole, observed
with exemplary propriety notwithstanding the temptations incident to a
state of high and luxurious refinement; and that religion was spreading,
even amid scepticism and false philosophy.

I was in consequence continually making efforts for a series of years, to
visit the Western World, with a view to satisfy myself on those subjects by
personal experience. I ultimately succeeded in surmounting the obstacles
to my purpose . . .; and having sailed from Calcutta on the 19th of November, 1830, I arrived in England on the 8th of April following.[4]

Ram Mohan's departure was as much an event in India as his arrival
was in England. Though two Bombay *Brahmins* had visited England
forty years earlier, Ram Mohan was the first Indian of distinction to
cross the "black waters"; and hence, he stirred waves at both ends. In
editorial remarks the *Samachar Darpan* assured its readers that the
Raja's journey to England would be productive of benefit to all of
them. It says that though differences of opinion exist in the Hindu
community in regard to his religious ideas, "all will admit that he is one
of the ablest men of the age, and that no one is more capable of advis-
ing measures for the benefit of India." It is considered fortunate that
his journey to England has coincided with the time "when the momentous question of the future settlement of Indian affairs" is being discussed, and "his profound knowledge and sound judgment may prove
of the highest service to this country."[5]

In a similar vein, the *India Gazette* considered it "novel" that a native
of India should be asked to appear before the Parliament to give his
opinion upon "the character of the system of Government in this empire."[6]

On September 19, 1831 Ram Mohan submitted his frank sentiments
with respect to seventy-eight questions connected with the internal
administration of British India.

In answer to the query whether the judicial system in India is calculated to secure justice, the Raja states that the system established in
1793 under Lord Cornwallis is "certainly well adapted to the situation
of the country, and to the character of the people as well of the Government," but he considers the practical operation of the system defective.

One defect is the want of a sufficient number of judges and magistrates. Since there are but few courts, many of the inhabitants who live
at a distance from them, especially the poorer classes, are unable to
seek redress against the oppressions of wealthier neighbors possessing
local influence.[7]

A second defect is the want of due qualifications in the judges to discharge their duties in foreign languages. The judicial officers themselves are men of the "highest talents, as well as of strict integrity, and earnestly intent on doing justice." However, being unfamiliar with the laws and language of the people, "they must either rely greatly on the interpretation of their native officers, or be guided by their own surmises and conjectures."[8]

A third obstruction to the administration of justice is the want of a better code of laws. The annual publication of regulations by the local government since 1793, which supply the courts with instructions, are poor guides. Equally unclear are the Muslim and Hindu laws which are administered in conjunction with the above regulations. Since the indigenous codes are found in books of varying authority, the judges must depend entirely upon the interpretations of native lawyers "whose conflicting legal opinions have introduced great perplexity into the administration of justice."[9]

Many other impediments to the fair administration of justice were also pointed out. These include: lack of a common language between administrators and the public; the absence of all cultural communication between the two; unequal relations between the native pleaders and the judge as compared with the British bar and the bench; insufficient publicity to monitor public opinion; the prevalence of perjury and forgery; inadequate publicizing of the regulations which presently function as a code of law; and dishonorable conduct among the ranks of the judicial officers.

Confronted by such evils, the Raja states that the respectable and intelligent natives generally do not have confidence in the purity of the Company's courts or in the accuracy of their decisions; neither do they have confidence in the integrity of the subordinate judicial officers.[10]

Ram Mohan then proceeds to suggest modes of removing the several defects he had underscored in the administration of justice.

Inasmuch as European judges are dependent on native assistance for a knowledge of the language, customs, habits, and practices of the people; and inasmuch as the native officers do not possess inherent power to command respect, the best remedy is to "combine the knowledge and experience of the native with the dignity and firmness of the European."[11]

To guard against the possibility of a native assessor unduly influencing a European judge of insufficient qualification, "it is necessary to have recourse to trial by jury, as being the only effectual check against corruption, which, from the force of inveterate habit, and the contagion of example, has become so notoriously prevalent in India."[12]

To remedy the evils arising from want of publicity of the regulations, "two or three copies in each of the principal native languages used in that part of the country should be kept in a building in the populous quarter of the town."[13]

To remedy the evils arising from the distance of the courts from the poorer inhabitants, "the Sudder Ameens [superior commissioners] should be stationed at proportionate distances in different parts of the district, so that suitors may not have to travel far from their homes to file their bills and afterwards to seek and obtain justice."[14]

Ram Mohan also recommends the adoption of the ancient *Panchayat* system (elected village assembly) which is analogous to the Western jury system. It is worthy of adoption since

> A Punchayet composed of the intelligent and respectable inhabitants, under the direction of a European judge to preserve order, and a native judge to guard against any private influence, is the only tribunal which can estimate properly the whole bearing of a case, with the validity of the documentary evidence, and the character of the witnesses, who could have little chance of imposing false testimony upon such a tribunal.[15]

In certain respects the *Panchayat* system has more to commend it than the established judicial system. First, fully understanding the native character and the language of the parties, "it would not be so liable to error in its decision." Second, the judge and his assessors would not unduly be able to influence the jury. Third, "it would guard the assessor from the use of undue influence." Fourth, it would expedite business, make appeals unnecessary, and check perjury and forgery.[16]

Ram Mohan is of the opinion that natives selected from "retired pleaders (*Wakils*) and retired judicial officers, from agents employed by private individuals to attend the court (*mukhtars*)" were eminently qualified to serve as jurors in all judicial situations; not merely subordinate ones.[17]

He considers the recent combination of the office of revenue officer with that of circuit judge quite incompatible and injurious. The judge presides over major criminal cases and is also responsible for law and order over extensive territory. "It is morally impossible, therefore, that he can fulfill the expectation of Government and the public if his attention be at the same time engrossed and distracted by political, commercial, or revenue transactions."[18]

The remedy is "to separate the duties between two distinct sets of officers, and double the jurisdiction of each."[19]

Turning to the problem of the backlog of cases, Ram Mohan remarks that a case may be pending on an average of two to three years in the Zillah courts and from four to five years in the Courts of Appeal and in the *Sadar Diwani Adalat*, to say nothing of the appeals to the King in Council. The cause of delays is mainly due to irregular work habits in attending to judicial duties, and a lack of control over judicial officers. "These daily growing evils in every branch of the judicial establishment have, in a great measure defeated the object which the government had in view in establishing it."[20]

Among the remedies for the above delays, Ram Mohan suggests a reduction in the number of appeals to the superior courts; and as a substitute for appeal to the King in Council, which he considers "a great source of evil," he proposes the creation of a specific court of appeal "expressly for Indian appeal causes above 10,000 pounds."[21]

A fundamental desideratum, according to the Raja, was the framing of a code of criminal law suitable to the wants of the entire country:

> A code of criminal law for India should be founded as far as possible on those principles which are common to, and acknowledged by all the different sects and tribes inhabiting the country. It ought to be simple in its principles, clear in its arrangement, and precise in its definitions; so that it may be established as a standard of criminal justice in itself, and not stand in need of explanation by a reference to any other books of authority, either Mohammedan or Christian.[22]

Persons of high political standing who are treated preferentially by the prevailing judicial system, would not be exempt from the law, according to the proposed code. Blind to political and social distinctions, government would try such persons by "a special commission, composed of three or more persons of the same rank."[23]

The final question put to him asks: "Can you offer any other suggestions for the improvement of the Judicial Establishment?" He recommends: (1) that the salaries of the judicial officers should be such that they will be above temptation; (2) with the additional help of joint native judges, assessors, and juries, as proposed, the civil courts of appeal may be dissolved, barring the supreme civil court (Sadar Diwani Adalat); and (3) by the gradual introduction of natives into the revenue departments and into the judicial department, under European supervision, "the natives may become attached to the present system of government, so that it may become consolidated, and maintain itself by the influence of the intelligent and respectable classes of the inhabitants, and by the general goodwill of the people, and not any longer stand isolated in the midst of its subjects, supporting itself merely by the exertion of superior force."[24]

In conclusion he avows that his answers have been unaffected by any bias, and that the opinions expressed have been his own: "I have been guided only by my conscience and by the impressions left on my mind by long experience and reflection." He has kept the interests of both the governors and the governed in mind; and without losing sight of economics, he states: "I have been actuated by a desire to see the administration of justice in India placed on a solid and permanent foundation."[25]

It should be pointed out that at the same time when Ram Mohan compiled his answers he was not cognizant of the recent administrative changes in the judicial system passed by the Bengal government. For instance, Regulation V of the Bengal Code (1832) made provision for the appointment of natives to various judicial offices, stating that "it is desirable to employ respectable natives in more important trusts connected with the administration of the country."[26] A second regulation created a Court of *Sadar Diwani Adalat* and *Nizamat Adalat* to function as the chief court of civil and criminal jurisdiction for the Western provinces. It was to be an open court. A third regulation empowered the governor-general to invest three Zillah judges with added authorities so as to speed the process of criminal justice. However, the revenue officer still had the dual role of functioning as a circuit judge too.

These recent changes in the judicial system were the result of Lord William Bentinck's liberal reforms. It is a tribute to the Raja that the policies he recommended both preceded and went beyond the *most progressive thinking* of his time.

Next, we turn to the reformer's recommendations for the improvement of the revenue administration of the land.

Though himself a member of the landed gentry, Ram Mohan attacked the corruptions of the zamindary system with a mental acuity and missionary ardor which was almost absent in his times. Yet, being a staunch constitutionalist, he did not incite the workers of Hindustan to arise. Instead, diplomat that he was, he endeavored to rouse the Christian conscience of the British to loose the laborers from their chains. Officially he came to England as the envoy of the Moghul King; but, in a truer sense, he was the self-appointed ambassador of the poor. It was in this capacity that he submitted his evidence on the administration of the Revnue System in India. He supplied answers to fifty-four questions put to him by the Select Committee of the House of Commons.

The first question deals with land tenure. Ram Mohan states that in the provinces of Bengal, Bihar, and parts of Orissa, land is held by a "class of persons called *Zamindars* (i.e., landholders), who are entitled to perpetual hereditary possession, on condition of paying to government a certain revenue, fixed on their respective lands. This is termed the *Zamindary* system."[27]

By contrast, in the Madras Presidency there is the *Ryotwari* system wherein revenue is collected directly from the cultivators (*ryots*) by the government revenue officers.

As conceived by the Marquis of Cornwallis, the revenue system based on Permanent Settlement was calculated to operate beneficially for all concerned, but in practice the cultivator got the worst of the bargain.

This is true in the rate of rent. In theory the cultivator pays fifty per cent of the produce to the landholder, "out of which half, 10-11ths or 9-10ths constitute the revenue paid to Government, and 1-10th or 1-11th the rent of the landholder." This payment is a great burden upon the cultivator, considering he must bear all of the seed and labor costs. In practice, since the Permanent Settlement of 1793, "the landholders have adopted every measure to raise the rents by means of the power put into their hands."

In answer to question nine, he affirms that tenants are subjected to frequent rent increases in spite of Regulation VIII of 1793 which declares that "no one should cancel the *Pattahs* (i.e., the title deeds), fixing the rates of payments for the lands of the *Khud-kasht Ryots* (peasants cultivating the lands of their own village)."[28]

Theoretically, the proprietors of the land regulate the rate of rent paid by the tenants according to certain standards; but, in practice, there is "no fixed standard to afford security to the cultivators for the rate amount of rent demandable for them."[29]

In the event of the tenants falling into arrears with their rent, the proprietors "distrain their moveable property with some exceptions by the police officers and get it sold by means of the judicial authorities."[30]

Answers to subsequent questions make it clear that the lot of the cultivator under the *zamindari* system of Bengal and the *ryotwari* system of Madras is that of a helpless pawn, manipulated by greedy and conniving forces beyond his control. In the *zamindari* system, "they are placed at the mercy of the zamindar's avarice and ambition." In the *ryotwari* system, "they are subjected to the extortions and intrigues of the surveyors and other government revenue officers." The Raja continues:

> I deeply compassionate both; with this difference in regard to the agricultural peasantry of Bengal that there the landlords have met with indulgence from government in the assessment of their revenue, while no part of this indulgence is extended towards the poor cultivators. In an abundant season, when the price of corn is low, the sale of their whole crops is required to meet the demands of the landholder, leaving little or nothing for seed or substance to the labourer or his family.[31]

This strong and irrefutable indictment is followed by the proposal for improving the state of the cultivators and inhabitants at large. Ram Mohan states that in view of the fact that the existing system has made it possible for the landholders, over a period of forty years, to keep raising the rents of the cultivators to a breaking point, "the very least I can propose and the least which the government can do for bettering the condition of the peasantry, is absolutely to interdict any further increase of rent on any pretense whatsoever; particularly on no consideration to allow the present settled and recognized extent of the land to be disturbed by pretended remeasurements; as in forming the Permanent Settlement (Reg. I of 1793, Sec. 8, Art. I), the government declared it to be its right and its duty to protect cultivators as being from their situation most helpless."[32] By the same legislation the government acknowledged the principle of the *Khud-kasht* whereby cultivators are given perpetual rights in the lands they have cultivated and can only be dispossessed in certain specific cases. To realize all of these rights which are already in the law books, the Raja suggests: "If government can succeed in raising a sufficient revenue otherwise by means of duties, etc., or by reducing their establishments particularly in the revenue department, they may then, in the districts where the rents are very high, reduce the rents payable by the cultivators to the landholders, by allowing to the latter a proportionate reduction.''[33] He then refers to a paper (Appendix A) he had drawn up on this subject which provides all of the details of his proposal.

In addition to the *zamindar*, two other sources of pestilence are laid bare—the middlemen and the government officers.

It was common practice for the *zamindars* to farm out their estates to middlemen for the purpose of collecting rent from their tenants in an aggregate sum. The treatment frequently meted out to the cultivators by these middlemen was even "much less merciful than the Zamindars."[34] When the cultivator seeking redress from such oppression approaches the legal authorities, he finds no relief because they are plainly incompetent. The witness explains:

> The judicial authorities being few in number, and often situated at a great distance, and the landholders and middlemen being in general possessed of great local influence and pecuniary means, while the cultivators are too poor and too timid to undertake the hazardous and expensive enterprize of seeking redress, I regret to say that the legal protection of the cultivators is not at all such as could be desired.[35]

Ram Mohan then suggests six possible changes in the administration to safeguard the cultivator: First, there is the suggestion that "no further measurement or increase of rent on any pretence" be allowed. Second, these two points should be publicized in every village, under police supervision, for a period of one year. Third, native judicial officers empowered to sell distrained property for the recovery of rent, should first ascertain that the *zamindar's* demands were not in excess of rates paid in the preceding year. Fourth, judges should set one day a week aside for the purpose of hearing such cases, and should hand out severe punishments if the *zamindar* is guilty of raising the rent illegally, or if the police or native commissioners are culpable of complicity or negligent of duties. Fifth, district magistrates should make annual tours to make sure that these laws for the protection of the poor peasantry are being followed. Sixth, the collector should draw up a register containing the names of all cultivators, a description of their land, and the rents fixed permanently according to the proposed system.[36]

The sad plight of the cultivator is further highlighted in question thirty-five. Whereas the condition of the proprietors of the land has improved under the present system of assessment, and whereas the government has not incurred any loss by concluding the Permanent Settlement of 1793, only the condition of the cultivator has deteriorated.

As an illustration: The cultivators have no means whatsoever of accumulating capital under the present system. Often when the supply of grain is plentiful and the price is cheap, the cultivators are obliged "to sell their whole produce to satisfy the demands of their landholders, and to subsist themselves by their own labour. In years of scarcity they may be able to retain some portion of the crop to form part of their subsistence, but by no means enough for the whole. In short, such is the melancholy condition of the agricultural labourers," says the Raja, "that it always gives me the greatest pain to allude to it."[37]

Not only do the cultivators have no means of getting rich, they have little means to prevent themselves from getting poorer. Unfair assessments of their land make them "dirt poor" because they are victims of collusion, embezzlement, and oppression in the valuing and measuring of their lands. These evils cannot be prevented under the present system because it is engineered by "a vast number of individuals who are generally poor, and have no character to support." The mismanagement also hurts the government through reduced revenues "under a system that at once presses down the people and exhausts the resources of the country."[38] The only way to rectify the situation is for the government to set up a standard based on the survey and assessment of a preceding year, and disallow any future measurement and assessment.

The final question asked is: "Can you suggest any improvement which might secure the revenue to government and protection to the people?" Ram Mohan replies:

> The regulations already in force are fully adequate to secure the government revenue. But to secure the people against any unjust exactions on the part of the revenue officers, I would propose, first, that the collectors should not by any means be armed with magisterial powers. Secondly, that any charge against the revenue officers should be at once investigated by the judicial courts to which they are subject, without reference to the number of cases on the file of the court, as has been the practice with regard to causes in which the collectors are prosecutors; so that both parties may have an equal chance to legal redress. This, under existing circumstances, seems to be the best remedy that presents itself; but with the present system, I must repeat my fears that redress will not always be attainable.[39]

The remaining questions on the Revenue System of India touch on the thorny subject of admitting European settlers on Indian soil. This carries us into a discussion of economic matters to which we next turn.

# CHAPTER 11

# Economic Reform

The final frame in which we view the moral profile of Raja Ram Mohan Roy is economic. His concerns in this area are expressed along two lines of agitation: European colonization and the Salt Monopoly of the East India Company.

On December 17, 1829, one hundred and sixteen men representing "the entire wealth and intelligence of Calcutta," assembled in the town hall to express their unanimous opinion "that all subjects of His Majesty should have 'a legal right' to establish themselves and remain in this part of his dominions, subject only to the restraints of just and equal laws duly administered in open tribunals."[1]

The current policy was to deny British subjects any such rights, and in place of just laws and open tribunals, their residency was contingent upon tacit permission which could be arbitrarily withdrawn in secret conclave, followed by deportation. To remedy this situation the inhabitants of Calcutta met to solicit from Parliament the abolition of restrictions against colonization in India. A Petition was drawn up and speeches were made in its support.

Ram Mohan supported a resolution made by Dwarkanath Tagore, saying that from personal experience he was impressed with the conviction that increased native intercourse with the Europeans will bring about greater productivity in literary, social, and political matters, "a fact which can be easily proved by comparing the condition of those of my countrymen who have enjoyed this advantage with that of those who unfortunately have not had that opportunity; and a fact which I could, to the best of my belief, declare on solemn oath before any assembly."[2]

The *Samachar Chandrika* denounced the above meeting, declaring that "if colonization be introduced into this country, the natives will be subject to many disadvantages." This was counterveiled by a letter appearing in the *Sambad Kaumudi* which claimed that wherever the number and intelligence of the peasantry is raised in their diverse occupations, agriculture is improved, and the rents of the *zamindars* is increased, and no land is left uncultivated; "whence it is certain that industry, skill and a numerous population are required for the improvement of the country,"[3] regardless of the color of the inhabitants. The writer infers from this assertion that by the introduction of European skill and industry into India, and by permitting Europeans to reside freely in the land and to superintend its cultivation, "there will be great benefit to the community at large."[4]

Through the press and by every other means, Ram Mohan canvassed the ideas of free trade and open settlement. He was not blind to the specters which the *Chandrika* kept conjuring up before the public eye, but he calculated that on the whole, colonization would be good for the people in every sense—economic, political, social, and moral. He takes, as an instance, the case of the indigo planters. He observes that he has travelled through several districts in Bengal and Bihar and has "found the natives residing in the neighbourhood of Indigo plantations evidently better clothed and better conditioned than those who lived at a distance from such stations." He concedes there may be some amount of injury done by the planters, "but, on the whole, they have performed more good to the generality of the natives of this country, than any other class of Europeans whether in or out of the Service."[5]

Ram Mohan's campaign for colonization not only roused the ire of the *Samachar Chandrika*, expressing the sentiments of the Orthodox community; it also stirred up the *John Bull*, representing Tory opinion. These two groups came together to counteract Ram Mohan's campaign. They drew up a Petition to Parliament sponsored by the Orthodox Hindus. Eighteen hundred persons lent their signatures.

The Petitioners argued that the unrestricted settlement of Europeans would upset the stability of the empire and injure the economic, social, and religious bases of Indian society. The indigo planters are cited for "taking possession of lands by force, sowing indigo by destroying rice-plant (which is the cause of diminution in the produce of rice, and dearth of the articles of consumption), detaining cattle of, and extorting money from, poor individuals." The Petitioners warn: "if they be permitted to hold any zemindary, or landed property here, the native zemindars and their ryots must be unavoidably ruined."[6]

This Petition was presented, along with the *sati* Petition, to Parliament.

Despite opposition from the Orthodox wing, Ram Mohan forged ahead with his plan. His position was significantly strengthened when Lord William Bentinck came out in favor of his views. In his Minute on Colonization (May 30, 1829), the governor-general states: "various and important national advantages will result from there being a considerable body of our countrymen, and their descendants, settled in the country."[7] He predicted that European skill and machinery would advance the prosperity of India by introducing modern industry and har-

nessing "the vast productive powers of the country, now lying inert."
He also believed that the people's lives would be enriched by "the diffusion of European knowledge and morals."

Bentinck dismissed the so-called dangers attendant upon colonization
by disproving the theory that the natives are "exceedingly jealous of
any interference by strangers, and singularly averse to change." To the
contrary, historical circumstances show that the Indians "would profit
largely by a more general intercourse with intelligent and respectable
Europeans, and would promptly recognize the advantage of it."[8]

Insisting that there were no grounds for fear that the Englishmen
would stir up a turmoil among the populace, the governor-general
demonstrates that earlier instances of violence were based on the
"weakness of the law" and that "the occasional misconduct of the
planters is nothing when contrasted with the sum of good they have diffused around them."[9]

He also finds no reason to consider the interests of the two parties
distinct. "Have we not hitherto found, that where the field has been
equally open, the accumulation of wealth by the natives has fully kept
pace with that of our countrymen; nay, that the former, as being the
most necessary to their joint concerns, and the most keenly alive to
the means of forwarding his private interests, has generally had the
advantages?"[10]

Having considered all the pros and cons, Bentinck concludes that
India stands to gain from the free resort of Englishmen in its territories. Only on one supposition does he entertain the apprehension of
danger. The presence of Englishmen and the diffusion of knowledge
will make the people more politically conscious. But this, he holds, is no
real danger.

> Were our purpose to pursue a course of injustice, to withold from the
> people the privileges they may fairly claim and could advantageously ex-
> ercise, to sport with their lives, their properties or their feelings, by arbi-
> trary acts, by grinding extortion, or by capricious innovation, we should
> act most unwisely in permitting one British subject to enter the country,
> excepting as an accomplice in the scheme; we should be acting madly in
> spreading abroad the lights of knowledge. But our designs being benevo-
> lent towards India, let us not withold what best would serve her. Our
> duty being to maintain the dominion of England, let us not reject the best
> means of confirming it. Our care being equally the interests of both
> countries, let us not exclude those who would best promote and combine
> them.[11]

With such statements Bentinck was anxious that the existing laws be
amended so as to facilitate the settlement of Britishers in the interior.
All inhabitants must equally be under the authority of the local courts.
The doubts and misgivings of both parties must be fully aired and re-

moved by appropriate legislation. "It would be the height of absurdity
to argue, from the inefficiency of our existing institutions, against the
admission of Europeans." The patent remedy, he thinks, "is not the
exclusion of these, but the reform of the system."[12]

Bentinck's sentiments, so strikingly similar to those of Ram Mohan,
were the most "advanced thought of the age." But, in spite of the
weight of his office and the cogency of his testimony, the Court of Directors, in their dispatch of April 6, 1831, denied any relaxation of restrictions barring Europeans from settling in the interior of the
country. However, what the governor-general failed to achieve
through the power of his office, Ram Mohan, possessed only of his reputation as a sincere, knowledgeable, and objective patriot, secured
through his persuasive testimony before the Select Committee.

Let us now look at the evidence. Our sources are the concluding
questions on the Revenue System, and his *Remarks on the Settlement of
India by Europeans*.

First, Ram Mohan addresses himself to the question whether it would
be beneficial to allow Europeans of capital to purchase estates and settle on them. Typically, his analysis of the economic situation touches on
its moral dimensions as our italicizing of his answer indicates. He states:
"If Europeans of *character* and capital were allowed to settle in the
country . . . it would greatly improve the resources of the country, and
also the condition of the native inhabitants, by shewing them superior
methods of cultivation, and the *proper mode of treating their labourers and
dependents*."[13]

Secondly, his answer to question forty-nine makes it clear that the
type of European settler he has in mind is one who belongs to the
higher, educated classes, and is possessed of wealth. This group has already given evidence of respect for the differences which characterize
the two races and cultures. On the other hand, "common Europeans
are often disposed to annoy the native inhabitants." Besides, without
capital, the lower and uneducated Europeans could not, "in a hot country, compete with the native labourers." Consequently, this class of settler "would not find his situation at all improved, but the very reverse
by emigrating to India."[14]

Thirdly, echoes of Bentinck's Minute are heard in his answer to the
question whether the present judicial system would be sufficient to control the European settlers in the interior. He answers that under the
present system British subjects are not amenable to the Company's
courts, barring minor fines (Rupees 500). Consequently, the courts as
now established "are by no means competent to exercise any adequate
control over British-born subjects in the interior." Like Bentinck, Ram
Mohan would want the laws to be amended to safeguard the native
community. This end could be accomplished either by extending the
jurisdiction of the king's courts already established in the presidencies,
or to augment their number. Should expenses render this plan imprac-

ticable, it is advisable that greater power be given to Company's judges over the European settlers.[15]

The last important question asks: "How would the settlement on a large scale of Europeans of capital in the country improve its resources?" His answer is that inasmuch as major funds are currently withdrawn from India by Europeans retiring from it with fortunes minted there, "a system which would encourage Europeans of capital to become permanent settlers with their families, would necessarily greatly improve the resources of the country."[16]

We now turn to our second source: *Remarks on the Settlement in India by Europeans*. Originally, this document appeared in the General Appendix to the Report of the Select Committee of the House of Commons on the affairs of the East India Company, 1832. In characteristic style, Ram Mohan lists the pros and cons on the subject, weighing them clearly and objectively. He confronts the chief arguments of the anticolonists, offers his rebuttals, and indicates how some legitimate abuses can be rectified. Since we have already summarized this document in connection with Ram Mohan's attitude toward the British, we shall pass on.

On the basis of the evidence presented by Ram Mohan and others, the new Charter Act of 1833 declared Europeans, without benefit of license, to be eligible to settle freely in territories acquired by the Company prior to 1800. Immigration to territories secured after 1800 required the obtaining of a license from local authorities.

In the estimation of Jatindra Kumar Majumdar, these provisions served to ameliorate the condition of the people through improvements in agriculture, industry, and commerce, much of which was to the credit of Ram Mohan and his band of liberal followers. Chief among these was Prince Dwarkanath Tagore who showed "the way to his timid and unenterprising countrymen of how to avail themselves of the opportunity of the application of European skill, capital and enterprise for the accomplishment of the purpose for which they had pleaded." Since their time, Majumdar continues, demand for the industrial, agricultural, and commercial development of India has been increasingly felt, and "the names of those who amongst their countrymen first realised it and made the pioneering efforts in the direction, which has gradually ushered in a new age in this country, can never be forgotten."[17] Majumdar, it should be noted, is writing as a Liberal toward the end of the British period.

We now turn to a second agitation in which Ram Mohan became involved—agitation against the East India Company's salt monopoly as practiced in Bengal.

Once again Ram Mohan came to the rescue of the underdog. His sympathies for the *ryot* were only rivalled by his compassion for the *molungee*. Some 125,000 of these native laborers slaved in the manufacture of salt. The marshy *Sunderbuns* in which the factories were located were hot-beds of disease and were infested with fierce tigers. Only the hardiest of humans survived, but none could escape the economic strangle-hold which the Company had on these unfortunate creatures. To keep the wolf from the door, they had to work for the Company, but once inside the Company they could not leave, for they were irredeemably in debt to this all-encompassing octopus. So the laborers were damned when they did not work, and they were damned when they did.

The way the salt business was run by the government was actually a monopoly within a monopoly. The government itself did not have a hand in the production or retailing of salt—those responsibilities were relegated to Company agents. The total produce fell into the laps of a few Calcutta merchants whose monopolistic powers enabled them freely to manipulate the market. The combination of hoarding and high prices spawned the twin evils of black marketeering and the downgrading of quality. Buyers were trapped by this cartel because the Company and its surrogates saw to it that foreign salt was kept out of the country by heavy import taxes.

Among the anti-monopolists who decried the evils of the system were J. Crawford who authored the book: *Inquiry into Some of the Principal Monopolies of the East India Company* (London, 1830), and R. Richards who entitled his exposé: *India* (London, 1829). Ram Mohan Roy attacked the salt monopoly on two fronts: while he was in Bengal, and before the Select Committee in England.

Writing under the pseudonym of Ram Horee Doss, his pen quivers with outrage against the moral obtuseness of a typical salt officer. With shouting words he headlines his letter to the *Government Gazette*: "RESPECT US! WE ARE YET A PEOPLE—A NATION." The letter is addressed to the "Covenanted Salt Officer," and reveals some of the evils of the business. It reads:

> My name is Ram Horee Doss. I pay annually to Government a sum of 120 rupees. I am therefore a ten pound freeholder, as you call it. *My son was one of those who assisted to thrash the palkee of an honourable Covenanted Salt Officer*, and returned home triumphant to tell of how he had seen the To-pee Walla run for his life. Why did he do all this? Why should more of us not repeat it? If *we find* that insult is added to injury, may *you* not one day *find that the worm will turn when it is trodden upon*!

> Let us leave the declamation and come to facts. Did it never occur to you that 325 Rs. per 100 maunds . . . was *somewhat* too dear when the smugglers would furnish it at 1 rupee 8 annas? And then, too, your . . . salt was augmented here to 8 Rs. per maund of two-thirds salt and one-third sand . . . . And did it never strike you, Sir, amidst your heartless gibes, that when a people so notorious for submission as we are, even to the very shadow of power, were driven (I say *driven*, for I aver that the Bengalee *must* be driven ere he ventures on such remedies)—*driven* then, to attack

a Company's officer of high rank, and one so generally beloved for his many excellent qualities, in the manner we so notoriously did in the very suburbs of Calcutta,—I may say under the guns of Fort William—did it never occur to you, that there must have been some pressing demand for that which could render its smugglers so bold in its defence as to make the very women of a *reward "for the head of Topee Wallah?"* Have you, with all your esprit, so little judgment as not to discern something in this?

. . . You assert that, we do not purchase more, we have *therefore* enough! Was there no professor, Sir, in the College in which you were reared (at our expence) to teach you that in an argument we should never *assume* that which it is the object of the argument to *prove?* You wish to prove that our supply of Salt is ample, and to do it you *assume* that it is so *because* we do not buy it at your monopoly price! Fie upon you, Sir! to call this argument. Show us the period when Salt has been sold at its natural price. Supply ten families in any village with it. Give your starving workmen at home a full supply of bread and meat, at the price they would obtain it without your Corn Laws, and see *then* if they would consume more of it or not . . .

. . . When you next mean to sport with our sufferings, let me counsel you to ask your medical adviser if he thinks the miserable ryot and his squalid children have a sufficient supply of salt. Ask him if he does not believe that to the want of it is probably to be attributed much of the mortality and suffering which prevails amongst them from worms and mesentric obstructions . . .[18]

In closing, Ram Horee Doss bluntly states: "I am of those who look upon the whites as intruders into our country, and who think they might in decency refrain from mockery of our 'miseries molungian.' " With stinging sarcasm he informs the salt officer he has a talent for writing critically of the people. "You *have* talent, Sir. Believe me there are far better ways in which to employ it than this which you have chosen, even if you consulted your interest only. *It is not possible that you might receive an order to be silent?* If you do not, there are those amongst us who *may* solicit one."[19]

The above writing is not only revelatory of the evils of the monopoly, but the indignation of the man. It shows that the follower of the *Precepts of Jesus* was not prepared to keep turning the other cheek. After a certain point, neither was Jesus. There was a bottom line of indignity which people could take and yet keep faith with their humanity. *These forceful but forgotten sentiments must be carefully considered by critics who characterize Ram Mohan as a lackey of the British, and as one whose economic interests prevented him from emphathising with his hungry countrymen.* We now shift scenes from "under the guns of Fort William" to the English Parliament where Ram Mohan answered queries pertaining to the salt monopoly, either in person or by communication (March 19, 1832).

First, he quotes the retail price of adulterated salt in Calcutta as eight seers to the rupee, and pure English salt as five seers to the rupee. The price differential indicates that only the well-to-do can procure the imported product, while the poor must pay good money for bad quality.

Salt is highly necessary, he points out, for the Bengalis because of the insipid nature of their food. Therefore, its deprivation becomes a dietary burden which is difficult to bear.

If the price of salt were reduced and quality improved, its consumption would markedly increase. Its use may be extended by villagers "in seasoning the food of cattle, for which purpose formerly in large quantities were used. The poorer classes at any rate would not in this case be compelled to sacrifice any other comfort in order to procure it."[20]

One way to alleviate the problem would be to import fine English salt. Only a few Brahmins might abstain from its usage on the grounds of religious scruples.

The importation of salt at a cheaper price than that manufactured in Bengal would not precipitate mass unemployment among the *molungees* because they could be absorbed into other lines of work in which there is a dearth of man-power.

As compared with the *ryots*, the working conditions of the *molungees* are more pathetic. The danger from tigers had been diminished since the Sunderbuns have been partially cleared. "But the *molungees* suffer chiefly from the humidity of the soil and the dampness of the atmosphere where they are obliged to continue during the manufacturing season. The agriculturists are better situated than the *molungees* in respect to both health and personal freedom, from not being, like the latter, liable to be detained during the working season, though the agriculturists are not equally sure of regular employment and wages."[21]

Natural causes aside, the *molungees* also suffer at the unjust hands of subordinate officers of the salt agencies. When the officers practice extortion at the expense of the head *molungees*, they, in turn, "indemnify themselves by defrauding the inferior *molungees* in respect to the wages allowed to them, and the work exacted from them."[22]

Regulations have been passed to protect the *molungees*, but bureaucracy has nullified them; not to mention "the insuperable difficulties under which a humble individual generally labours in endeavouring to get redress against those in power, or superior to himself in wealth and influence."[23]

The end product of all this blood, sweat, and tears is a mixture of what is euphemistically called "salt." "The adulteration of the salt is carried to an enormous extent, by mixing it with one-third or even one-half of earth, until, instead of being like salt, it more resembles the earth of which it is composed. Persons in comfortable circumstances generally purify it by manufacturing it over again before they use it, or purchase it already refined, often at double the common price; but the poorer classes cannot afford the expense of either."[24]

Ram Mohan's testimony delivered March 19, 1832, revealed the error and hypocrisy of government claims sent by letter to the Court of Directors on the subject of Salt Revenue, dated April 2, 1832. With a view to appeasing the anxieties of the Court on mismanagement, the Bengal Government, making use of a report from the Board of Customs, *Salt and Opium* (dated January 28, 1832), tried to establish that: the supply of salt was adequate to meet all needs; that its price was within the reach of the poorest classes; and that if there were any agitation, it came only from Europeans who were hostile to the Company.

Interestingly, the Bengal government considered lack of intensity in Ram Mohan's opposition (as they assessed it), proof of the validity of their position—a back-handed compliment to the Raja. They say: "If now and then a native of talent and education, as Rammohun Roy, for instance, raises an objection to the monopoly, it is weakly urged as compared with the strong mode in which other assumed evils are commented upon, and then not from any actual experience or observation of the mischief it is said to produce, but because it is contrary to some general principle of political economy."[25]

How wrong they were! Ram Mohan's testimony dealt not with "general principles" but with rupees, annas, and pies that were being wrung from the hands of the little people whose staple of rice and *turkari* (curried vegetables) could only be rendered palatable by common salt made by miserable *molungees* who had sold their soul to the Company's store!

The Raja's testimony carried the day. The Parliamentary Select Committee recommended changes advocated by him and other anti-monopolists. Among these measures they recommended an excise duty on salt produced in Bengal, and a duty on salt that was imported. Against the option of opening up the manufacture to free enterprise, fear of loss in revenues persuaded the Committee to recommend continuance of the present system. However, they pushed for a scheme of progressively graduated imports. It was their expectation that in the remodelled system, domestic manufacture might lessen, starting with those areas in which costs were highest, until foreign salt became so large a part of consumption that it could be imported free under a custom duty. Such a plan could materially reduce the price of salt, "which would prove of the greatest advantage to the Native population of India, to whom a cheap supply of this necessary of life is of the utmost importance."[26]

How do we evaluate Ram Mohan's economic reforms? First, it would be incorrect to conclude on the basis of our list of economic events in which he was involved that his ethics were *episodic*; that his intense humanism forced him to react intuitively to *specific* situations as they happened to arise, but that there was *no infrastructure* to his reforming activity. On the contrary, we can discern a certain plan of action within an *overarching economic philosophy* that was *aimed at developing a modern economy*. B. N. Ganguli defines as follows the strategy that he finds implicit in Ram Mohan's economic philosophy:

Widely disseminated Western education; assimilation of Western science
and technology; growth of an enlightened *bourgeois elite* with a spirit of
enterprise and rationality and continuously vigilant about social justice,
amelioration of the social and economic conditions of underprivileged
masses and vulnerable groups and any threat to human rights that came
from alien administrators; partnership, on the basis of enlightened interest, between foreign capital, skill and enterprise and whatever enterprise
was left amongst the masses of the population, in order to raise the latter
to a higher level of economic efficiency; removal of legal barriers to the
development of a free enterprise system, which was either the result of an
antiquated social system or the consequence of ill-conceived administrative measures; and lastly, moderating the excesses of a colonial economy.[27]

On the last point Ram Mohan's judgment faltered. He and his fellow
Liberals failed to see that despite its fine ideology, the basic business of
the Imperial policy was to make money for the betterment of the English social order. To be sure, he was oppressively aware of the enormous drain of wealth from India. He calculated that in the period
between 1765 and 1820, India lost approximately 110,000,000 sterling
pounds by the way of stock dividends of the E.I.C., commercial profits,
and Company salaries. He sought, therefore, to offset this depletion of
national wealth through proposals for European settlement and by the
infusion of foreign capital and technical expertise, especially in the area
of agriculture. He fought side by side with free traders against the
monopolistic privileges of the East India Company. The Utilitarian
ethic of the "greatest good of the greatest number" was their guiding
ideology. Native landlords and merchants who considered the East
India Company effete and reactionary also joined him. Together,
they formed a band of "enlightened patriots who sought a modernised
economy and polity by aligning themselves with 'progressive forces' released by the Industrial Revolution in England. They thought, perhaps
*naïvely*, that the ultimate social, economic and political emancipation of
India would come about through rapid socio-economic transformation
on the basis of partnership of foreign capital, skill and enterprise supported by the enlightened self-interest of a liberal British
administration."[28]

One creation of the "enlightened self-interest" of the government
was the Permanent Settlement of 1793. By conferring exclusive ownership rights on the *zamindars*, the Court of Directors had hoped that
"the magic touch of property would set a certain productive principle
in operation, which would abundantly recompense them in future for
the sacrifices they had then made."[29]

The conferment of property rights did succeed in advancing the colonial objectives of bringing wastelands under cultivation and instilling
a strong sense of loyalty in Bengal's new middle class, but, as Asok Sen
points out, "it failed miserably in one sphere, the sphere one would

consider to be extremely vital for the building of the bases of a viable economy. The 'magic touch of property,' as it had been administered, could never bring in operation 'a certain productive principle' about which the Court of Directors made so eloquent anticipations."[30]

The failure of the system lay in the development of "a class of pure rentiers" who became fat at the expense of the poor *ryots* who worked their land. Originally, Cornwallis had hoped to preserve the rights of the *ryots*, but the need for revenue to support the stability and security of the Empire, gave rise to a series of regulations which made rack-renting the basis of the agricultural economy. Ram Mohan, as we recall, exposed this problem during his testimony before the Select Committee.

However, Radicals at home thought that Ram Mohan was too soft on the *zamindars*. The *Hurkaru*, quoting the old Spanish proverb, "One must be hammer or anvil in this world," declared, "Rammohan Roy . . . belongs to the hammers, and his evidence is taken at home for that of anvils."[31]

Contemporary critics quote the *Hurkaru* in charging that Ram Mohan's support of the *ryots* was weak, but what is forgotten is that the *Samachar Chandrika* blasted the *babu* for having injured the *zamindars* in his evidence.[32] This is more in keeping with the evidence we have surveyed above. It is not our purpose to get caught between this cross-fire, because the more important point is that whereas Ram Mohan thought the system could be salvaged by his recommendations; in fact, as a tool of the colonial policy, it could never achieve the ideological goal of enhancing the production system of the land.

Turning from the agricultural economy to the industrial economy, the picture is just as bleak, and that not surprisingly because the two were closely connected and mutually affected one another.

Prior to their victory in 1813, British free traders sought the aid of the Bengali bourgeoisie in their battle against the East India Company. Ram Mohan led this group of native capitalists which included Dwarkanath and Prasanna Kumar Tagore who had indigo interests, and ship-builders such as Ramdulal Dey, Panchoo Datta, Ramgopal Mullick, and Mandan Dutt. The role and ideology of this group characterized it as "a *comprador* group which expected a dependent but nevertheless substantial development of Indian capitalism in collaboration with the free trader merchants and bankers."[33]

Their capitalist dreams only gave the illusion of reality during the faint dawn of the mercantile enterprise, but soon the harsh light of the rising colonial sun awakened them to their subservient state. Their former English partners dumped them once they had achieved their objectives, and the fledgling businesses they had started proved unequal to the unfair competition of the colonial market. Ashok Sen discusses this topic in terms of the "Deindustrialization" of Bengal, a term which N. K. Sinha also employs.[34] He points out that from 1765 onwards, Indian silk and cotton manufacturers paid exorbitant import duties to the British which were exceeded only by the tariff on raw materials which were imported from India for British textile manufacture. In keeping with this colonial brand of "free trade," the Indian market became a happy dumping ground for the sale of cheap British commodities. Once the Charter Act of 1813 went into effect and the East Indian trade was opened to private enterprise, the Indian cotton industry was squeezed out of existence. Its obituary was found in the 1822 report of the governor-general. "Cotton piece-goods, for so many ages the staple of manufacture of India, seem thus forever lost."[35] In time, the silk industry, the sugar industry, and the salt and shipping industries suffered similar collapse.

Their dreams of free trade shattered, the Bengali bourgeoisie took to money-lending and land investment which, as we have seen, feathered the beds of the landlords through the terms of the Permanent Settlement.

Sen is flabbergasted by the turn of events which marked the industrial debacle of Bengal between 1800–1833—events, it is charged, which Ram Mohan witnessed at close hand but never challenged. He wonders why in his many writings on numerous topics there is scant allusion to this calamity of deindustrialization.

> It appears that *Sambad Cowmoody*, his own paper, gave little importance to the increasing plight of the country's weavers and spinners. Some vital questions are thrown up in this sphere; the questions we cannot really square up with what Rammohun wrote about the benefits of expanding British trade, about the identity of his country's interests with the liberal stances of the British industrial revolution, or even about the prospects of his reformed Permanent Settlement. This was the sphere again where the attempt to rationalize the civilizing effects of English rule would turn out to be most untenable.[36]

Rajat K. Ray thinks that Sen overdoes his case for the "deindustrialization of Bengal." He grants that artisan industries such as cotton manufactures declined, "but surely such handicrafts could not supply the basis for rapid industrialization of the country. Nor was the disappearance of urban Bengalis in the *comprador* type of trading and business activities as sudden and as complete as Sen seems to think."[37]

Citing the case of Dwarkanath Tagore, Sen states that the liquidation of his business enterprises "in course of only one generation and of the maintenance of the *zamindars* alone" is supportive of his thesis of "deindustrialization." Again, the case seems to be somewhat overdrawn. Factors other than colonial handicaps are overlooked. It must be remembered that Dwarkanath won immense wealth through his versatility and commercial acumen. But when he died at the early age of fifty-two, there was no one in the family who had matching skills to enable the various firms to continue prospering. Hiranmay Banerjee points out that "his eldest son was given to piety and had no aptitude for business as he himself admitted. In consequence, the Carr Tagore Company failed in 1848. The Union Bank founded by him failed even earlier in 1847. The Carr Tagore Company went into liquidation and the assets of the family were also seized for meeting the claims of the creditors."[38]

However, due to Dwarkanath's business astuteness, some rental estates were left untouched by creditors. Prior to his departure for Britain, he had set up a trust which gave legal immunity against seizure to four *zamindary* estates. Debendranath utilized the income from these holdings to liquidate the family debts, thereby enabling the family once more to "live comfortably without being affluent."[39]

Citing the story of other capitalist families who prospered, notwithstanding great risks, Rajat Ray concludes that economic development did take place, but it was "a limited development that was very different from industrialization of the type that occurs after a genuine takeoff." Native entrepreneurs were not all wiped out, nor was wealth simply invested in non-productive schemes. The real problem, as Ray sees it, was that "all entrepreneurial activities tended to be subordinated to the import-export bias of the economy and served only to strengthen the colonial aspect of the relationship between the economies of Britain and India."[40]

In the light of these facts, Ray maintains that it is a shaky assumption, which is at odds with actual developments, to say Bengal's entire industrial economy was obliterated during Ram Mohan's lifetime "and then to pose the question why in his so many writings there is no reference to the phenomenon of deindustrialization and the causes reponsible for this calamity. The calamity was not apparent to Rammohun Roy because he genuinely believed that the country was proceeding on the path of economic development, and while he could not possibly appreciate the limited character of this growth, 'deindustrialization' is hardly a suitable term for it."[41]

Sen concludes his critique of Ram Mohan's economic perspective by drawing attention to the anomalous situation in which he found himself. Despite the genuineness of his intentions, his magnanimity, his patriotic love, and his motive of modernizing India with British help, "Rammohun could not break through the false premises of a perspective which went to believe: 'Divine Providence at last, in its abundant mercy, stirred up the English nation . . . to receive the oppressed Natives of Bengal under its protection.' "[42] That, says Sen, is the oddity and the abnormality of Ram Mohan's position, "particularly when so much was happening in his environment, in the production economy of his own land to raise doubts about the validity of those premises."[43]

The anomaly resides more in the mind of the writer than that of Ram Mohan. This becomes clear when we read the above quotation in its immediate context. As Ram Mohan uses the word Providence, it is, precisely, to be understood *environmentally*, as Sen would plead. Providence was "no pie in the sky," while the hungry masses salivated for salt. Against the Muslim environment in which property was plundered, religion insulted, and blood wantonly shed, the British environment bore all the "marks of favour, as a free people would be expected to bestow, in establishing an English Judicature, and granting to all within its jurisdiction, the same civil rights as every Briton enjoys in his native country; thus putting the natives of India in possession of such privileges as their forefathers never expected to attain, even under Hindu Rulers."[44] Furthermore, "under the cheering influence of equitable and indulgent treatment, and stimulated by the example of a people famed for their wisdom and liberality, the natives of India, with the *means of amelioration set before them, have been gradually advancing in social and intellectual improvement*" (italics supplied).[45]

Of course, the environment could be suddenly changed, as the *Appeal for the Freedom of the Press* apprehended; but in that context, Providence would be null and void. If the British had a "Mandate" from "Heaven," it must be *demonstrated* in all "means of amelioration," and when the latter is absent, the former is non-existent, for the former is only a religious label for the latter. Even more. When oppression reigns, and no one listens to the cry for justice, one must see the devil in evil events, and the people have the moral responsibility to rise up and cast out the demons, whether they wear cross or crescent, or be white or brown. Ram Mohan did not distinguish between demons!

Sen would have avoided this *faux pas* on which he bases his economic criticism had he examined the Raja's statement about Providence in the context of his theological presuppositions. In his theology, there is no room for acts of divine Providence. History, like nature, is governed by law. Religions may claim acts of supernatural intervention to show that God is on their side, but history is the scene of human causality. In history, karma alone is king. In keeping with this theology, Ram Mohan rejected the Christian notion of a divine Messiah sent by Providence; how much less amenable would he have been to the notion of a British Messiah, for the latter were often less than Christian! All talk of Providence must therefore be understood as the rhetoric of religion to describe a state of affairs which was heaven *compared to* the previous hell. Of course, heaven was no land of milk and honey, as the *ryots* and *molungees* knew only too well, but it was good by comparison and had all the elements of hope.

Also, when Ram Mohan talked about Providence he was employing a psychological device to remind the British to live up to their own ideology of divine destiny. The British had rationalized their colonial ambitions in terms of the White Man's Burden. Ram Mohan understood this very well and took every opportunity to use this rationalized morality to keep them moral!

## CHAPTER 12

# Visit to England and Journey's End

The dominating concern of Ram Mohan during his stay in London was the welfare of his country. We have just perused the care with which he answered the many questions of the Select Committee of the House of Commons. He was always on hand to supply the government with any information they required and he studiously followed legislative developments. "Frequently was the noble form of the illustrious stranger seen within the precincts of our Houses of Parliament," notes one Londoner.

He pulled many Tory strings in connection with legislative deliberations on the *Sati* Petition, and was at hand when the Privy Council delivered its judgment against the Orthodox Petition. Writing to a friend, Mrs. Woodford, he says: "You will, I am sure, be highly gratified to learn that the present Governor-General of India has sufficient courage to afford them [Hindu widows] protection against their selfish relations, who cruelly used to take advantage of their tender feelings in the name and under the cloak of religion."[1]

He also functioned as the envoy of the Emperor of Delhi who had invested him with the title of Raja, and was able to secure satisfactory reparations for the sovereign. So successful was he in these direct negotiations with the English authorities that other Indian royalty sought his services.

Turning from affairs of India to British politics; when Ram Mohan arrived in England, the country was buzzing with excitement about the Reform Bill. Ram Mohan was sufficiently familiar with British history and political institutions to know the far-reaching effects of this bill, not only for England, but India as well. He says: "The struggles are not merely between the reformers and the anti-reformers; but between liberty and oppression throughout the world; between justice and injustice, and between right and wrong."[2]

With the passage of the Reform Bill, he writes an animated letter to a friend:

> I am *now* happy to find myself fully justified in congratulating you and my other friends at Liverpool on the *complete* success of the Reform Bills, notwithstanding the violent opposition and want of political principle on the part of the aristocrats. The nation can no longer be a prey of the few who used to fill their purses at the expense, nay, to the ruin of the people, for a period upwards of fifty years. The Ministers have honestly and firmly discharged their duty, and provided the people with means of securing their rights. I hope and pray that the people, the mighty people of England, may now in like manner do their's, cherishing public spirit and liberal principles, at the same time banishing bribery, corruption and selfish interests, from public proceedings.[3]

So strongly did the Raja feel about the principles of justice involved in the above legislation that he "publicly avowed that in the event of the Reform Bill being defeated," he would renounce his connection with England.[4] All of this speaks eloquently of his internationalism and his concern for social ethics, even though the politics of another nation was involved.

When Ram Mohan was not discussing politics, he was talking theology. The Unitarians awaited the arrival of the "Apostle of the East," with eager anticipation. A meeting of the Association in London was arranged "where the enlightened Brahmin was welcomed as a fellow-labourer and received with every mark of deep and heart-felt respect."[5] Spirits were so high at the meeting that it seemed they were being honored with the presence of "a Plato or a Socrates, a Milton or a Newton."[6]

Sir John Bowring took the floor and proposed the following resolution:

> That the members of the Association feel a deep interest in the amelioration of the condition of the natives of British India; and that we trust their welfare and improvement will never be lost sight of by the Legislature and Government of our country; that we have especial pleasure in the hope that juster notions and purer forms of religion are gradually advancing amongst them; and that our illustrious visitor from that distant region, the Rajah Rammohun Roy, be hereby certified of our sympathy in his arduous and philanthropic labours, of our admiration of his character, our delight at his presence amongst us, and of our conviction that the magnanimous and beneficent course which he has marked out for himself and hitherto consistently pursued, will entitle him to the blessings of his countrymen and of mankind, as it will assuredly receive those of future generations.[7]

The motion was seconded by Dr. Kirkland (late President of Harvard University) who observed: "It is well known that the Rajah is an object of lively interest in America; and he is expected there with the greatest anxiety."

Though fatigued from excessive socializing, with becoming modesty the Raja thanked all present for their cordial welcome and said he did not deserve any of the encomiums bestowed upon him. He acknowledged that he had labored under many disadvantages. His theistic movement based on belief in one God, not only incurred the wrath of the Hindus, but the hostility of the Christians. He declares:

> I have honour for the appellation of Christian; but they always tried to throw difficulties and obstacles in the way of the principles of Unitarian Christianity. I have found some of these here; but more there. They abhor the notion of simple precepts. They always lay a stress on mystery and mystical focal points, which serve to delude their followers; and the consequence is, that we meet with such opposition in India that our progress is very slight; and I feel ashamed on my side that I have not made any progress that might have placed me on a footing with my fellow-labourers in this part of the globe. However, if this is the true system of Christianity, it will prevail, notwithstanding all the opposition that may be made to it. Scripture seconds your system of religion, common sense is always on your side; while power and prejudice are on the side of your opponents. There is a battle going on between reason, scripture and common-sense; and wealth, and power and prejudice.[8]

He concludes with thanks for all the kindness conferred on him, and says he shall never forget it "to the last moment" of his existence.

In spite of his personal and theological affinities with Unitarianism, Ram Mohan did not identify himself with this or any other church group. It was his practice to visit churches of all denominations.

In social intercourse, Ram Mohan endeared himself to the cosmopolitan community of London, and to all segments of society. The following extracts from letters of Lucy Aikin show how he captured the social limelight of London and commandeered the respect of its intellectual elite. Writing to Dr. Channing, dated Hampstead, June 28, 1831, she says:

> All accounts agree in representing him as a person of extraordinary merit. With very great intelligence and ability, he unites a modesty and simplicity which win all hearts. He has a very great command of the language, and seems perfectly well versed in the political state of Europe, and *an ardent well-wisher to the cause of freedom and improvement everywhere* (italics supplied).[9]

Aikin's next letter is dated Hampstead, September 6, 1831. It is clear that in the short space of three months the Raja has won the writer's heart, as with freed feelings she exults in her great discovery:

He is indeed a glorious being, a true sage, as it appears, with the genuine
humility of the character, and with the genuine sensibility, a more engag-
ing tenderness of heart than any *class* of character can justly claim.[10]

An intellectual celebrity who called on Ram Mohan on the very first
night of his arrival in London was the venerable philosopher, Jeremy
Bentham. Another celebrated Londoner whom Ram Mohan engaged
in discussion was Robert Owen, "the father of British Socialism."
Other distinguished persons thronged to his lodgings at 125 Regent
Street. There was a steady flow of visitors from eleven a.m. to four
p.m., until this "constant state of excitement drove him to a state of
exhaustion."

Ironically, the Anglo-Indian officials who had snubbed him in India,
now vied with socialites to be seen in his company. In place of the cava-
lier treatment afforded him in Calcutta, the same officials feted him
with a grand dinner fit for governors on their way to India.

The highest honor paid to Ram Mohan was his presentation to the
King of England, making him the first Indian to be received at the British Court. "The ceremony was the picturesque token of a significant
moment in the evolution of the empire."[11]

The stately figure that caught the eye of king and commoner must
now be fully described:

The Rajah, in the outer man, was cast in nature's finest mould; his figure
was manly and robust; his carriage dignified: the forehead towering, ex-
pansive and commanding: the eye dark, restless, full of brightness and animation, yet liquid and benevolent and frequently glistening with a tear
when affected by the deeper sensibility of the heart; the nose of Roman
form and proportions: lips full and indicative of independence; the whole
features deeply expressive, with a smile of soft and peculiar fascination
which won irresistibly the suffrages to whom it was addressed. His manners were characterized by suavity blended with dignity, verging towards
either point according to the company in which he might be placed. To
ladies his politeness was marked by the most delicate manner, and his fe-
licitous mode of paying them a compliment gained him many admirers
among the high-born beauties of Britain. In conversation with individuals
of every rank and of various nations and professions, he passed with the
utmost ease from one language to another, suiting his remarks to each
and all in excellent taste, and commanding the astonishment and respect
of his hearers.

It was in argument, however, that this exalted Brahmin was most con-
spicuous: he seemed to grapple with truth intuitively, and called in invec-
tive, raillery, sarcasm, and sometimes a most brilliant wit to aid him in
confuting his opponent; if precedent were necessary, a remarkably reten-
tive memory and extensive reading in many languages supplied him with
a copious fund; and at times with a rough, unsparing, ruthless hand he
burst asunder the meshes of sophistry, error and bigotry, in which it
might be attempted to entangle him.[12]

For a brief stretch under ill-advice, Ram Mohan occupied an aristocratic abode in Cumberland Terrace, Regents Park, where he lived like a maharaja. It was not long before he abandoned the life of pomp and show and took up residence at 48 Bedford Square, in company with the brother of his old friend, David Hare. "He kept a plain chariot, with a coachman and a footman in neat liveries; in fact adopted and adhered to the style of a private gentleman of moderate fortune, though still courted by the first men in the kingdom."[13]

The scaling down of his style of life was also necessitated by the failure of his family to make remittances from India.[14] These pecuniary difficulties proved highly embarrassing for one who had always known wealth.

Of equal embarrassment was his betrayal by Sanford Arnot whom Ram Mohan had employed as his secretary. H. H. Wilson informs Babu Ram Comul Sen in a letter written three months after the Raja's demise (December 21, 1833), that Arnot "importuned him for the payment of large sums which he called arrears of salary, and threatened Rammohun if not paid, to do what he has done since his death—claim as his own writing all that Rammohun published in England. In short Rammohun had got amongst a low, needy, unprincipled set of people, and found out his mistake, I suspect, when too late, which preyed upon his spirits and injured his health."[15]

By all mental and physical signs Ram Mohan was in need of some rest and recreation. In the beginning of September 1832, his Unitarian friends arranged for a vacation in Bristol, through the generous hospitality of Miss Castle, residing at Stapleton Grove.

On September 11 a large party was given in the Raja's honor. It is described by Dr. Carpenter:

> In the conversation at Stapleton Grove were men fully competent to judge of intellectual power and one and all admired and were delighted by the clearness, the closeness, and the acuteness of his arguments, and the beautiful tones of his mind. In the second of the two conversations at which Mr. Foster was present, the Raja continued for three hours, standing the whole time, replying to all the inquiries and observations that were made by a number of gentlemen who surrounded him, on the moral and political state and prospects of India, and on an elucidation at great length of certain dogmas of the Indian philosophers.[16]

A week later, September 19, the Raja was stricken with fever. Progressively, his pulse grew weak; he developed spasms and headaches; and by the following week he was paralyzed on his left side. His friends were deeply troubled by his condition and did everything in their power to relieve him. Since the problem seemed to be located in the head, leeches were applied under the watchful eyes of three attending physicians. Ram Mohan had great faith in his doctors, saying that were he to die, he had the satisfaction of knowing he had the best medical advice in Bristol.

His faith was also in the Divine. He sensed the end was near, and told his friends so. One of the last words he uttered was the sacred syllable *Om*—the root syllable of origination and dissolution. As a student of the *Veda*, Ram Mohan had learned that the recitation of *Om* at the beginning of a lesson and end of a lesson guaranteed that the wisdom grasped would not be dissipated. Also, as a devotee he had learned that the utterance of this eternal syllable helps meet all one's needs, including the need of *moksha* which is final liberation. Lessons learned in life were affirmed in death, as with his last breath Ram Mohan uttered the imperishable sound—*Om!*

The death scene is touchingly memorialized in the journal of Dr. J. B. Estlin:

> It was a beautiful moonlight night; on one side of the window, as Mr. Hare, Miss Kiddell and I, looked out of it, was the calm rural midnight scene; on the other, this extraordinary man dying. I shall never forget the moment. Miss Hare, now hopeless and overcome, could not summon the courage to hang over the dying Raja, as she did while soothing or feeding him ere hope had left her, and remained sobbing in a chair near; young Raja was generally holding his hand. I doubt if he knew any since morn yesterday. About half-past one, to please Miss Kiddell, as life was fast ebbing from our admired friend, and nothing but watching the last breath remained for those around, I lay down on my bed with my clothes on. At half past two, Mr. Hare came into my room and told me it was all over; Ram Rotun was holding the Raja's chin, kneeling by him. Miss Hare, young Raja, Miss Kiddell, Mr. Hare, my mother, Miss Castle, Ram Hurry, and one or two servants were there also; his last breath had been drawn at twenty-five minutes past two a.m.[17]

As the body was being prepared for interment it was plain that Ram Mohan Roy died as a Hindu for "his Brahminical thread was over the left shoulder and under the right, like a skein of common brown thread."[18]

Caste rites were also observed in Ram Mohan's obsequies. He requested that he be not buried in a Christian cemetery by Christian rites. The reason for his explicit instructions that his caste standing be kept inviolate was two-fold. First, it established him as a member of the Hindu community. Secondly, it secured his property which was bound by Hindu codes of inheritance.

The problem of burial was solved by Miss Castle's offer to donate a beautiful and sequestered spot in the shadow of tall elms, to become his resting place. Dr. Estlin's mother gives her vivid recolleciton of the interment:

The scene was truly affecting and impressive. We all followed the coffin along the broad gravel walk, and through a winding path between the trees, which led to the beautiful spot selected, and consecrated indeed by being his resting place! Here we all stood around the open grave, in solemn silence, and watched with intense interest his sacred remains deposited in their last abode.

We remained fixed to the spot for a considerable time, our minds filled with such thought as the awful scene could not but suggest, and I felt that no *words* were wanting to increase the proper feelings of our hearts. When at length an intention of retiring was manifested, a burst of grief was observed from those most nearly connected. The two Hindoo attendants who closed the funeral procession, stood leaning against the trees and sobbed aloud, as they took their last look at the grave of their late kind master.[19]

John Hare impressed upon Ram Rotun to inform friends and family back in India, that in strict compliance with the Raja's wishes, he was buried in a plot by himself and that no religious ceremony was conducted at his interment.

Stapleton Grove was not to be the permanent site of Ram Mohan's mortal remains. Prince Dwarkanath Tagore, his beloved disciple and companion, made a pilgrimage to Bristol and built a beautiful mausoleum in the cemetery by Arno's Vale, at the entrance of the city, which is now the master's final resting place. In 1872 the following inscription was placed on his tomb:

Beneath this stone rests the remains of Raja Rammohun Roy Bahadoor. A conscientious and steadfast believer in the unity of the Godhead; He consecrated his life with entire devotion to the worship of the divine Spirit alone. To great natural talents he united thorough mastery of many languages, and early distinguished himself as one of the greatest scholars of his day. His unwearied labours to promote the social, moral and physical condition of the people of India, his earnest endeavours to suppress idolatry and the rite of suttee, and his constant zealous advocacy of whatever tended to advance the glory of God and the welfare of man, live in the grateful remembrance of his countrymen. This tablet records the sorrow and pride with which his memory is cherished by his descendants. He was born in Radhanagore, in Bengal, in 1774, and died at Bristol, September 27th, 1833.[20]

The monument enshrining these words is shaped like a Hindu temple which gracefully stands out among the other grave sites. It is a fitting symbol of the man as he was both in life and in death.

 *PART TWO*

# THE ETHICS OF
# RAM MOHAN ROY

 *CHAPTER 13*

# Foundations for Doing Ethics

## I. Ram Mohan's Ethical Insights

Our historical survey has shown that from the earliest period Ram Mohan devoted the greater part of his time and talents to dealing with moral issues. We have just read the inscription which tells of "his unwearied labours to promote the social, moral and physical condition of the people of India," and which permanently identifies him as "a conscientious and steadfast" individual. Though he was possessed of the finest mind of his time, he chose not to follow the lonely path of *jnana* (knowledge), but combined *jnana* with *karma* (work). By harnessing the energies of the intellect to the practical problems besetting the comfort and happiness of his people, he set the model for subsequent reformers, including Mahatma Gandhi.

Though ethics played a major role in the life and labors of Ram Mohan, no comprehensive study has been undertaken to develop the *ethical side* of his work. Indeed, excellent biographies of Roy have been published (Collet, Das, Dasgupta, Joshi, Majumdar, Parekh, Ray, N., Ray, A. K., Sarkar, Sen, Singh), but their chief purpose has lain elsewhere than in an exploration of ethics. Part of the reason why ethical studies have not been undertaken lies in the fact that though Ram Mohan was keenly involved in dealing with moral issues, nowhere does he develop a coherent system of ethics. Fragments of ethical insights are spread all over his writings, but he does not come to grips with giving them a systematic frame of reference.

The task before us is therefore an archeological one: to bring to the surface hidden elements of moral reasoning, and to provide the missing links which would seem to be justified by his attitude and activities.

When this task is done we shall discover that we have not merely recovered the ethics of a pioneer who belongs to India's past, but a

191

prophet who points to India's future. Six generations have come and gone since the Raja's death, but time has not relegated him to antiquated obscurity. He remains the source of all modernizing movements in India.

Charles H. Heimsath substantiates our point. He states that "until the Gandhian Congress pre-empted all other national leadership, at least for Hindus, the social reformers, whether or not they acknowledged it, followed the guidelines of Rammohun Roy in carrying the intellectual burden of advancing modernity." He mentions three "touchstones of conviction" which all the reformers have held in common—rationalism, humanism, and "reform from within."[1]

Take the first touchstone—rationalism. Ram Mohan's fundamental conviction was that man is essentially a rational being. "India's modern culture, along with the social reform movement, rises from this new faith in man's 'innate' capacity to reason, whether in religious and social affairs or in economic and political and scientific pursuits."[2]

Next we turn to humanism. Ram Mohan was also convinced about the dignity of the person, derived from his religious beliefs, which he dressed in the Utilitarian jargon of "comfort" and "happiness." "Roy's castigation of the inhuman treatment of women and the lower castes and his plea for higher ethical standards among Hindus formed the basic tenets of the reformer's programme in the modern era."[3]

A third conviction which has uniquely enabled India to undergo change without the agony of revolution was Ram Mohan's strategy of cultural grafting.

> This facet was what later reformers called "reform from within," or the application of new ideas to old values. Roy, who eschewed conversion to Christianity and managed to blend Indian and Western modes of life, exemplified this remarkable dimension. Whether a Keshub Chunder, or a Dayananda, or a Tilak, or a Ranade, or a Gandhi, reformers of various dispositions—and their intellectual opponents as well—selected some Indian traditions as vehicles for transforming the others. Roy provided one formula, the Brahmo Samaj, and many more styles of reform followed, each suited to its own time, locale, and the predispositions of its leaders. Reformers, however Westernised, seldom failed to phrase their lessons in the manner of Rammohun, who quoted a respected Indian authority when he wanted his point to sink in.[4]

All of these points elevated Ram Mohan to "a man of a thousand years," and render his ethics worthy of inquiry. But, before we delve into his ethics, a prior task awaits us. We must first define the meaning of ethics.

## II. The Structure of Ethics

Ethics presupposes metaphysics. Ethical theories raise such questions as: How ought men to live? What is the good life for man? Some of the answers given in classical theoretical studies are that man's highest good lies in the accumulation of pleasure, of happiness, or that it is identical with doing one's duty. But why pleasure? Why happiness? Why duty? Each of these answers is preceded logically, though not always chronologically, by a particular view of what constitutes the ultimate reality of all things. The ethics propounded always presuppose a philosophical allegiance to something or someone that is assumed to be ultimately real, ultimately true, ultimately good. Hence the derivative character of ethical systems.

Early Christian ethics furnishes us with one example of the above point. Among the many forces which shaped the moral thinking of the first Christians was a certain devaluing of the material world. Pessimism about life in the world—particularly the value of physical existence—was a dominant element in the religious consciousness of large segments of Mediterranean societies.

> In this atmosphere, where the world was regarded as evil or valueless, and man's only hope lay in escaping from it or rendering himself, as far as possible, impervious to its influence, moral striving for objectives and ideals within the world lost all point. Ethical argument ceased to have that stable background of significant experience which is a condition of its seriousness. To proclaim human ideals was to utter meaningless cries in a mocking or unheeding universe. Salvation could only come from without. come from without. No process of self-improvement within the world, with its relationships and its intricacies of behaviour, could possibly contribute to this outcome, for the divine, the only source of salvation, had not one whit of concern for the fabric and setting of human life.[5]

An examination of the New Testament literature reveals ample evidence for this influence. However, the early Christians did not adopt the path of strict asceticism (or extreme libertinism) favored by the rising gnostic sects because of their strong Jewish theology. Genesis affirmed for them the goodness of the Creator, and derivatively, the goodness both of nature and of man.

Marxism provides us with a modern illustration of the derivative character of ethics. Smith and Hodges observe:

> Marxist systems demand that the major portion of human effort be directed toward economic production. This demand is a moral judgment in that it presumes to declare what *ought* to be done. But behind this judgment is the presupposition that the final meaning of human life is to be found in the production and distribution of goods. This is a judgment

about what is ultimately real, and therefore good, in the world. It is a metaphysical judgment, not an ethical one, and it is the assumption on which the morality of Marxism is based.[6]

This leads us to ask: On what assumption is the morality of Ram Mohan based? What was his apprehension of Ultimate Reality? And, how do man and the universe fit into the big picture?

## III. Metaphysical Assumptions: God, Man, and World

In the *Abridgement of the Vedanta* Ram Mohan discusses the nature of Reality described as *Brahman*. The *Upanishads* declare that "an accurate and positive knowledge of the Supreme Being is not within the boundary of comprehension."[7] In the words of the *Mundaka*: "The Supreme Being is not comprehended by vision, or by any other organ of sense; nor can he be conceived by means of devotion, or virtuous practices."[8] But though the finite capacities of man cannot define the Infinite in his *essence*, it is possible to understand him through his effects. Drawing on natural theology, Ram Mohan states:

> We see the multifarious, wonderful universe, as well as the birth, existence, and annihilation of its different parts; hence, we naturally infer the existence of a Being who regulates the whole, and call him the Supreme: in the same manner as from sight of a pot we conclude the existence of its artificer.[9]

In a similar vein the *Taittiriya* states: "He from whom the universal world proceeds, who is the Lord of the Universe, and whose work is the universe, is the Supreme Being."[10]

*Brahman* is the efficient cause of the universe—"as a potter is of earthen pots"; and is also its material cause—"as the earth is the material cause of different earthen pots."[11]

The *Veda* commences and concludes with the following mysterious epithets of *Brahman*: (1) *Om*—signifying "*That* Being which preserves, destroys and creates"; (2) *Tat*—implying "*That* only Being which is neither male nor female"; (3) *Sat*—meaning "*The True Being*." Collectively these terms affirm: "that One Unknown, True Being is the Creator, Preserver, and Destroyer of the Universe."[12]

In sum, the *Vedanta* announces that the Supreme Being is "the Soul of the universe, and bears the same relation to all material extensions that a human soul does to the individual body with which it is connected."[13]

The nature of the above relationship between God, man, and the world is fully explicated in a key passage found in the *Brahmanical Magazine*.

First, on the relation of the world to God, Ram Mohan interprets the Vedanta as teaching that the world is material and is the effect of *maya*.

> The term Maya implies, primarily, the power of creation, and secondarily, its effect, which is the Universe. The Vedanta, by comparing the world with a misconceived notion of a snake, when a rope really exists, means that the world, like the supposed snake, has no independent existence, that it receives its existence from the Supreme Being. In like manner the Vedanta compares the world with a dream: as all the objects seen in a dream depend on the motion of the mind, so the existence of the world is dependent upon the being of God.[14]

This is to say that the world is ultimately an illusion, but it does have practical existence and serves as an arena for the nurture of the soul. But due to ignorance, the *jiva* (self) perceives the world as a superimposition upon *Brahman* and thinks this mayic world is independently real. Thus, matter is opposed to intelligence (*chit*) in a dualistic relationship. Only when the intuition of Oneness dawns does the *jiva* realize the world is only a dependent entity.

The *Brahmin* bard declares the same ideas in musical thought:

> The Eternally Pure, Primeval Cause,
>   prevading this home, the universe,—
>   Immutable, Impassible, Intangible forever,
>
> Letter without a beginning, Paragon
>   amongst the best, the Self inscrutable—
>   Omniparency, Omnipotent, Omnipresent,
>
> ever unrued or undaunted of, the Irreducible,
>   Sole Healer, Benignity to all,
>   upholder of the three worlds—Truth the Cardinal,
> unsulled Omniscience, unmoving Sanctity,
> *Parabrahman* immanent—insurmountable His glory,
> infinitely incomprehensible, witness of all,
>   indestructible!
>
> The sun and the moon, the winds and the stars
>   move to His call;
> on bubbles His patterns form wondrously well.
>
> The countless lives, the many birds and beasts
>   are all His creations;
> the fixed and the flux, to rule, keep their shape.
>
> Food He grants to all, the source of life,—
> as sap in the wound, milk in the teats,
> He causes the world to shape itself.
>
> Existence, birth and death—the ways of beings—
>   follow but His divination;

He is the Noblest: meditate on Him always.[15]

Secondly, on the relation of the soul to God, Ram Mohan states that according to the *Vedanta*:

> God is mere spirit, whose particular influences being shed upon certain material objects are called souls in the same manner as the reflections of the sun are seen on water placed in various vessels. As these reflections of the sun seem to be moved by the motion of the water of these vessels without effecting any motion in the sun, so souls, being, as it were, the reflections of the Supreme Spirit on matter, seem to be affected by the circumstances that influence matter, without God being affected by such circumstances. As some reflections are bright from the purity of the water on which they are cast, while others seem obscure owing to its foulness, so some souls are more pure from the purity of the matter with which they are connected, while others are dull owing to the dullness of matter.
>
> As the reflections of the sun, though without light proper to themselves, appear splendid from their connnection with the illuminating sun, so the soul, though not true intellect, seems intellectual and acts as if it were a real spirit from its actual relation to the Universal Intellect: and as from the particular relations of the sun to the water placed in different pots, various reflections appear resembling the same sun in nature and differing from it in qualities; and again as these cease to appear on the removal of the water, so through the peculiar relation of various material objects to one Supreme Spirit numerous souls appear and seem as performing good and evil works, and also receiving their consequences; and as soon as that relation ceases, they, at that very minute cease to appear distinctly from their original.[16]

Here, too, separateness is an illusion and constitutes bondage. In truth, the individual *atman* is none other than the universal *Brahman*, and it is the destiny of the soul to realize its oneness with God.

The poet asks:

> Whom do you search for?
>   Why these hymns and rites,
>   These devices, worship meditation and
>     contemplation?
>
> By turns you raise or renounce Him
>   pervading the universe, a pefect whole.
>
> Who shall realize Him? Not the senses.
>   He is the cause of all,
>     the *Parabrahman*, unattributable.
>
>     Not caring for wisdom,
>         you accept the elements as final.
>   Don't you know these to be illusory, mind?

Again,

> Turn inward, mind!
>     Why such confusion?
>     The object of your search
> is the Quintessence in all beings.

>     Manifest as the heat in the sun
>         and the chill in the moon
>             are his ways.

>     Expressed as Atman in you
>         is the Universal.[17]

The doctrines of God, man, and the world provide the bases upon which Ram Mohan does his ethical thinking. This is to say, his is an acknowledging ethic. It acknowledges a certain dimension of reality and responds to it through appropriate conduct. He does not use his reason independently to set up some system of morality in accordance with preconceived values, but starts with what is already here. *Brahman* is here. It is One. All duality is false. The discovery of these truths is then brought to bear upon what he considers to be a person's duty in the world.

## CHAPTER 14

# The Principle of
# Ethical Decision-Making

It is our purpose in this chapter to ascertain the principle in Ram Mohan's ethics which is directly connected to the metaphysical beliefs described above. Our search for this ethical principle requires that we examine the process by which souls in estrangement through ignorance are finally restored to their Source.

The *Vedanta* declares "that it is absolutely necessary for mankind to acquire knowledge respecting the Supreme Being."[1] The essence of this knowledge is that "God is indeed one and has no second."[2]

The *Vedanta* also describes the path by which life's goal is reached. Worship of the Supreme Being is an essential step along the way. The *Veda* illustrates the mode in which worship should be made: "To God we should approach, of him we should hear, of him we should think, and to him we should attempt to approximate."[3] Ram Mohan elucidates these three components of worship—*shravana* (hearing), *manana* (reflection), and *dhyana* (meditation):

> These three are in reality included in the first (as the direction for col- lecting fire in the worship of fire), for we cannot approach to God with- out hearing and thinking of him, nor without attempting to make our approximation; and the last, viz., attempting to God, is required until we have approached him. By hearing of God is meant hearing his declara- tions which establish his unity; and by thinking of him is meant thinking of the contents of his law; and by attempting to approximate to him is meant attempting to apply our minds to that true Being on which the dif- fusive existence of the universe relies, in order that by means of the con- stant practice of this attempt we may approach to him.[4]

The adoration of God includes *shraddha*—a strong "faith in the only God." Adoration also has an ethical aspect—it is a life lived by "moral principle." Ram Mohan says:

199

The Vedanta shows that moral principle is a part of the adoration of God, viz., "A command over our passions and over the external senses of the body and good acts, are declared by the Veda to be indispensable in the mind's approximation to God, they should therefore be strictly taken care of, and attended to, both previously and subsequently to such approximation to the Supreme Being"; i.e., we should not indulge our evil propensities, but should endeavour to have entire control over them. Reliance on, and self-resignation to, the only true Being, with an aversion to worldly considerations are included in the good acts alluded to.[5]

By constantly practicing *sadhana*, the true worshipper becomes a *jivanmukta* (liberated in this life). He says:

The adoration of the Supreme Being produces eternal beatitude, as well as all desired advantages; as the Vedanta declares: "It is the firm opinion of Vyasa 'that from devotion to God all the desired consequences proceed' "; and it is thus represented by the Vedas, "He who is desirous of prosperity should worship the Supreme Being."[6]

Thus, the end of worship is becoming one with *Brahman* and being freed from the cycle of transmigration. This is the *summum bonum*, the highest good of all ethical endeavor. But, until that apotheosis takes place, one can enjoy all the good that this life in the world has to offer.

The view of what it means to be human envisaged in the above scheme is within the framework of the four *purusharthas* (values of life) —*kama* (any pleasure derived through the five senses, under the control of the mind); *artha* (value pertaining to economic and political needs governed by law); *dharma* (performance of right action out of a consciousness of moral law); and *moksha* (the supreme value of liberation from the cycle of rebirths).

Espousal of the *purushartha* doctrine shows that Ram Mohan perceived human personality as a complex organism. He recognized an empirical side to life, represented by the first three *purusharthas*, having natural desires and social aims. He conceived of the human being as naturally craving sex, and all other pleasures, as well as social recognition and the realization of the common good. He also recognized a spiritual side to life marked by other worldy-hungers. Moreover, both these sides were integrated within a holistic view of being human. Thus, he allowed no schism between desire and aspiration, or the demands of the kingdom of earth and of heaven. Both were good when viewed relationally. Correctly pursued, *kama, artha,* and *dharma* lead to *moksha. Moksha* is not the denial of these values but their fulfillment. That person is free indeed for whom *kama* is regulated by *artha*; *artha* by *dharma*; and *dharma* by *moksha*.

The single value which dominates this total scheme of life is freedom. Ram Mohan took this ancient Hindu value and gave it a modern ring. Through all of his multifarious reforms, Ram Mohan called for the making of free individuals, living in free societies, in free nations, and in a free world.

All forms of bondage—spiritual, cultural, political, and economic were categorically evil and had to be stamped out. He stood firmly by the ancient belief that freedom is a person's birthright. It is not a value that is tagged on to that person by a utilitarian society. It *is* that person. Thou *art* That. And *That* is *free!* There is only bondage in ignorance—all types of ignorance. And the fundamental purpose of his reforms was to free people from the evils of ignorance.

How harmoniously *Vedantic* idealism was seen to blend with the revolutionary mood which had spread over Europe with its proclamation of the "natural rights" of the individual! The slogans heard in the capitals of Europe were consonant with the insights of the Indian *rishis*. It was easy to pick up the modern tempo for it harmonized well with the heart-beat of his ancient people.

The axiom by which Ram Mohan sought to promote the value of freedom may be formulated thus: Act always so as to maximize freedom both in the individual and in society. The exact words are missing, but as we see him measure the worth of an action, the hidden yardstick always is the capacity of that action to help or hinder the interests of freedom. The good is that which fulfills and furthers freedom, whereas evil frustrates it.

The centrality of freedom both as foundational value and procedural principle is best illustrated by the man himself. Freedom was not a matter of logic but of life. He was not just a moral philosopher who held this view; the view held him. William Adam who knew Ram Mohan intimately has left us this unforgettable portrait of a free man. He reflects:

> I was never more thoroughly, deeply, and constantly impressed than when in the presence of Rammohun Roy and in friendly and confidential converse with him, that I was in the presence of a man of natural and inherent genius, of powerful understanding, and of determined will, a will determined with singular energy and uncontrollable self-direction, to lofty and generous purposes. He seemed to feel, to think, to speak, to act, as if he could not but do all this, and that he must and could do it only in and from and through himself, and that the application of any external influence, distinct from his own strong will, would be the annihilation of his being and identity. He would be free or not be at all . . . . Love of freedom was perhaps the strongest passion of his soul, freedom not of action merely, but of thought . . . . This tenacity of personal independence, this sensitive jealousy of the slightest approach to an encroachment on his mental freedom was accompanied with a very nice perception of the equal rights of others, even of those who differed most widely from him.[7]

## CHAPTER 15

# Freedom in the Practice of Ethical Decision-Making

In this chapter we shall examine the practical bearing of Ram Mohan's metaphysical views and of the principle of freedom upon some of the moral issues with which he struggled and which continue to vex us today.

## I. Freedom and Religion

A reciprocal relationship exists between religion and ethics. Ram Mohan considers the two disciplines autonomous but interdependent. Whereas religion provides ethics with a foundation for the moral life, ethics authenticates religion by keeping it moral. In both instances the goal is freedom.

First let us look at the contribution of religion to ethics. Religion invests ethics with an authority it cannot command in and of itself. Belief in the spiritual structure of Reality provides ethics with the assurance that its moral strivings are not subjective and ephemeral, but objective and permanent.

The *Vedanta* posits the continuity of life with its ultimate source. When it declares that "God is everywhere, and everything is in God," it means that "nothing is absent from God, and nothing bears real existence except by the volition of God, whose existence is the sole support of the conceived existence of the universe, which is acted upon by him in the same manner as a human body is by a soul."[1]

In a similar vein, the *Isha Upanishad* declares that the Supreme Being "pervades the internal and external parts of the whole universe," and that "he, who perceives the whole universe in the Supreme Being (*that is, he who perceives that the material existence is merely dependent upon the existence of the Supreme Spirit*); and who also perceives the Supreme Being in the whole universe (*that is, he who perceives that the Supreme Spirit extends over all material extension*): does not feel contempt *towards any creature whatsoever.*"[2]

Religion thus serves as the authority for an ethic which affirms and celebrates the sacredness of all life. Ram Mohan argues that a consistent belief in the unity and universality of *Brahman* "forbids, positively, treating with contempt or behaving ill towards any creature whatsoever."[3]

Secondly, while religion "sacralizes" ethics, the latter "ethicizes" religion. We shall examine this in two aspects: positive and negative.

Positively stated: Ram Mohan's idea of an ethically valid religion incorporates two elements—faith in *Brahman*, and love for one's fellows. Faith without love is empty, and love without faith is blind. The proposition is first stated in the *Tuhfat*.[4] It is repeated in his *Brahmopasana* (1828), and it is incorporated in the Trust Deed of the *Brahmo Samaj*. The Deed stipulates that there shall be no sermon, hymn, or prayer used in worship, "but such as have a tendency to the promotion of the contemplation of the Author and Preserver of the Universe, to the promotion of Charity, morality, piety, benevolence, virtue, and the strengthening the bonds of union between men of all religious persuasions and creeds."[5]

The nature of a cause is present in its effects; therefore, the authenticity of a religion should be known by its social consequences. It consists of "attending to social life" with "mutual love and affection" of all fellow creatures regardless of "shape, colour, creed and religion." All this is "a pure devotion acceptable to God." Faith is active in love.

It is clear, then, that the ethical or horizontal dimension in the natural religion of Ram Mohan is as important as the theological or vertical dimension. As a matter of fact, the vertical only stands upright as long as it is supported by the horizontal. This is confirmed by Ram Mohan's quotation from Hafiz at the close of the *Tuhfat*: "Be not after the injury of any being and do whatever you please. For in our way there is no sin except it (injuring others)."[6]

Negatively evaluated: A religion that is short on moral content is unauthentic and unfree. Two specimens stand out: sectarianism and idolatry.

Ram Mohan distinguished between religion and religions, i.e., the bona fide impulse and the bogus institutions. Essential religion was rooted in human nature and was the common core of Hinduism, Islam, Christianity, Judaism, and all other faiths. All people everywhere tend towards "one Being who is the source of creation and the governor of it." Underlying this subjective unity of the mind and heart there is objective diversity of theology and precept. The theological and moral formulations have an "excrescent quality" inasmuch as they are the products of historical conditioning. Regretably, sectarian proclivities manifest in all religions tend to absolutize the relative and relativize the absolute. Hence, falsehood and arrogance are common features of all religions without distinction.

Christianity exemplifies the process whereby the down-to-earth religion of a founding genius, centered around faith in God expressed through love of man, is immediately institutionalized into a body of dogma by lesser followers. The metamorphosis is possible because people's spiritual ideas and feelings are not insulated against secular associations and interests. When the secular dominates the spiritual, religion becomes exclusive, imperialistic, arrogant, and intolerant. Truth perishes, and upon its remains a temple of marble is raised to some cultic god with name and form bearing an interesting resemblance to the principals involved. The trouble with this type of institutionalized and ecclesiastical religion is that it divides people when the real business of religion, as the word suggests, is to bind. Such phenomena are not worthy of the pure impulse of religion which is ideally expressed in a community of concern.

Ram Mohan's moral critique of religions is echoed in the twentieth-century by William James. He argues that "the baseness" which is often blamed on religion is "not chargeable at all to religion proper" but such wicked associates as "the spirit of corporate dominion." Similarly, most of the bigotries are chargeable to religion's wicked intellectual associate, "the spirit of dogmatic dominion, the passion for laying down the law in the forms of an absolutely closed-in theoretical system." Together, "the spirit of corporate dominion" and "intellectual dominion" constitute the ecclesiastical spirit, and James beseeches his readers "never to confound the phenomena of mere tribal or corporate psychology which it presents with those manifestations of the purely interior life."

By way of illustration, James cites the following acts of baseness which are commonly charged to religion's account:

> The baiting of the Jews, the hunting of the Albigenses and Waldenses, the stoning of the Quakers and ducking of Methodists, the murdering of Mormons and the massacring of Armenians, express much rather that aboriginal human neophobia, that pugnacity of which we all share the vestiges, and that inborn hatred of the alien, than they express the positive piety of the various perpetrators. Piety is the mask, the inner force is tribal instinct.[7]

While pure religion is not culpable for the many historic aberrations with which it has been identified, there is one side of religion which is prone to fault. This is the perennial religious tendency toward fanaticism. Ram Mohan describes the nature of this overzealousness which comes into play when devoutness loses its balance. He says:

Most of the leaders of different religions, for the sake of perpetuating their names and gaining honour, having invented several dogmas of faith, have declared them in the form of truth by pretending some supernatural acts or by the force of their tongue, or some other measure suitable to the circumstances of their contemporaries, and thereby have made a multitude of people adhere to them so that those poor people having lost sight of conscience bind themselves to submit to their leaders and think it to be a sin to make distinction between a real virtue and an actual sin in carrying out the injunctions of their religious leaders. Having a regard for their religion and faith, they think such abominable acts as murder, usurpation and torturing others, although they be of the same species and offspring of the same parents, acts of great virtue. And having an impression that a firm belief (lit. pure faith) in their spiritual leaders, notwithstanding the commission of most abominable deeds such as telling lies, breach of trust, theft, adultery, etc., which are heinous crimes in reference to future life as well as mischievous to society (lit. public) is the cause of salvation from sins, they always devote their valuable time to reading stories and legends which are full of *impossibilities* and which tend to strengthen (lit. increase) this faith in their past religious leaders as well as in the present expounders.[8]

William James has made a psychological study of religious fanaticism, a subject which is currently in the forefront of the news, and which threatens to mar the 1980s with international hostility and global insecurity as terrorism threatens to become the wave of the future. It is most interesting to hear James speak on this subject in terms that have already been expressed by Ram Mohan. He says:

When an intensely loyal and narrow mind is once grasped by the feeling that a certain superhuman person is worthy of its exclusive devotion one of the first things that happens is that it idealizes the devotion itself. To adequately realize the merits of the idol gets to be considered the one great merit of the worshipper; and the sacrifices and servilities by which savage tribesmen have from time immemorial exhibited their faithfulness to chieftains are now outbid in favour of the deity. Vocabularies are exhausted and languages altered in the attempt to praise him enough; death is looked on as gain if it attract his grateful notice; and the personal attitude of being his devotee becomes what one might call a new and exalted kind of professional specialty within the tribe. The legends that gather round the lives of holy persons are fruits of this impulse to celebrate and glorify.[9]

As does Ram Mohan, James illustrates his point by referring to the glorification of religious prophets in Buddhism, Christianity, and Islam. He concurs with his Indian predecessor that the divination of Jesus as God incarnate is a pathetic manifestation of people's misguided propensity to praise.

James continues his analysis with the same critical rigor we have seen demonstrated in the *Tuhfat*. He points out that the initial consequence of this propensity to glorify is jealousy for the honor of the deity. He asks if it is possible for the devotee to employ some better way to express his loyalty than through sensitiveness, and answers:

> The slightest affront or neglect must be resented, the deity's enemies must be put to shame. In exceedingly narrow minds and active wills, such a care may become an engrossing preoccupation; and crusades have been preached and massacres instigated for no other reason than to remove a fancied slight upon the God. Theologies representing the gods as mindful of their glory, and churches with imperialistic policies, have conspired to fan this temper to a glow, so that intolerance and persecution have come to be vices associated by some of us inseparably with the saintly mind.[10]

So much for sectarianism as an unauthentic expression of true universal religion. Its elevation of divisive doctrines over deeds that should be morally and socially conducive, render all forms of sectarianism monuments to human bondage.

A second expression of religious bondage, closely related to the first, is idolatry. The critique of idolatry is once again made on moral grounds.

The genealogy of "the fatal system of idolatry" is first analyzed. It is born of sensuousness, ignorance, and exploitation. Ignorant people are naturally inclined to "worship objects resembling their own nature." Anthropomorphism is the expression of limited consciousness. The more constricted consciousness is, the more apt it is to make the world in its own image. It follows that the rites employed in such anthropomorphic worship will both project and pander to their immediate feelings of sensuousness. Ignorant masses are exploited by "pretended guides" who follow double standards in pursuit of self-interest.

Idolatry is its own indictment; it is condemned by its own consequences. Ram Mohan refuses to be bogged down by unresolvable theological hair-splitting and says: Religion is what religion does. "By their fruits ye shall know them." Idolatry is evil because it induces "the violation of every humane and social feeling."[11]

Several illustrations are given of "exceptionable practices which are destructive of morals." There is frequent self-destruction as "at Prayaga, Ganga Sagar, and under the wheels of their car Jagganath."[12]

There is also human sacrifice of the lives of family and friends, as, for instance: "Persons, whose recovery from sickness is supposed to be doubtful, are carried to die on the banks of the Ganges. This is practised by the Hindoos of Bengal only, the cruelty of which affects even Hindoos of Behar, Illahabad, and all the upper provinces."[13]

There is female murder in the practice of *sati*.

Then, there are the ceremonies instituted under the pretext of honoring nature's God, which are in fact of "a tendency utterly subversive of every moral principle." He first cites Krishna worship:

> His worship is made to consist in the institution of his image or picture, accompanied by one or more females, and in the contemplation of his history and behaviour, such as his perpetration of murder upon a female of the name of Putana; his compelling a great number of married and unmarried women to stand before him denuded; his debauching them and several others, to the mortal affliction of their husbands and relations; his annoying them, by violating the laws of cleanliness and other facts of the same nature. The grossness of his worship does not find a limit here. His devotees very often personify (in the same manner as European actors upon stages do) him and his female companions, dancing with indecent gestures, and singing songs relative to his love and debaucheries. It is impossible to explain in language fit to meet the public eye, the mode in which Mahadeva, or the destroying attribute, is worshipped by the generality of the Hindoos: suffice it to say, that it is altogether congenial with the indecent nature of the image, under whose form he is most commonly adorned.[14]

Next, there is the worship of Kali in whose celebration, "human sacrifices, the use of wine, criminal intercourse, licentious songs are included: the first of these practices had become generally extinct; but it is believed there are parts of the country where human victims are still offered."[15]

Thus, whereas learned Brahmins zealously supported idolatry as conducive to morality, Ram Mohan demonstrates that it is rejected by the *shastras*, "but must also be looked upon with great horror by common sense, as leading directly to immorality and destructive of social comforts."[16] If the test of a religion be, in the words of Ashoka's Edicts, "Doing as little harm as possible, in doing good in abundance, the practice of love, of compassion, of truthfulness and purity, in all walks of life," then, the absence of these moral qualities in idolatrous Hinduism betokens this brand of religion as bondage.

## II. Freedom and Morality

Various facets of Ram Mohan's thinking upon the nature of morality are refined and reinforced by contemporary scholars such as Paul Tillich, the late philospher/theologian, and Erich Fromm, the humanistic psychologist.

In his *Theology and Culture*, Tillich makes useful distinctions between three key words dealing with the subject: moralism, moralisms, and morality.

*Moralism* designates a widespread attitude which is a "distortion of the moral imperative into an oppressive law." It is seen in many varieties—puritan, evangelistic, and most commonly as conventional moralism. It is a negative attitude against which Tillich recommends that theology and psychology should wage a common war.[17]

*Moralisms*, on the other hand, are free of the above negative connotations. The word designates the systems of moral imperatives as they have taken shape in diverse cultures and are contingent upon all the relativities and limitations of those cultures. However, Tillich points out an essential relation between moralism and moralisms.

> Moral systems, just because of their intimate connection with a cultural system, have a tendency to become oppressive if the general cultural scheme changes. They tend to produce moralism as a negative attitude. The distinction between moralisms as ethical systems and moralism as a negative attitude is identical with the distinction between the creative and the oppressive character of moral imperatives, and each ethical system has both characteristics.[18]

The third term Tillich examines is *morality*. Primarily, it is the experience of the moral imperative. Morality is a human function in the absence of which a person would no longer qualify as a person. It is the consciousness of a moral demand which constitutes our personhood.

> If a feeble-minded child behaves as if he were unaware of any demand, he is sub-human, which does not mean that he is an animal. He is both more and less than an animal. In contrast to him, a criminal is aware of the moral imperative, while defying its commands. He is human although he fights against an essential element in human nature. For man as man has the potential to contradict himself.[19]

Tillich's clarification of the above terms helps us appreciate the Raja's reforms. His chief contribution lies in freeing unconditioned morality from the destructive and demonic consequences of conditioned moralism.

Immanuel Kant gave a classical description of the unconditioned morality when he called it the "Categorical Imperative"—the moral command which tell us unconditionally what we "ought to be." Ram Mohan, too, maintained a notion of the "Categorical Imperative." It was experienced as that inner law of our being "which teaches that man should do unto others as he would wish to be done by."[20] This moral code is "well fitted to regulate the conduct of the human race in the discharge of their various duties to God, to themselves, and to society."[21]

It is clear from the above quotation that the word "moral" is being used in an inclusive sense—a point which the missionary critics overlooked in their debates. In the moral lexicon of Ram Mohan, *dharma* sees with compound eyes in all directions. The most "appropriate mode of performing our duty to the Almighty power" is by serving our fellow creatures.[22] This teaching is the common denominator of all religions.

However, there is no guarantee that the moral imperative will develop in the free way described above. People are free to contradict the humanity that is within themselves. The reason for this is that whereas the *form* of the moral imperative is unconditional, its *contents* are conditioned and are relative to time and place. If, for example, the environment is rigid and authoritarian, morality will be impeded because of the constriction of individual freedom. This is more generally the case than our facile rhetoric about freedom is prepared to admit. The fact is that most people fall into one of three categories: (1) deceivers, "who in order to attract the people to themselves wilfully invent doctrines of creeds and faith and put the people to troubles and cause disunion amongst them"; (2) deceived people, "who without inquiring into the fact, adhere to others"; and (3) people who are both deceivers and deceived, "who having themselves faith in the saying in another induce others to adhere" to their doctrines.[23] It is clear from this that freedom is a rare commodity in this world, especially when it comes to religion and morality. Most people are mere echoes and shadows of others who tell them what to think and do. We all imagine that we are free agents but in fact we are all victims of authoritarianism.

Erich Fromm wrestles with the same problems today in his book, *Man for Himself*, doing battle against modern authoritarian ethics. He defines authoritarian ethics as a system in which "an authority states what is good for man and lays down the laws and norms of conduct."[24]

The sources of this irrational authority over people are invariably power and fear. Physically and mentally, the "Grand Inquisitors" of all times bully their followers into toeing the party line. "Criticism of the authority is not only not required but forbidden."[25] Similar analysis runs through the *Tuhfat*. Ram Mohan observes:

> If by chance sometimes any one through want of prudence makes any question against any principles of faith of his religion, his co-religionists in case of having power, make over that inexperienced fellow to the tongue (point) of the spear (i.e., kill him), and in the case of their having no such opportunity make him over to the spear of the tongue (i.e., overload him with reproaches and slanders).[26]

Both authors trace the genesis of the authoritarian conscience back to early childhood:

According to Ram Mohan, "during the time of boyhood when his faculties were susceptible of receiving impressions of ideas conveyed to him," the growing lad, indoctrinated by his elders, "acquires such a firm belief in religious dogmas that he cannot renounce his adopted faith although most of its doctrines be obviously nonsensical and absurd." The youth goes through life with this built-in bias, observing only the rites and ceremonies of his own religion and thereby becomes more firmly attached to it. His critical faculties are thus not given a chance to develop, and the consequence is that when he becomes an adult his mind is "insufficient to discover the real truth."[27]

Fromm finds a similar pattern at work. He says: "The foundations of our ability to differentiate good from evil are laid in childhood." First there is the acquisition of a sense by which good is distinguished from bad, prior to knowing the difference by reason. This way of categorizing and viewing things is picked up by the child from the adults who make up his world. "Good" is what is praised, "bad" is that for which one is punished. "The fear of disapproval and the need for approval seem to be the most powerful and almost exclusive motivation for ethical judgment. This intense emotional pressure prevents the child, and later the adult, from asking critically whether 'good' in a judgment means good for him or for the authority."[28]

Ram Mohan's critique of authoritarian ethics has important sociopolitical ramifications that are applicable to our time. Whenever people abdicate the use of reason and autonomous conscience, they lay themselves open to two dangers. Not knowing for themselves what to do or think, they will do what others do, which is the danger of *conformism*. Or else, they will do what others tell them to do and think, which is the danger of *totalitarianism*.

The antidote to either form of irrational authority is an ethic which is rational, empirical, and open. Appealing to the good sense of his countrymen, Ram Mohan asks:

> Whose advice appears the most disinterested and most rational—that of those who, concealing your scriptures from you, continually teach you thus, "Believe whatever we may say—don't examine or even touch your scriptures, neglect entirely your reasoning faculties—do not only consider us, whatever may be our principles, as gods on earth, but humbly adore and propitiate us by sacrificing to us the greater part (if not the whole) of your property": or that of the man who lays your scriptures and their comments as well as their translations before you, and solicits you to examine their purport, without neglecting the proper and moderate use of reason; and to attend strictly to their directions, by the rational performance of your duty to your sole Creator, and to your fellow creatures, and also to pay true respect to those who think and act righteously.[29]

The fact that he could make the above appeal and anticipate some change in the entrenched habits of his countrymen, indicates that while Ram Mohan accepted behavioral determinism, it was not to the forfeiture of human autonomy. Rather, both are combined within a scheme of developmental morality based on the insights of the Bhagavad Gita.

Using the terminology of the Gita, the key to Ram Mohan's psychology of conduct lies in his view of personality as embracing both *prakriti* and *purusha*. *Prakriti* is the psychical apparatus with which a man is endowed at birth, being a carryover from his mental development in a previous existence.[30] The effects of one's past *karmas* are so potent that repression is useless.[31]

At the same time, difficult though the task of sense-control may be, it is not unattainable. The resources of man's higher nature can help him gain mastery over *prakriti*. The lower faculties must progressively be brought under the higher faculties until *purusha* (spiritual essense) is in complete control. The evolutionary character of the discipline is explained thus: "The senses, they say, are great; greater than the sense is the mind (*manas*); greater than the mind is the reason (*buddhi*); and greater than reason is He."[32]

Elsewhere I have explained:

> The rationale behind this discipline is that freedom is correlative to consciousness—the greater the consciousness the greater the freedom. The outward life of sense is least free because consciousness is constricted by the sway of the senses. Freedom emerges when the senses are made dependent on the mind. Freedom is enhanced when the mind is yoked with intelligence. Greatest freedom is achieved when intelligence is informed by the consciousness of the Self. Thus, starting from the bondage of the outward life of sensations, the *yogin* moves inward and upward until he discovers the central and greatest reality of his own being. This is the highest level of consciousness, and with it, the maximization of freedom.[33]

It was this faith of the *Bhagavad Gita* in the power of the *purusha* to prevail progressively over *prakriti* which provided Ram Mohan with the necessary impetus to launch his moral reforms. With psychological precision, the following passage clearly delineates the tension between determinism and autonomy, and the resources—mental and spiritual—by which freedom may be achieved. He says:

> I have never ceased to contemplate with the strongest feelings of regret, the obstinate adherence of my countrymen to their fatal system of idolatry, inducing, for the sake of propitiating their supposed Deities, the *violation of every humane and social feeling*. And this in various instances; but more especially in the dreadful acts of self-destruction and the immolation of the nearest relations, under the delusion of conforming to sacred religious rites. I have never ceased, I repeat, to contemplate these practices with the strongest feelings of regret, and to view in them the *moral debasement* of a race who, I cannot help thinking, are *capable of better things*; whose susceptibility, patience, and mildness of character, render them *worthy of a better destiny*. Under these impressions, therefore, I have been impelled to lay before them genuine translations of part of their

scripture, which inculcates not only the *enlightened worship of one God*, but the *purest principles of morality* (italics supplied).[34]

Placed in the context of contemporary moral philosophy, Ram Mohan's moral orientation may be described as a clear specimen of Meliorism. In the lexicon of William James, "Meliorism implies a world that is open-ended, where the past does not exhaustively determine what will be the case in the future, and where man's present conscious awareness has power and freedom to move in a variety of ways."[35] However, whereas with James conscious awareness can rise in freedom to the level of *buddhi* (intellect), with Ram Mohan, and with Indian moral psychology, it can ascend to the level of *purusha* (spiritual essence).

## III. Freedom and Society

Ram Mohan derived his social ethics from the notion subscribed to by Sankara of the identification of the atman with *Brahman*. Social service was tantamount to *self-service* because all life was unified in the Being of God.

Metaphysical presuppositions aside, Ram Mohan believed that a strong case for social ethics could be made on empirical evidence. Writing to the French ambassador in England, he protested his having to obtain a passport to enter France. "Such restrictions against foreigners," he complained, "are not observed even among the nations of Asia," and was, therefore, "quite at a loss to conceive how it should exist among a people so famed as the French are for courtesy and liberality in all other matters." He went on to plead for the removal of all travel restrictions "in order to promote the reciprocal advantage and enjoyment of the whole human race," and held that "not religion only but unbiased common sense as well as the accurate deductions of scientific research lead to the conclusion that all mankind are one great family of which numerous nations and tribes are only various branches."[36]

Elements present in Hinduism which contradicted human solidarity were frankly exposed and openly attacked. He branded the caste system as anti-social because the least departure from its ceremonial codes was not only visited upon the offender with "the severest censure, but actually punished by exclusion from the society of his family and friends."[37] There were many other social liabilities to *Varna-dharma* which were brought before the public eye.

*Ashrama-dharma*, the second branch of Hindu social organization, was also shown to be in need of immediate overhauling. For instance, though participation in the different *ashramas* or stations in life is urged by the scriptures as a means of acquiring true knowledge of God, these same scriptures declare the performance of the Brahmanical rites and cermonies only helpful, but not necessary. The same end can be

achieved by faith in God alone. Even so, both *shruti* (revealed literature) and *smriti* (traditional literature) recommend the combination of
*karma* (works) and *shraddha* (faith). Contrary to *Vedantic* preference,
it is Ram Mohan's position that a man's social and spiritual ends are
better served when the observance of "rules and rites prescribed by the
*Veda* applicable to different classes of Hindoos" is kept merely optional.[38] It is not difficult to see that his own preference lies with
*shraddha*.

The authority of *shraddha* is also justified in disregarding social taboos, such as pertain to eating habits. Though the *Veda* says: "He who
has true faith in the omnipresent Supreme Being may eat all that exists," the "Vedanta limits" this freedom by giving the text a situational
meaning, i.e., taboos may be disregarded only in emergency circumstances. Ram Mohan would seem to prefer *shraddha* as the basis on
which one decides the merits or the demerits of concrete social actions.
Considering his whole lifestyle, it appears that he would rather expand
the situational component of Hindu ethics into a more prominent option, guided by faith, than to limit it to emergency situations. It is clear,
for instance, from his own eating habits that he made liberal use of the
emergency clause.

*Shraddha* also liberates one from what society thinks is the proper
place in which one must worship, or the most auspicious time at which
one may die. The *Vedanta* says: "In any place wherein the mind feels itself undisturbed, men should worship God," and "Anyone who has
faith in the only God, dying even when the sun may be south of the
equator, his soul shall proceed from the body, through Sushumna (a
vein which, as the Brahmans suppose, passes through the navel up to
the brain), and approaches to the Supreme Being."[39]

So far we have looked at the objective side of traditional Hindu ethics, represented by *Varnashrama dharma*, to discover Ram Mohan's own
social ethics within the framework of that system. Now we shall look at
the subjective side of Hindu ethics which is known as *cittashuddhi* or purification of the mind.

*Cittashuddhi* is considered a moral advance over *Varnashrama dharma*
because "virtues are superior to duties." The first represents internal
sanctions; the second, external sanctions. One is related to experiences
of preference; the other to experiences of prohibition and fear. The
morality of one is individualistic; that of the other, tribalistic. In sum:
"while Objective Ethics springs from a sense of duty, usually entailing
an element of coercion, Subjective Ethics springs from virtue which is
always a labour of love."[40]

Ram Mohan sees this love as flowing from the understanding and
experience of the oneness of all life which, in turn, merits care, responsibility, respect, and knowledge.

Love presupposes freedom. Only a free agent can act responsibly out
of respect and knowledge. But freedom seems to be questioned or con-

tradicted by belief in the law of *karma*. Ram Mohan endorsed belief in this aspect of Hinduism's conception of moral law as also being part of the *Vedantic* teaching.[41]

In the opinion of some scholars, belief in the law of *karma* is a "formidable barrier to radical social change," and they are therefore happy that the reformer did not accept the *karma* doctrine, even though he "came very near."[42] But this is a double error. Ram Mohan not only espoused the doctrine, but found no contradiction between karmic law and social change. The reason lies in his mode of interpreting *karma* which has its roots in the *Bhagavad Gita*.

Along with the ancient *rishis* who beheld the cosmos as governed by *rita* (cosmic order), Ram Mohan believed that the universe is morally structured. Nothing happens capriciously, or even miraculously, for all is governed by just law. *Karma* is therefore not a strange, extraneous force which determines what happens to us. It is us, formed by our own past.

There is no element of fatalism in Ram Mohan's concept of *karma* anymore than there is in the *Gita*. As I have explained in *The Evolution of Hindu Ethical Ideals*, "Fate signifies a contradiction of freedom, but *Karma* signifies a polar correlation. *Karma* is not the opposite of freedom but points to the conditions and limits of freedom. *Karma* is the ground of freedom; and freedom participates in moulding *karma*."[43]

Radhakrishnan has the same notion in mind when he says: "The cards in the game of life are given to us. We do not select them. They are traced to our past Karma, but we can call as we please, lead what suit we will, and as we play, we gain or lose. And there is freedom."[44] For Ram Mohan, *karma* was a reality. He could see its stranglehold upon millions of his countrymen who were held prisoners of their past. But life's game must go on. New victories must be won. Freedom, however limited, is here. Indians must therefore heed the *Gita's* clarion call which challenges us to raise the self by the self!

Harking back to the subjective stage of Hindu ethics, we find that though the quality of ethical activity is progressively free and is characterized by *vairagya* (detachment), its main preoccupation is with individual perfection through *cittashuddhi* or purification of mind. For instance, social welfare is a minor theme in Vatsyayana's list of *dharma* or virtue.[45]

However, it would be incorrect to conclude with some that the higher flights of Hindu ethics are anti-social. What we have here is a pre-industrial type of thinking which reasons that the best way to change society is to change the individuals in that society.

Furthermore, ancient Hindus would be expected to fulfill their own *dharma* by assuming the role of Good Samaritan. But, by Ram Mohan's time, the religion once vigorous, in a country once prosperous, had grown effete and tired. Social welfare was as neglected as it was needed.

Ram Mohan accepted the ideal of subjective ethics in the prevailing scheme, but insisted that the spiritual cultivation of the individual can take place in and through society. The ascetical ideal of renunciation is maintained, but it is not renunciation *of* action, but renunciation *in* action. Thus, the quietism of the East is synthesized with the activism of the West, and the result is an ethic of disinterested performance of duty. This ethical stance, of course, is identical with that of the Gita which, in its own time, had synthesized the positive elements of *pravritti* (active life) and *nivritti* (quietism) in the ideal of *karma-yoga* (detached activism).[46] In the spirit of the Gita, Ram Mohan emphasizes that in order to realize *moksha* (liberation), one must not only practice *upasana* (duties of meditation and worship), but *nishkama karma* (disinterested social duties).[47]

In the performance of *nishkama karma*, the actor is completely free. Whereas *karma* binds a person to the fruit of his actions through feelings of pleasure and pain, *nishkama karma* liberates because *karma* without *kama* (desire) has no potency for rebirth. A person who lives by this ethic is truly free. Happy in the possession of the self, he works for the welfare of the world and thereby attains perfection.

Janaka, the philosopher-king of Mithila, was a household example of self-realization through selfless activity. He obtained the unique position of *acarya* (preceptor) in *yoga-viddhi* (selfless action). The Gita cites his reputation and adds: "Thou shouldst do works also with a view to the maintenance of the world."[48] The distinctive word used here is *lokasamgraha* or world-maintenance. It points to the fragile web of life of which we are all a part, and signifies that without social action on the part of the individual, there can be no welfare in the world.

Ram Mohan was the Janaka of the nineteenth century. He elevated work for the world to the realm of *dharma*. He demonstrated that one does not have to become a *yogi* (one who practices *yoga*) and retreat to the forest to achieve self-realization. *Work in the world is worship*. The business of religion is not to evangelize the "heathen," or to dominate education, economics or politics. Religion must free the people to become themselves and help create the family of man on earth. For Ram Mohan the concept of the world was more than a world of uni-sex, uni-culture, or uni-politics; it was a polymorphous world. It included males and females, Christians and Hindus, *Brahmins* and *Shudras*, Asiatics and Westerners. As a son of Sarasvati (goddess of eloquence), Ram Mohan spoke the languages of the world—Arabic, Persian, Sanskrit, Latin, Greek, Hebrew, and more. Those who heard him speak their native tongue knew at once, that he cared.

One who has such an inclusive world has everything, and has nothing; has everyone and has no one. *Lokasamgraha* is the elimination of all sense of "mineness," for *kama* is displaced by *karma*; desire is displaced by the deed. It is said that when the news was broken to Janaka that his capital was on fire, the teacher of *yogaviddhi* exclaimed: "If Mithila is on fire nothing that is mine is on fire."[49]

In addition to the ideal of *nishkama karma*, the practical ethics of the Raja incorporated the Golden Rule which teaches that "man should do unto others as he would wish to be done by."[50] This is not mere moral pragmatism; it is natural law.[51] As the common core of universal moral experience, "it is taught in every system of religion," and is "principally inculcated by Christianity."[52] His remarks on this point require a critical look.

In our recollection of Indian thought, one ancient ethical treatise in which the Golden Rule is found is the *Dhammapada*. Here is the basis of *ahimsa* (non violence), as the following verse attests:

> All fear punishment, all love life.
> Therefore, do not kill, or cause to kill.
> Do as you would want done.[53]

The theme also appears in the *Mahabharata* where we are told: "Good people do not injure living beings; in joy and sorrow, pleasure and pain, one should act toward others as one would have them act toward oneself."[54] More broadly stated, the *Mahabharata* says: "Whatever one would wish for oneself, that let one plan for another."[55]

In *Vedantic* ethics, when the *jivan-mukta* (one who is liberated while still living) discovers, "Thou art That," there dawns upon him a sense of cosmic consciousness or the feeling of universal belonging. This unitive sense is expressed ethically in the Golden Rule. The metaphysical insight and its corresponding ethical expression is articulated well in this verse from the *Gita*;

> This highest Godhead hath his seat in every being, and liveth though they die; who seeth him, is seeing, and he who everywhere this highest God hath found, will not wound Self with self.[56]

On the basis of the above evidence, Ram Mohan was patently incorrect in saying that the Golden Rule was only "partially taught" in the Hindu tradition. It seems his ardor for ecumenical dialogue, plus the prominence attained by the Golden Rule in Western social reform movements of the time, influenced his evaluation. The above texts with which he was all too familiar, and numerous other citations and references of his own, would suggest that the Raja's own evaluation must be contextually evaluated. The truth of the matter is that whereas the New Testament formulation of the Golden Rule is *socially oriented*, in Buddhism and Hinduism it includes "hurting or killing sentient beings."[57] Within the Indian tradition, the scope is thus enlarged to include *all forms of life*.

Critical comments aside, the social reformer firmly believed that "this simple code of religion and morality is so admirably calculated to elevate men's ideas to high and liberal notions of God," and that it is "well fitted to regulate the conduct of the human race in the discharge of their various duties to themselves, and to society."[58]

Moving from practical ethics to social polity, Ram Mohan held that it is the duty of civil administration to secure for the citizenry their natural rights and freedoms. These included the fundamental rights of life and property and the freedoms of speech, opinion, conscience, and association. Together, these constituted happiness, and, therefore, Ram Mohan more commonly referred to happiness as the goal of organized society. Happiness comprised a balance between individual rights and the common good. Obviously, the formulation of such sociopolitical concepts as the "natural rights of man" were Western. Among Western social and political theorists, Bentham, in particular, had a formative influence upon Ram Mohan's liberalism and rational critique of social problems. But while the formulas were foreign, the *spirit* of the principles was not alien to Hindu *dharma*, thus making it possible for Ram Mohan to insert "his humanitarian religion as a motive power to the organisation of social polity."[59]

One factor which attracted the venerable Bentham to Ram Mohan was the latter's zeal for reform.

For his part, Ram Mohan did not presume any pretentious roles, especially those which would cast him as an innovator in matters religious and social; but he did consider himself an unrelenting friend of human rights. He remarks in a letter to an associate; "The struggles are not merely between the reformers and anti-reformers, but between liberty and oppression throughout the world; between justice and injustice; and between right and wrong."[60] He could valiantly endure the struggle because he also believed that liberty would triumph over oppression. He says: "From a reflection on the past events of history, we clearly perceive that liberal principles in politics and religion have been long gradually but steadily gaining ground notwithstanding the opposition and obstinacy of despots and bigots."[61]

Two areas in which the oppressors still held the field were the twin social evils of racism and sexism.


## A. Racism


Racism was a phenomenon of British society. It was related to British imperialism both as cause and effect. The British regarded themselves as the best specimens of humanity. Indians, who were not endowed by nature with the same biological characteristics, were somehow lesser people. With ethnocentric pride in his blue eyes and blonde hair, the young British captain could look down his waxed mustache and feel a decided superiority over the dark-skinned *babu* who bowed to his every command.

Not only did the white man justify his humanity by virtue of his physical features, he used racism as a strategic weapon in subjugating the Asiatic masses. The British developed their own version of the caste system. It, too, was based on color. The white man was the Brahmin and the *kala admi* (blackman) was the lower caste.

The stratagem worked. Social indoctrination supported by a system of rewards and punishments produced an army of sycophants for whom, as for their masters, racism was a "pigment" of the imagination.

Not all Indians were prepared to do political *puja* (worship), and Ram Mohan stood tall among the rebels. He believed the British were as much victims of racism as the natives. From a surface point of view there were the oppressors and the oppressed. The natives suffered because of various deprivations, and knew what had been taken away from them. The oppressors could not feel the suffering all around them because they allowed material gain and political power to obstruct their vision. Loss of vision entailed the loss of their own humanity. Thus, the oppressors were themselves oppressed. Of the two, the masters were more bound than the slaves. Ram Mohan therefore sought not only to free the oppressed, but the oppressors, also. The master must die so that the brother may be born. This two-fold concern makes Ram Mohan unique among the reformers.

Now let us examine the nature of his reform. First, since the psychological warfare of the oppressor only succeeds to the extent that the oppressed allow themselves to become servile, Ram Mohan went about creating a new self-consciousness and self-confidence in his people. His object was to liberate Indians from their debilitating sense of personal and national inferiority. As one article states it, "Personal self-respect and national self-respect were the most powerful forces that worked behind the Raja's relations with people of other races and cultures."[62]

On the matter of personal self-respect, the Raja bowed to no man, no matter how high and mighty, as Sir Frederick Hamilton was shocked to discover. Flouting colonial protocol, Ram Mohan refused to descend from his palanquin in deference to the Englishman, leaving him furious at native insolence and insubordination. Ram Mohan might well have said with George Fox (1624–1691), "When the Lord sent me forth into the world, He forbade me put off my hat to any high or low." He was able to keep his head high because he was at all times in touch with his spiritual roots. He had an inner dignity which impressed all those who came in contact with him. The governor-general perceived this quality in the Raja and was quick to honor it. He recognized soon that to obtain the cooperation of this man, he must not command him from the pedestal of "his Excellency," but must solicit his help as "Mr. William Bentinck."[63]

On the matter of national self-respect, Ram Mohan reminded Indians and foreigners alike that India had a civilization second to none. The world was indebted to India for the first dawn of knowledge, in science, literature, and religion, India was only indebted to the English in the area of mechanical arts.

The Raja exploded the myth of "Asiatic effeminacy," pointing out that Jesus and the prophets were all Asiatics.

The strategy was thus to fight the myths of racism with the realities of race. Racial prejudice is spawned by prejudgment with no basis in fact. Therefore, to curb the spread of racism there must be a ban on the lower, ignorant class of English settlers, and only those belonging to a select cadre of enlightened landlords would be welcomed.

Enlightenment was necessary but was not enough. Appeals to the conscience of individual parties was also not enough. Individuals do not change institutions; institutions change individuals. That is to say, behavioural change precedes attitudinal change. To accomplish this, and with enormous faith in his people, Ram Mohan recommended before the parliamentary committees that offices presently segregated by race be opened to all qualified persons. He testified that Indians are capable of functioning as Collectors and were qualified to discharge all judicial duties.

With such pride in his country, Ram Mohan evinced a unique style of patriotism. Unlike geographic loyalties which spout pernicious sentiments such as "my country right or wrong," the rational loyalty of the Raja was such that where the country was right, he worked to keep it right, and where it was wrong, he worked to make it right. At the same time, he loved India sufficiently to wish that she become a model for Asia and the world. This type of patriotism is what Mahatma Gandhi called, "love of humanity." He proved that patriotism need not be chauvinistic when love of country is a nationalistic expression of love of humanity, just as love of humanity is a tangible expression of love of God.

Today, the principle of human solidarity which Ram Mohan established on religious, scientific, and rational grounds, and by which he combated the evils of racism, is worthy of social investigation. India's basic problem at this time is the ". . . threat to its unity." The threat is both external and internal. Of the two, the internal threat is by far the more serious. Fully allowing for inevitable diversity in a land so vast and variegated as India, there are certain differences which threaten the integrity of the nation. Prominent among these are regionalism, linguistic diversity, and friction in the relations between the Centre and the States. But the most sinister among them are the cancer of caste and communalism.

Addressing the thirty-ninth convocation of the Tata Institute of Social Sciences, Bombay in 1979, Shri K. R. Narayan gave his opinion that the atomization of Indian society into castes, sub-castes, and tribes was a "colossal social and economic problem," and unless it were remedied soon, "there might well be convulsions which will disturb the unity and stability of India."[64]

On the question of communalism, the speaker singled out the mistreatment of Muslims as a second "potentially explosive" area. He speculated that though Indian Muslims would probably remain unaffected by the resurgence of Islam in neighboring states, what would produce an incendiary reaction in the community would be "intolerant and obscurantist attitudes on the part of the majority of the community and the inability of the government to give protection in such situations."[65] The communal riots in Jamshedpur in the spring of 1979 witness to the build up of communal hostilities and lend credence to the prophecy of Jawharlal Nehru when he said in 1947, that unless Muslims are given complete democratic freedom, "we shall have a festering sore which will eventually poison the whole body politic and probably destroy it."[66]

Indian Christians also feel the rising tide of communalism which treats them as if they are another race within their own country. They are impatient with being looked upon as second-class citizens. The introduction on December 22, 1978, in the Lok Sabha, of "The Freedom of Religion Bill, 1978," by O. P. Tyagi, a Jana Sangh member of Parliament, sent shock waves through the Christian community. Ostensibly the bill was aimed at curbing wrongful conversion, but actually it placed a ban on all conversions and thereby restricted legitimate religious freedom. G. S. Reddy, Congress (1) M. P. from Andhra Pradesh and chairman, Extension Service, Catholic Union of India, summed up Christian feelings: "They [the RSS] are afraid of Muslims, but not Christians. The Christians are peaceful so they think anything can be done against them . . ."[67]

The current threat to Indian unity arises from unresolved issues affecting the Sikh community. The outbursts of fury, culminating in the assasination of Prime Minister Indira Gandhi, raise serious doubts about the viability of democracy in a land which is so violently divided against itself.

It is high time the Indian people buried all the differences which divide and weaken their national solidarity—racial, religious, regional and linguistic. All of them are infected by the same pernicious pattern we have described in the case of racism which contradicts the declared democratic ideals of the nation. The solution to the problem of Indian unity is not going to be simple. We quote once more from Shri Narayan as he addresses himself both to the problem and to the solution:

> The fragmentation of our social system is such that one may say that the social mind of India is like a broken mirror. The many-coloured dome of India is shattered into thousands and thousands of fragments. In each broken piece, it is possible to see tiny reflections of the countenance of India and each caste, sub-caste, group or tribe may believe that what it sees is the total image. The problem of Indian unity is to see India steadily and as a whole in all its baffling dimensions and diversities, to put all the diminutive images in the broken pieces into the giant reality that is

India. Such a concept of unity can only be the product of many factors—political, social, economic, cultural, educational and psychological. It can be brought about only through major changes in society, through greater equalisation of the social order, through the establishment of an easy and effective system of inter-communication among the various strata of society and regions of the country and above all through a *spirit of tolerance prevailing among the people as a whole* (italics supplied).[68]

If tolerance be the key to the survival of India's national integrity, then, there is no greater architect or exemplar of the spirit of tolerance than Raja Ram Mohan Roy. Nag and Burman say of him:

> In that age of controversies when east and the west clashed on so many fundamental points, Rammohun by his thought and action, left us a *record of tolerance and philanthropy rarely paralleled among his contemporaries* . . . . this could be nowhere better illustrated than with his controversies with the contemporary Christian European writers (italics supplied).[69]

Ram Mohan's tolerance was not a matter of "live and let live," nor must it be taken for moderation which could be a subtle form of intolerance. Rather, it was tolerance born of profound love. Through love he could empathize with the experience of others; be one with the many and yet be himself. He considers such a spirit not only possible for Indians, but regards it as the Hindu's greatest asset. He says: "It is well-known to the whole world, that no people on earth are more tolerant than the Hindoos, who believe all men to be equally within the reach of Divine beneficence, which embraces the good of every religious sect and denomination."[70] This is heady Vedantic doctrine which must be translated into social action, but if this is a time when religion is being politicized negatively, its obverse is equally possible.

## B. Sexism

A second form of oppression Ram Mohan tackled was masculine sexism. Western social analysts define sexism as:

> The mastery of men over women on the basis of the privileges that they see in their manhood . . . a masculine pride in one's own sex, favoring the special characteristics of masculinity in culture, the conviction that these characteristics are fundamentally of a biological nature and therefore are determined, combined with the depreciation of women to the "weaker sex," the devaluing of the presumed "feminine" attributes, and the exclusion of women from full participation in the life of society.[71]

As in the case of racism, sexism is a group phenomenon. Males justify themselves by the characteristics of their male sexuality. To be fully human is, primarily, to be male; females are not that completely evolved. The sexist self-image is, therefore, negative and aggressive. "A man defines himself by saying that he is 'not a woman' and by not allowing himself to be 'feminine,' as in all sorts of fraternal organizations."[72]

Sexism is also the weaponry employed for dominating women through psychological warfare. The total upbringing of a female in a patriarchal society is aimed at developing in her a dependency on the opposite sex. She has a uniqueness all of her own, but it is biologically defined as wife and mother. This in turn provides the framework for her role and status which is domestically understood.

The biological legitimation of sexism is only one side of the coin; the other is theological. God himself is conceived in the image of man, whereas woman is the temptress. Man is therefore given charge over her, so that by his wise protection the "weaker vessel" will come to good.

Ram Mohan does not use the word "sexism," but the social and psychological acuity with which he describes male dominance renders his analysis refreshingly up to date.

He points out that for the Hindu male, the full meaning of humanity is to be found in masculinity. Physical prowess, mental agility, and moral integrity are all male attributes. In the gods these attributes are writ large. By contrast, women are considered the "weaker sex." Not only are they physically weak, "women are by nature of inferior understanding, without resolution, unworthy of trust, subject to passions, and void of virtuous knowledge."[73] The constitutional weakness of the woman justifies the diminution of her rights and privileges, and disbars her from participation in public affairs. The only safe place in which she can live a virtuous life is within the protective walls of her home; first under the tutelage of her father; then her husband; and finally, her sons. All of these encroachments upon her freedom make life for women one long misery from girlhood to the grave.

As children, women are sometimes made the victims of infanticide. The Rajputs, in the neighborhood of Doab, "are accustomed to destroy their infant daughters."[74] The lot of the survivors is hardly enviable. Modern legislators twist the scriptures to deprive daughters of their meagre inheritance.[75] Lower *Brahmins* and *Kayasthas* of high caste "frequently marry their female relations to men having defects and worn out by old age or disease, merely from pecuniary considerations."[76]

As wives, women suffer much distress. Ceremonially, she is considered "half of her husband," but once formalities are over, the wife is "treated worse than inferior animals."[77]

For the woman is employed to do the work of a slave in the house, such as, in her turn, to clean the place very early in the morning, whether cold or wet, to scour the dishes, to wash the floor, to cook night and day, to prepare and serve food for her husband, father, mother-in-law, sisters-in-law, brothers-in-law, and friends and connections . . . . If in the preparation or serving up of victuals they commit the smallest fault, what insult do they not receive from their husband, their mother-in-law, and the younger brothers of their husband? After all the male part of the family have satisfied themselves, the women content themselves with what may be left, whether sufficient in quantity or not. Where Brahmans or Kayasthas are not wealthy, their women are obliged to attend to their cows, and to prepare cow-dung for firing. In the afternoon they fetch water from the river or tank, and at night perform the office of menial servants in making the beds. In case of any fault or omission in the performance of those labours they receive injurious treatment. Should the husband acquire wealth, he indulges in criminal amours to her perfect knowledge and almost under her eyes, and does not see her perhaps once a month.[78]

In homes that are polygamous, the wives are "subjected to mental miseries and constant quarrels."[79] Preference for one wife usually takes the form of cruelty toward another. Among lower classes, "on the slightest fault, or even on bare suspicion of her conduct," a wife is "chastised as a thief."[80]

As widows, women are deprived of their ancient scriptural rights of inheritance by modern interpretations of the law. According to this late exposition of the law, a widow "can receive nothing when her husband has no issue by her; and in case he dies leaving only one son by his wife, or having had more sons, one of whom happened to die leaving issue, she shall in these cases, also have no claim to the property."[81]

Further, in case a husband "leave more than one surviving son, and they, unwilling to allow a share to the widow, keep the property undivided, the mother can claim nothing in this instance also. But when a person dies, leaving two or more sons, and all of them survive and he inclined to allot a share to their mother, her right is in this case only valid. Under these expositions, and with such limitations, both step-mothers and mothers have, in reality, been left destitute in the division of her husband's property, and the right of a widow exists in theory only among the learned, but unknown to the populace."[82]

The consequence is that when a widow loses her husband, she also loses all authority in the home. She must depend upon the whims and fancies of her sons and their wives who can be very cruel. Step-mothers, who are numerous in polygamous housholds, "are still more shamefully neglected in general by their step-sons, and sometimes dreadfully treated by their sisters-in-law who have fortunately a son or sons by their husband."[83]

The prospects of such a life of daily insults, drive women to choose immolation over ignominy, which makes *sati* into glorified suicide.

All of this inhumanity stems from masculine sexism. With courage and insight rare even in this time and place, Ram Mohan exposes the myth of male superiority and lays the spiritual and social foundations for women's liberation. He makes his brief on the basis of *shastra* and common sense.

In effect he says to the male chauvinists: Men are bullies; you are victims of your own strength. Taking advantage of the "corporeal weakness" of women, you first deny them the freedom to develop their natural excellence, and then, when nothing is produced, you turn around and say that women are unproductive![84]

In point of fact, what you consider to be the constitutional bankruptcy of women is a projection of your own weaknesses. You and the whole "Hindu community look down upon them as contemptible and mischievous creatures," but what you see is a reflection of yourselves. You hate them because you despise yourselves. When you point one finger at women for lack of understanding, of resolution, of trustworthiness, of virtuous knowledge, and subjection to passions, you point three fingers at yourselves.[85]

On the question of their supposed intellectual inferiority, "when did you ever afford them a fair opportunity of exhibiting their natural capacity? How then can you accuse them of want of understanding? If, after instruction in knowledge and wisdom, a person cannot comprehend or retain what has been taught him, we may consider him deficient; but as you keep women generally void of education and acquirements, you cannot, therefore, in justice pronounce on their inferiority."[86]

Could it be that you are afraid that should you give them opportunity, they might prove your equals? The *shastras* do show that for every enlightened husband, there is an enlightened wife. *Kalidasa* is complemented by *Bhanumati*, and *Yajnavalkya* by *Maitreyi*.[87]

As to moral qualities, men shudder at death, but women resolutely burn themselves with the corpses of their deceased husbands. Whereas men are ten times more promiscuous than women, women are cast in the role of temptress because men are the managers and manipulators of public information.[88] "The medium is the massage," and that medium is always male. Whereas wives desire one husband, the husband desires many wives, and the quintessence of each passion is pure selfishness.

As to the accusation that women are in want of virtuous knowledge:

Observe what pain, what slighting, what contempt, and what afflictions their virtue enables them to support! How many Kulin Brahmans are there who marry ten or fifteen wives for the sake of money, that never see the greater number of them after the day of marriage, and visit others only three or four times in the course of their life. Still amongst these women, most, even without seeing or receiving any support from their husbands, living dependent on their fathers or brothers, and suffering much distress, continue to preserve their virtue; and when Brahmans, or those of other tribes, bring their wives to live with them, what misery do the women suffer?[89]

On all counts, male superiority is a myth. The narrow identity of masculinity must be exchanged for the expanded identity of humanity. We are all humans who happen to be of different sexes; not sexes who happen to be human.

For females to realize their full human potential, men must give them equal opportunities in all areas—religious, social, and educational. Most important is freedom from want for Hindu widows, which means that the Hindu law of inheritance must be changed. As long as women themselves are thought of as property, there is little recognition for their need for property.

Finally, the consciousness of women must be raised. They have been brainwashed into believing all the prejudices against their sex and therefore do not believe that society owes them a better deal in life. The very scriptures that are dished out to them cater to the lower levels of their consciousness. No wonder some of them are prepared to embrace *sati*, thinking they reap rewards in heaven. On the other hand, if they are brought up along the path of *Vedantic* consciousness, they will develop a more positive self-appreciation, for they will discover that the Divine is found equally in males and females everywhere, and in all times.

Turning to the present, Renuka Ray, well-known civic leader and former Member of Parliament, states: "The role and status of women in modern Indian society flows to a great extent from the cherished objective and ideals that inspired the renaissance in India and the awakening of women was an integral part of it."[90] Raja Ram Mohan Roy was the progenitor of the women's movement. "It was his activities and of those who followed in his wake, that brought into existence the women pioneers of the 19th century in India."[91]

The attitude and approach of the Raja and his followers are still relevant for Indian women today. They involve two foci: (1) the removal of dehumanizing traditions and; (2) education and opportunities on par with men.

In respect to the first point, India's women are still bound by tradition. Their's is a man-centered world of father, husbands, and sons. Dr. Manashi Das Gupta, eminent educator and social scientist, remarks: "Traditionally women are considered so much to be 'the shadow' of their husbands that their separate identity is hardly recognised."[92] Presently, they only have a minority status, standing somewhere between men and children. They do have power, but it does not flow from their femininity. "A woman may be able to dominate when she is old because old people traditionally dominate the younger ones within specific limits. A young wife might, however, dominate her poor mother-in-law because she is a rich man's daughter and her father continues to support her even after marriage. Dominance and superior status thus depend on several factors. It is not a simple function of femininity."[93] The creative principle in the universe represented by the female deity, may be acknowledged, but "has not found any direct expression in Hindu social institutions."[94] Mother, of course, is highly respected in Hindu society, but is only potentially dominant. "Had she been actually so the social situation would have been different. The mother is eulogised not because she dominates but because she gives the succour as does the sacred cow."[95]

Even those women who are successful in the public sector become dependent when they return home because they have been long conditioned into depending on the men in their household. The old feminine social values of reliance-on-others and submission-to-authority are therefore very much alive today and are rewarded by "protection and support within the family."[96]

There are hopeful signs that a new genre of women is emerging who refuse to submit to oppressive traditions. In Poona in the spring of 1979, a seminar was held commemorating the birth of Lord Rama. The venue was the Rama temple in Sadashiv Peth, a bastion of Orthodox Brahmanism. Participating in the seminar was a wide range of middle-class women. The subject under discussion was whether it was possible to observe the traditional code of wifely duties (*Pativrata dharma*) in the present situation. The *Poona Herald* made the following report:

> All the speakers narrate different tales with the same substance that woman is treated as an inferior being at home as well as in society. And they are all one in their demand that society must now change its outlook and liberalise its attitude towards women. They say that until the last generation woman was a virtual slave in the family. Whether as wife or mother or sister or daughter, her role was always subservient to man. She had lost her identity and had no existence as an individual. Now the times have changed but the old fetters have not gone. Today, woman has come out of the home and shares work with men in office and industry. But she is still expected to observe the same rules of conduct which were imposed on her when she was confined to the hearth and cradle within the four walls of the home. Let man be assured that today's woman has not forsaken her conscience and sense of responsibility; nor has she broken the accepted norms of social behaviour. But the new role which she has begun to play as a citizen demands that she be treated with equality by man at home and in society. Her dignity and status as an individual must be accepted and respected.[97]

The equal rights of women have been written into the Indian Constitution. This was to be expected, both on account of the declared equality of women in the Vedas, as Ram Mohan and all the nineteenth-century reformers pointed out, and also because of the courageous role assumed by Indian women in the Freedom Movement against the British. Ram Mohan was the first to fight for women's rights under law; but for all its achievements he recognized that effective law is contingent upon moral consciousness and the commitment of society. Former United States Chief Justice, Earl Warren confirms this view:

> In civilized life, Law floats in a sea of Ethics . . . . Without ethical understanding, the Law, as a Ship of State, would be stranded on dry land. When there is no ethical commitment to observe the Law, the judicial and police systems are really helpless, and the Law often ceases to operate at all.[98]

To develop this moral awareness, Ram Mohan showed the men of his day how they must step out of their egos and feel as females feel. Interchanging with another person's feelings dissolves ignorance and selfishness and produces true community. One can almost hear the Raja say to the millions of Indian males who make a daily hypocrisy of the rights granted to women by virtue of the Indian Constitution: "What I lament is, that, seeing the women thus dependent and exposed to every misery, you feel for them no compassion."[99] The word compassion means, "suffer with." As long as the traditional sexist attitude prevails, and men somehow consider themselves different beings with special rights marked off by masculinity, there can be no compassion which, as the Buddha taught, is the basis if all ethical relationships.

The need for education and commensurate opportunities is the second point emphasized by Ram Mohan. True, the schools he founded were for boys, as circumstances dictated, but his concern for female enlightenment is unequivocal. His educational emphasis was continued by the Brahmo Samaj and subsequently by the Arya Samaj. But, for all these and other efforts of subsequent activists, the educational picture for females in modern India is bleak.

Dr. Aleyamma George, specialist in the fields of Statistics Demography, and Director of the Centre for Mathematical Sciences, Vazhuthacaud, Trivandrum, has collated some revealing statistics. In regard to the progress of female literacy, 1901–1971, figures supplied by the Ministry of Education show that whereas in 1901 the percentage of female literacy in relation to the total female population was 0.69, in 1971 that figure had merely crawled to 18.72. On the other hand, male literacy for the same period rose from 9.83 to 39.45—more than double the percentage for females in 1971. The growth rate of female literacy since independence has been a mere ten per cent. We agree with Dr. George that "it is not an easy task for a nation which has emerged from the clutches of foreign rule to eradicate illiteracy of the teeming millions completely within a short period,"[100] but not enough is being done even to bridge the gap between female and male levels of attainment. The disparity is as unhealthy as the sexist attitudes behind it are pervasive.

It is not popular to mention, but underlying the disparity between male and female levels of education is a warped sense of values found on all levels of society. Gita Mukharji, prominent for her social activities, points out that in all areas of life, including education, boys are given preference over girls. "In the less educated or uneducated families belonging to the lowest income group, girls, even if enrolled in primary or pre-primary school, are taken out before completion of the term to help in domestic work, or in the family trade or to earn for the family."[101] At the other end of the social spectrum, some wealthy families oppose female education on traditional grounds.

The gap is being shortened today among lower income groups and among the middle class, primarily for economic considerations and the desire for upward social mobility.

Returning to the Ministry of Education statistics, in respect to school enrollment in 1972, out of a total of 83 million students in primary, middle and higher secondary grades, thirty-six per cent were girls. This means that for every seventeen male enrollments there were only ten females enrolled.

The record is still more depressing in rural areas where the literacy rate is approximately twenty-nine per cent below that of urban areas, and literacy growth among females is even lower.

In regard to the enrollment of females in the universities, the figures for 1972 are somewhat encouraging. Continuing the above statistics, 660,871 girls (twenty-six per cent) enrolled in general education. 61,046 (10 per cent) enrolled in professional education. The highest percentage (thirty-eight per cent) of girls was in teacher training followed by medicine (twenty-one per cent), commerce (five per cent), and engineering, technology, etc., (one per cent).

All of these figures have a direct bearing on the status of the Indian woman. Dr. George laments the fact that though women are the social equals of men in a theoretical and legal sense, the three decades following independence still find women under male dominance, eking out their existence in the "grip of traditional roles." To liberate themselves from the stigmas that have been attached to their sex, women should come to know their constitutional rights; should become economically self-sufficient; improve their living standards; and the key to all these closed doors is education.

> Various studies conducted in India reveal that the social status of women is significantly related to their aspirations, opportunities for education and employment and improvement of their standard of living. Education affects employment opportunities and the decision-making role is influenced by the education and employment of the wife. These are the factors which are most often related to the status of women. It is of no doubt

that *the cultural progress of a country can be judged by the status accorded to women in society* (italics supplied).[102]

The concluding line is significant. All of the social sciences affirm that a woman's place in society is the clearest index of its civilization. A society in which women are taught nothing but how to cater to men and to bear and bring up children is a society in decline.

Ram Mohan had this same insight, but perceived even greater ramifications. He saw women in the context of the nation, and the nation in the context of an international order of civilization. This vision produced in him feelings of national embarrassment because of the mistreatment of women by his countrymen. He attacked the problem with the fervor of a patriot, and when the fight over *sati* was successfully ended, we hear him offer up thanks to heaven, "whose protecting arm has rescued our weaker sex [only in a physical sense] from a cruel murder, under the cloak of religion, and *our character, as a people*, from the contempt and pity with which it has been regarded, on account of this custom, by all civilized nations on the surface of the globe." (italics supplied).[103]

 *CHAPTER 16*

# Conclusion

Yousuf Karsh, the photographer, has been described as the "legend who captures legends."[1] He has made some of the most expressive portraits of outstanding personages of our time. "Statesmen, tycoons, artists, musicians, actors, physicians, kings, popes and presidents have been 'karshed' for all time in their own environments, with an uncanny light seeming to play against their facial features, hands and clothing."[2] The list of legends includes Albert Einstein, George Bernard Shaw, Pablo Picasso, Charles De Gaulle, Ernest Hemingway, Albert Schweitzer, Pablo Casals, Igor Stravinsky, and Jawaharlal Nehru. "I seek to photograph people who make their mark on society," he says, noting that he tries to catch the "inward power" of the subjects.

Asked if he can recognize a person's extraordinary qualities immediately; if greatness is visible, Karsh replies:

> Intuitively you sense that you are in its presence, but I cannot tell you how. At times, you can tell by someone's conversation and compassion. But not all great people are articulate or verbal enough to express it. Nevertheless you feel that it's there.
>
> But I have found that great people do have some things in common. One is an immense belief in themselves and in their mission. They also have great determination as well as an ability to work hard. At the crucial moment of decision, they draw upon their accumulated wisdom. But above all they have integrity.
>
> I've also seen that great men are often lonely. This is understandable, because they have built such high standards for themselves that they often feel alone. But the same loneliness is part of their ability to create. Character, like photography, develops in darkness.[3]

Karsh could well have been describing the legend that is Raja Ram Mohan Roy, because he has brought into sharp focus everything we have been saying about this man. "Above all they have integrity"—as if Karsh had photographed the Raja himself! Were the artist speaking the language of the *Gita*, he would have summed up his subjects as the bearers of *dharma*. This is the aura of their presence and the source of their "inward power."

In the noblest tradition of his people, Ram Mohan was a man of *dharma*. We stated this at the beginning of this study, and more confidently do we state it now. He was a good man, not because he was a great man, but he was great because he was good. Throughout Indian tradition, the one presupposes the other, and the two cannot be separated.

It is part of our common moral understanding that a person must be good for something, or he is good for nothing—such seems the moral structure of life and the source from whence we derive its higher meanings. In the case of Ram Mohan, "something" equalled everything! Our survey of his era has shown that everything that could possibly promote human progress and happiness—religion, morality, education, economics, politics—was part of his mission; often a lonely mission. There was nothing human that was alien to him, and whatever was alien, he tried to humanize.

Thus, as F. Max Muller, the eminent Indologist has pointed out, the Raja lived up to his name, and walks as a king among men.[4] The sphere of service to his people was as complete as his dedication. Such a king must ever be enthroned within the hearts and minds of his people for in his greatness lies their own strength. The *Bengal Herald*, dated January 17, 1841, observes:

> The character of a nation is always in a great degree dependent upon the character of individuals. Names of men such as Shakespeare and Milton and Bacon and Newton, give a more distinct idea of England's mental greatness than could be produced by an elaborate essay on the subject, and an Englishman proud of his country always points to these glorious specimens of human nature when the character of English intellect is the subject of discussion. The single name of Rammohun Roy is cherished by the more enlightened of his countrymen with gratitude and veneration because they feel how much they owe him.[5]

The *Upanishads*, the source of the Raja's "inward power," echo the same sentiments in their poetic way:

> When the wick is aflame at its tip,
> The whole lamp is said to be burning.

# Notes

## PREFACE

1. See Rajat K. Ray, "Introduction," in *Rammohun Roy and the Process of Modernization in India*, ed. V. C. Joshi (Delhi: Vikas, 1975), p. 1.
2. Sir Brajendra Nath Seal, "Rammohun Roy: The Universal Man," in *The Father of Modern India*, ed. Satis Chandra Chakravarti (Calcutta: Rammohun Roy Centenary Committee, 1935), pp. 106, 107.
3. Ray, *op. cit.*, p. 2.
4. R. C. Majumdar, "*On Rammohun Roy*," Asiatic Journal, 1973, p. 40.
5. David Kopf, "Rammohun Roy and the Bengal Renaissance: An Historiographical Essay," in Joshi, *op. cit.*, pp. 21, 22.
6. Richard Wasserstrom, *Today's Moral Problems* (New York: Macmillan Publishing Company, 1975), Preface.
7. James Russell Lowell, "The Present Crisis," *A Treasury of Favorite Poems* (New York: Avenell Books, 1978), pp. 272, 273.
8. *London Daily News*, November 26, 1885.
9. A. T. Brown, *Half-Lights on Chelsfield Court Lodge* (Liverpool, by the Author, 1933), p. 43.

## CHAPTER 1

1. Vincent A. Smith, *The Oxford History of India*, ed. Percival Spear (3d. edition; Oxford: Clarendon Press, 1958), p. 733.
2. *Ibid.*, p. 451.
3. *Ibid.*, p. 453.
4. *Ibid.*
5. *Ibid.*, p. 454.
6. *Ibid.*, p. 453.
7. *Ibid.*, p. 454.
8. Battle of Plassey, 1757, or 1761, the year of Panipat.
9. *Vide Bhagavad Gita* IV.7.
10. *Father of Modern India, op. cit.*, p. 3.
11. *Ibid.*, p. 28.
12. *Ibid.*, p. 9.

13. *Ibid.*
14. Sophia Dobson Collet, *The Life and Letters of Rammohun Roy*, eds. Dilip Kumar Biswas and Prabhat Chandra Ganguli (3d. edition; Calcutta: Sadharan Brahmo Samaj, 1962), p. 4.
15. *Ibid.*, p. 7.
16. *Ibid.*, Supplementary Notes, p. 13.
17. *Ibid.*, Supplementary Notes, p. 12.
18. *Ibid.*, p. 8.

## CHAPTER 2

1. Collet, *Ibid.*, Supplementary Notes, p. 14.
2. *Ibid.*, p. 15.
3. *Ibid.*, p. 10.
4. *Ibid.*
5. Rammohun Roy, *Tuhfatul Muhwahhiddin*, Tr. Moulavi Obaidullah El Obaide (Calcutta: Adi Brahmo Samaj, 1889), p. 68.
6. Iqbal Singh, *Rammohun Roy* (Bombay: Asia Publishing House, 1958), p. 68.
7. Roy, *op. cit.*, p. 11.
8. *Ibid.*, p. 12.
9. *Ibid.*, p. 19.
10. *Ibid.*, p. 21.
11. *Ibid.*, p. 22.
12. *Ibid.*
13. *Ibid.*, p. 24.
14. *Ibid.*, p. 25.
15. Krishna R. Kripalani, "Rammohun: A Biographical Sketch," in *Rammohun Roy*, ed. Niharranjan Ray (Dehhi: National Book Trust, India, 1974). p. 11.
16. *The Dabistan*, cited by Ajit Kumar Ray, *The Religious Ideas of Rammohun Roy* (New Delhi: Kanak Publications, 1976), p. 22.
17. *Ibid.*
18. *Ibid.*, p. 23.
19. *Ibid.*, pp. 25–6.
20. Collet, *op. cit.*, Supplementary Notes, p. 41.
21. Vide Brajendranath Banerji, *Rammohun Roy*, p. 32. Quoted by Biswas and Ganguli, *Ibid.*
22. *Ibid.*, Supplementary Notes, p. 55.
23. J. K. Majumdar ed., *Raja Rammohun Roy and Progressive Movements in India* (Calcutta: Art Press, 1941), p. 267.
24. Collet, *op. cit.*, p. 31.
25. *Ibid.*, Supplementary Notes, p. 54.
26. Quoted in *The Father of Modern India*, Supplementary Notes, p. 32.
27. Collet, *op. cit.*, p. 27.
28. *Ibid.*, quoted.
29. *Ibid.*
30. *Ibid.*, Supplementary Notes, p. 57.
31. Pandit Sivanath Sastri, "Rammohun Roy: The Story of His Life," in *The Father of Modern India*, ed. Satis Chandra Chakravarti (Calcutta: Rammohun Roy Centenary Committee, 1935), p. 11.

## CHAPTER 3

1. Stat. 53, Geo. 111, cl. 155, Sect. 43. Quoted in Smith, *op. cit.*, p. 650.
2. *Ibid.*, p. 525.
3. *Ibid.*, p. 526.
4. Edmund Burke, *Works* (Boston, 1865), Vol. IX, p. 455.
5. *Ibid.*, Vol. X, p. 450.
6. "Warren Hastings," 6th. Day, Feb. 19, 1788, VII, 230–231: quoted in Gerald Chapman, *Edmund Burke* (Cambridge: Harvard University Press), 1961, p. 273.
7. Speech, 15 February 1788, *The Speeches of Edmund Burke on the Impeachment of Warren Hastings*, 1 (1895), pp. 93–94.
8. Smith, *op. cit.*, pp. 525, 526.
9. George Bearce, *British Attitudes Towards India 1784–1858* (London: Oxford University Press, 1961), p. 13.
10. Smith, *op. cit.*, p. 580.
11. "Warren Hastings," 4th. Day, Feb. 15, 1788, VII, 43–47. In Chapman, *op. cit.*, p. 248.
12. Eric Stokes, *English Utilitarians and India* (Oxford: Clarendon Press, 1959), xvi.
13. A. L. Basham, *The Wonder That Was India* (New York: Grove Press, 1959), p. 5.
14. S. N. Mukherjee, *Sir William Jones: A Study in Eighteenth-Century British Attitudes to India* (Cambridge: Cambridge University Press, 1968), p. 2.
15. Basham, *op. cit.*, p. 5.
16. Mukherjee, *op. cit.*, p. 99.
17. *Ibid.*, p. 83.
18. "On the Hindus," *Asian Review*, Vol. I, pp. 422–423. In Mukherjee, *op. cit.*, p. 95.
19. *Ibid.*, pp. 115, 116.
20. *Ibid.*, p. 116.
21. John Teignmouth ed., *The Works of Sir William Jones* (Delhi: Agam Prakashan, 1977), Vol. III, p. 2.
22. "On the Philosophy of Asiaticks," *Asian Review*, Vol. IV, p. 174.
23. Charles Wilkins, *A Translation of a Royal Grant of Land by one of the Ancient Raajas of Hindostan, Asiatic Researches*, I (1788).
24. Stokes, *op. cit.*, p. 51.
25. *Ibid.*, quoted.
26. *Ibid.*, p. 52.
27. James Mill to Dumont: *The Work of David Ricardo*, R. Scraffa (ed.), Vol. VIII, "Letters 1819–21," p. 40n. In Stokes, *op. cit.*, p. 48.
28. James Mill, *The History of British India*, Abridged by William Thomas (Chicago: University of Chicago Press, 1975), p. 225.
29. *Ibid.*, p. 224.
30. *Ibid.*, p. 137.
31. *Ibid.*, p. 141.
32. *Ibid.*, p. 142.
33. *Ibid.*, p. 145.
34. *Ibid.*, p. 149.
35. *Ibid.*, p. 150.

36. *Ibid.*, p. 165.
37. *Ibid.*, p. 191.
38. *Ibid.*, p. 192.
39. *Ibid.*, p. 210.
40. *Ibid.*, p. 211.
41. *Ibid.*
42. *Ibid.*, pp. 212, 213.
43. Bearce, *op. cit.*, p. 78.
44. Charles Grant, *Observations on the State of Society among the Asiatic Subjects of Great Britain, particularly with respect to Morals and on the Means of Improving it. Written chiefly in the Year 1792* (privately printed, 1797), p. 25, India Office Library: European MSS E93.
45. *Ibid.*
46. *Ibid.*, p. 18.
47. *Ibid.*, p. 71.
48. Speech of Wilberforce, 22 June 1813, *Hansard*, First Series, Vol. xxvi, p. 8, cited by E. H. Howse, *Saints in Politics: The Clapham Sect and the Growth of Freedom* (Toronto: University of Toronto Press, 1952), pp. 89–90.
49. Grant, *op. cit.*, p. 220.
50. A. Embree, *Charles Grant and British Rule in India* (New York: Columbia University Press, 1962), p. 152.
51. *Ibid.*, p. 153.
52. *Ibid.*, p. 155, 156.
53. *Ibid.*, p. 156.
54. Smith, *op. cit.*, p. 647.
55. *Ibid.*
56. Quoted in M. E. Chamberlain, *Britain and India* (Connecticut: Archon Books, 1974), p. 70.
57. Embree, *op. cit.*, p. 156.
58. Smith, *op. cit.*, p. 580.
59. Rajat Ray, *op. cit.*, p. 7.

### CHAPTER 4

1. Smith, *op. cit.*, p. 581.
2. Chamberlain, *op. cit.*, p. 81.
3. Tara Chand, *History of the Freedom Movement in India* (Delhi: Ministry of Education, Government of India, 1967), Vol. 2, p. 244.
4. *Ibid.*
5. *Ibid.* p. 246.
5. Smith, *op. cit.*, p. 733.
6. *Ibid.*
7. *Ibid.*
8. *Ibid.*

### CHAPTER 5

1. *The English Works of Raja Rammohun Roy*, Part II, eds. Kalidas Nag and Debajyoti Burman (Calcutta: Sadharan Brahmo Samaj, 1946), p. 51.
2. *Ibid.*
3. *Ibid.*
4. *Ibid.*

5. *Ibid.*, p. 1.
6. *Ibid.*, p. 24.
7. *Ibid.*, p. 1.
8. *Ibid.*, p. 41.
9. *Ibid.*, pp. 41, 42.
10. *Ibid.*, p. 59.
11. Collet, *op. cit.*, Supplementary Notes, pp. 98, 99.
12. *Works*, *op. cit.*, pp. 23, 24.
13. *Ibid.*, p. 23.
14. *Goverment Gazette*, February 1, 1816. In J. K. Majumdar, *op. cit.*, p. 3.
15. *Calcutta Monthly Journal*, December 1817, *Ibid.*, p. 13.
16. *Ibid.*
17. *Ibid.*
18. *Missionary Register* (London), 1816, *Ibid.*, p. 6.
19. *Calcutta Journal*, October, 1818, *Ibid.*, pp. 14, 15.
20. *Ibid.*, p. xx.
21. Chamberlain, *op. cit.*, p. 54.
22. *Works*, Part II, p. 41.
23. Chamberlain, *loc. cit.*
24. *Father of Modern India*, *op. cit.*, p. 12.
25. *Ibid.*
26. *India Gazette*, quoted by *Asiatic Journal*, May 18, 1819, in Majumdar, *op. cit.*, p. 18.
27. *Asiatic Journal* (monthly Series), August 1819, *Ibid.*, p. 22.
28. *Asiatic Journal*, July 1820, *Ibid.*
29. *Father of Modern India*, *op. cit.*, p. 13.
30. *Friend of India* (Quarterly Series), September 1820, in Majumdar, *op. cit.*, p. 22.
31. *Encylopaedia Britannica*, quoted in George Howells, *The Story of Serampore and Its College* (Serampore, by the author, 1927), p. 1.
32. *Ibid.*, p. 3.
33. *Periodical Accounts relative to the British Missionary Society*, Vol. VI (Bristol, 1817) No. 31 (From June 1815 to January 1816), pp. 106, 107, in Collet, *op. cit.*, p. 114n.
34. *Works*, Part V, p. 3.
35. *Ibid.*
36. *Ibid.*, p. 4.
37. Collet, *op. cit.*, p. 115.
38. *Ibid.*
39. *Friend of India* (Quarterly Series), September, 1820.
40. *Ibid.*
41. *Ibid.*
42. *Ibid.*
43. *Works*, Part V, p. 57.
44. *Ibid.*, p. 59.
45. *Ibid.*
46. *Ibid.*
47. St. Matthew 22:37–40.
48. *Ibid.*, p. 60.
49. *Ibid.*, p. 62.

50. *Ibid.*
51. *Ibid.*, p. 63.
52. *Ibid.*, p. 65.
53. *Ibid.*, p. 66.
54. *Ibid.*, p. 67.
55. *Ibid.*, p. 71.
56. *Works,* Part VI, p. 1.
57. *Ibid.*, Advertisement.
58. *Ibid.*, p. 1
59. *Ibid.*, pp. 3, 4.
60. *Ibid.*, p. 4.
61. *Ibid.*, p. 5.
62. *Ibid.*, p. 10.
63. *Ibid.*, p. 22.
64. *Ibid.*, p. 19.
65. *Ibid.*, p. 20.
66. *Ibid.*, p. 21.
67. *Ibid.*, p. 25.
68. *Ibid.*, p. 29.
69. *Ibid.*, p. 31.
70. *Ibid.*
71. *Ibid.*, p. 33.
72. *Ibid.*
73. *Ibid.*, p. 34.
74. *Ibid.*, p. 35.
75. *Ibid.*
76. *Ibid.*, p. 36.
77. *Ibid.*, p. 42, 43.
78. *Ibid.*, p. 43.
79. *Ibid.*, p. 45.
80. *Ibid.*, p. 46.
81. *Ibid.*, p. 47.
82. *Ibid.*
83. James Hoby in his *Memoir of William Yates of Calcutta* (London, 1847), p. 167, in Supplementary Notes, Collet, *op. cit.*, p. 157.
84. Extracts of Rev. Marshman's Review of Ram Mohan Roy's "Final Appeal to the Christian Public in defence of the Precepts of Jesus," December 1823, In Majumdar, *op. cit.*, p. 50.
85. *Ibid.*, p. 52.
86. *Ibid.*, p. 54.
87. *Ibid.*, Part VI, p. 16.
88. *Ibid.*, p. 9.
89. *Ibid.*, p. 47.
90. *Ibid.*, p. 4.
91. *Ibid.*
92. *Ibid.*, p. 3.
93. *Ibid.*, p. 37.
94. Collet, *op cit.*, p. 137.
94a. Reginald Heber, 1783–1826, in *Worship Service Hymnal* (Chicago: Hope Publishing Company, 1957), No. 431.

95. *Calcutta Journal,* August 1, 1821, In Majumdar, *op cit.*, p. 30.

96. *Ibid.,* August 2, 1821, p. 31.

97. *Ibid.*

98. *India Gazette,* May 17, 1824, in Majumdar, *Ibid.,* pp. 71, 72.

99. The Rev. W. Adam's letter to Rev. William Yates, *The Unitarian Repository and Christian Miscellany* (May), quoted by *India Gazette,* May 17, 1824, in Majumdar, *Ibid.,* p. 65.

100. *Ibid.,* pp. 72, 73.

101. *Works,* Part VI, p. 43.

102. *Ibid.*

103. *Ibid.,* p. 44.

104. Quoted in Collet, *op. cit.,* p. 150.

105. *Ibid.*

106. *Ibid.*

107. Quoted in Collet, *op. cit.,* p. 122.

108. *Ibid.,* p. 122, 123.

109. *Ibid.,* p. 123.

110. *Works,* Part II, p. 193.

111. Rev. Adam's letter to R. Dutton, June 26, 1827, quoted in Collet, *op. cit.,* p. 132.

112. *Ibid.*

113. *Works,* Part VI, p. 87.

114. Bruce Carlisle Robertson, "Rammohun Roy and American Unitarians." Paper delivered at the Bengal Studies Conference, April 10, 1976, Ann Arbor, Michigan, for publication in 1976 Bengal Studies Volume, p. 1.

115. *Ibid.,* footnote 2.

116. *Works,* Part IV, p. 86.

117. *Ibid.*

118. *Ibid.*

119. *Ibid.*

120. *Ibid.*

121. Quoted in Robertson, *op. cit.,* p. 4.

122. Reported by Rev. Adam, in Collet, *op. cit.,* p. 125.

123. *Works,* Part II, p. 139.

124. *Ibid.,* p. 137.

125. *Ibid.,* p. 138.

126. *Ibid.,* p. 144.

127. *Ibid.*

128. *Ibid.,* p. 147.

129. *Ibid.,* p. 154.

130. *Ibid.*

131. *Ibid.,* p. 155.

132. *Ibid.,* p. 167.

133. *Ibid.*

134. *Ibid.,* p. 172.

135. *Ibid.,* p. 186.

135a. *Ibid.,* pp. 186, 187.

136. *Ibid.,* p. 187, 188.

137. *Ibid.,* p. 188.

138. St. Matthew 23, Tr. J. B. Phillips, *The Gospels* (London: Geoffrey Bles, 1952), p. 50.
139. *Works,* Part II, pp. 188, 189.
140. *Works,* Part VI, p. 57.
141. *Ibid.*
142. Also, see *Works,* Part VI, pp. 52, 53, 60, 76.
143. *Works,* Park VI, p. 65.
144. *Ibid.,* p. 58.
145. *Ibid.,* p. 59.
146. *Ibid.*
147. *Ibid.,* p. 61.
148. *Ibid.,* p. 70.
149. *Ibid.*
150. *Ibid.,* p. 72.
151. *Ibid.*
152. *Ibid.*
153. *Ibid.*
154. *Ibid.,* p. 73
155. *Ibid.*
156. *Ibid.,* p. 74.
157. *Ibid.* Part II, p. 200.
158. *Ibid.*
159. *Ibid.,* p. 201.
160. *Ibid.*
161. *Ibid.*
162. *Calcutta Journal,* March 15, 1823, in Majumdar, *op cit.,* p. 43.
163. *Ibid.,* p. 47, 48.
164. *Ibid.* Part II, p. 9.
165. *Ibid.*
166. *Ibid.,* p. 10
167. *Ibid.*
168. *Ibid.,* p. 16.
169. *Ibid.,* p. 47.
170. *Ibid.,* p. 24.
171. *Ibid.*
172. *Works,* Part II, p. 153.
173. *Works,* Part VI, . 73.
174. *Works,* Part II, p. 52.
175. William Theodore De Bary, ed., *Sources of Indian Tradition,* Vol II (New York: Columbia University Press, 1964), p. 28.
176. Mahanirvana Tantra.
177. Collet, *op. cit.,* p. 148.
178. *Works,* Part II, p. 200.
179. *Ibid.*
180. *Ibid.,* p. 194.
181. Collet, *op. cit.,* p. 220.
182. *Ibid.,* p. 222, 223.
183. Manilal C. Parekh, *Rajarshi Ram Mohan Roy* (Rajkot: B. Kesub Chunder Sen, 1927), p. 131.
184. Collet, *op. cit.,* p. 225.

185. *Ibid.*
186. *Ibid.*, p. 226.
187. *Ibid.*, p. 227.
188. In a private letter to the author.
189. To the editor of the *John Bull*, January 12, 1830, in Majumdar, *op. cit.*, p. 82.
190. *Ibid.*
191. *Ibid.*
192. *Bengal Chronicle*, January 14, 1830, *Ibid.*, p. 83.
193. *Father of Modern India*, *op. cit.*, pp. 18, 19.
194. Collet, *op cit.*, p. 276.
195. Vide Collet, Appendix IV, pp. 468–477.

### CHAPTER 6

1. *Father of Modern India*, *op. cit.*, p. 72.
2. Sumit Sarkar, "Rammohun and the Break with the Past," in *Rammohun Roy and the Process of Modernization in India*, ed. V. C. Joshi (Delhi: Vikas Publishing House, 1975), p. 53.
3. Chitra Ghosh, "Changing Role of Women Towards Emancipation—1947 to the Present Day," in *Role and Status of Women in Indian Society* (Calcutta: Firma KLM (P) Limited, 1978), p. 54.
4. *Works*, Part IV, p. 48.
5. *Works*, Part II, p. 51.
6. Rev. Adam to Dr. Tuckerman on the rites of Caste observed by Ram Mohan Roy as a Brahmin, in Collet, *op. cit.*, p. 212.
7. *Works*, Part II, p. 138.
8. Benimadhava Barua, "Rammohun from the Buddhist Standpoint," in *Father of Modern India*, *op. cit.*, p. 249.
9. Majumdar, *op. cit.*, p. 18.
10. *Works*, Part II, p. 16.
11. *Ibid.*
12. *Barua, loc. cit.*
13. *Works*, Part V, p. 4.
14. *Majumdar, op. cit.*, p. 289.
15. *Father of Modern India*, *op. cit.*, p. 75.
16. *Ibid.*
17. Collet, *op. cit.*, p. 213.
18. *Father of Modern India*, *op. cit.*, pp. 164, 165.
19. Piyus Kanti Das, *Raja Rammohun Roy and Brahmoism* (Calcutta: by the author, 1970), p. 116.
20. Rammohun Roy, *The Complete Songs*, tr. Nikhiles Guhas (Calcutta: Writers Workshop, 1973), No. 15.
21. Margaret and James Stutley, *Harper's Dictionary of Hinduism* (New York: Harper and Row, 1977), p. 273.
22. Atharva Veda, xviii.iii.2.
23. Rig Veda, x.xviii.8.
24. R. W. Frazer, "Sati," in *Encyclopaedia of Religion and Ethics*, ed. James Hastings, Vol. XI (New York: Charles Scribner's Sons, 1925), p. 207.
25. *Ibid.*

26. *Ibid.*
27. Smith, *op. cit.*, p. 454.
28. Rajat K. Ray, in Joshi, *op. cit.*, p. 3.
29. *Ibid.*, p. 173.
30. *Ibid.*
31. Collet, *op. cit.*, p. 79.
32. *Ibid.*, p. 80.
33. Quoted in A. F. S. Ahmed, *Social Ideas and Social Change in Bengal 1818–1835* (Leiden: E. J. Brill, 1965), p. 109.
34. *Ibid.*
35. *Ibid.*, p. 110.
36. Majumdar, *op. cit.*, p. 111.
37. Ahmed, *op. cit.*, p. 111.
38. *Ibid.*
39. *Ibid.*
40. Collet, *op. cit.*, p. 84.
41. *Ibid.*
42. Quoted in Ahmed, *op. cit.*, p. 112.
43. *Ibid.*
44. *Asiatic Journal*, March 1818, pp. 290–291.
45. Majumdar, *op. cit.*, pp. 115, 116.
46. *Ibid.*, p. 117
47. *Works*, Part III, Advertisement, p. 88.
48. *Ibid.*, p. 95
49. *Ibid.*, p. 96
50. *Ibid.*, p. 97
51. *Calcutta Gazette*, December 24, 1818, in Majumdar, *op. cit.*, p. 114.
52. *Ibid.*
53. *Works*, Part III, p. 126.
54. *Ibid.*, p. 127.
55. Ahmed, *op. cit.*, pp. 113, 114.
56. Vide K. Ballhatchet, *Social Policy and Social Change in Western India 1817–1830* (London: Oxford University Press, 1957), p. 275.
57. Minute dated January 13, 1829, P. P. H. C. 1830, 125, 178.
58. Smith, *op. cit.*, p. 648.
59. *Calcutta Monthly Journal*, July 27, 1829, in Majumdar, *op. cit.*, p. 138.
60. Sivanath Sastri, in *Father of Modern India, op. cit.*, pp. 21, 22.
61. In Majumdar, *op. cit.*, pp. 153, 154.
62. *Ibid.*, p. 142
63. *Ibid.*
64. *Ibid.*, p. 145.
65. Collet, *op. cit.*, p. 250; editorial comment.
66. Majumdar, *op. cit.*, p. 156.
67. *Ibid.*
68. *Ibid.*, p. 157.
69. *Ibid.*, p. 162, 163.
70. Collet, *op. cit.*, Appendix III, p. 464.
71. *Ibid.*
72. *Ibid.*, p. 466, 467.
73. Majumdar, *op. cit.*, p. 163.

74. *Works*, Part III, p. 131.
75. *Ibid.*, p. 132.
76. *Ibid.*
77. *Ibid.*, p. 136.
78. Majumdar, *op. cit.*, p. 204.
79. Ashis Nandy, "Sati: A Nineteenth Century Tale of Women, Violence and Protest," in Joshi, *op. cit.*, p. 169n.

## CHAPTER 7

1. Cf. Amitabha Mukherjee, *Reform and Regeneration in Bengal 1774–1823* (Calcutta: Rabindra Bharati University, 1968), p. 1.
2. F. W. Thomas, *The History and Prospects of British Education in India* (Cambridge, 1891), p. 1.
3. Chand, *op. cit.*, p. 173.
4. R. C. Majumdar, H. C. Raychaudhuri, Kalikinka Datta, *An Advanced History of India* (London: Macmillan, 1960), p. 816.
5. Howells, *op. cit.*, p. 3.
6. *Ibid.*, p. 19.
7. *Ibid.*, p. 8.
8. R. C. Majumdar, et al., *op. cit.*, p. 817.
9. Collet, *op. cit.*, p. 114.
10. *Ibid.*, p. 184.
11. *Works*, IV, p. 49.
12. Speech of Alexander Duff at the General Assembly, 25th May, 1835; quoted in Chand, *op. cit.*, p. 180.
13. *Ibid.*, p. 180, 181.
14. Mukherjee, *op. cit.*, p. 14.
15. *A Biographical Sketch of David Hare* (reprint; Calcutta, 1949) p. 6; in Collet, *op. cit.*, Supplementary Notes, p. 102.
16. *Bengal Chronicle*, January 10, 1828; in Majumdar, *op. cit.*, p. 264.
17. *Calcutta Gazette*, February 28, 1829; *Ibid.*, p. 271.
18. *Ibid.*, p. 272.
19. *Ibid.*, p. 273, 274.
20. R. C. Majumdar, *Glimpses of Bengal in the Nineteenth Century* (Calcutta: K. L. Mukhopadhyay, 1960), p. 23.
21. H. Sharp (ed.), *Selections From Educational Records 1781–1839*, Part 1 (Calcutta, 1920), p. 17.
22. A. Howell, *Education in British India* (Calcutta, 1872), p. 1.
23. Minute by Lord Minto, dated March 6, 1811. Vide A. N. Basu, *Indian Education in Parliamentary Papers*, Part 1 (1832), Bombay, 1952, p. 144.
24. Stat. 53, Geo. III, cl. 155, Sect. 43.
25. J. K. Majumdar, *op. cit.*, p. 250.
26. *Ibid.*, p. 250, 251.
27. *Ibid.*, p. 251.
28. *Ibid.*, p. 252.
29. *Ibid.*
30. *Father of Modern India*, *op. cit.*, p. 24.
31. *Ibid*, Supplementary Notes, p. 45.
32. *Works*, Part II, p. 138; Part IV, pp. 70–72.

33. Rev. William Adam, Writing July 27, 1826; in Collet, *op. cit.*, p. 189.
34. In J. K. Majumdar, *op. cit.*, p. 253.
35. R. C. Majumdar, et al. *op. cit.*, p. 818.
36. Quoted in Dr. George Smith's biography of Alexander Duff, in *Father of Modern India, op. cit.*, Supplementary Notes, p. 46.
37. Smith, *op. cit.*, p. 589.
38. Cited in Chamberlain, *op. cit.*, p. 73.
39. Cited in *Father of Modern India, loc. cit.*

## CHAPTER 8

1. Aristotle.
2. R. C. Majumdar et al., *op. cit.*, p. 813.
3. *Ibid.*
4. Extract from a letter to Mr. Digby, dated January 18, 1828, in *Selected Works of Raja Rammohun Roy* (Delhi: Publications Division, Ministry of Information and Broadcasting, Government of India, 1977), p. 296.
5. *Works*, Part II, pp. 37, 38.
6. *Works*, Part IV, p. 72.
7. *Works*, Part VII, pp. 177–178.
8. *Works*, Part I, p. 1n.
9. J. K. Majumdar, *op. cit.*, p. 458.
10. *Ibid.*, p. 460.
11. Extract from a letter to Mr. J. Crawford, dated August 18, 1828; in *Selected Works, op. cit.*, p. 297.
12. Quoted in Collet, *op. cit.*, p. 386.
13. *Asiatic Journal*, Vol. XII, New Series, September to December, 1833, p. 212.
14. Rev. William Adam, *A Lecture on the Life and Labours of Rammohun Roy*, delivered in Boston, U.S.A., 1845; ed. Rakhaldas Haldar (Calcutta: G. P. Roy and Co., 1845), pp. 26, 27. In Collet, *op. cit.*, Supplementary Notes, p. 388.
15. Rajani Kanta Guha, "Rammohun and Politics," *Father of Modern India, op. cit.*, p. 301.
16. *Ibid.*, p. 302.
17. *Ibid.*
18. Cited in Amiya Kumar Sen, *Raja Rammohun Roy: The Representative Man* (Calcutta: Calcutta Text Book Society, 1967), p. 41.
19. *Mirat-ul-Akhbar*, April 24, 1822, in J. K. Majumdar, *op. cit.*, p. 299.
20. Quoted in Sen, *op. cit.*, p. 47.
21. *Asiatic Journal*, quoted in *Calcutta Journal*, February 14, 1823.
22. *Calcutta Journal*, February 14, 1823.
23. *Ibid.*, April 5, 1823.
24. *Mirat-ul-Akhbar*, quoted by *Calcutta Journal*, March 1, 1823; in J. K. Majumdar, *op. cit.*, pp. 319, 320.
25. *Mirat-ul-Akhbar*, April 4, 1823, quoted in *Calcutta Journal*, April 10, 1823.
26. Collet, *op. cit.*, p. 177.
27. *Ibid.*, Appendix I, p. 428.
28. *Ibid.*, p. 428, 429.
29. *Ibid.*, p. 429.
30. *Ibid.*, p. 180.

31. *Ibid.*, p. 430–454.
32. *Ibid.*, Supplementary Notes, p. 206.
33. *Mirat-ul-Akhbar*, April 10, 1823, in J. K. Majumdar, *op. cit.*, p. 322.
34. *Edinburgh Magazine and Literary Miscellany*, September 1823, in Collet, *op. cit.*, Supplementary Notes, p. 162.
35. *Works*, Part IV, p. 93.
36. James Sutherland in *India Gazette*, February 18, 1834, reprinted in *Calcutta Review*, vol. 57, No. 1, October 1935; cited in Supplementary Notes, Collet, *op. cit.*, p. 307.
37. *Works*, Part IV, p. 94.
38. Sutherland, *op. cit.*, pp. 309, 310.
39. Sarojini Naidu, "Tribute to Rammohun," *Father of Modern India, op. cit.*, p. 236.
40. Chand, *op. cit.*, p. 260.
41. Sumit Sarkar, "Rammohun Roy and the Break with the Past," in Joshi, *op. cit.*, p. 59.
42. Collet, *op. cit.*, Appendix VIII, p. 497.
43. Mufakharul Islam, *Rammohun Royer Agnyatatas-Itihas* (Dacca, 1969), cited by Sarkar, *Ibid.*
44. Sarkar, *loc. cit.*
45. *Samachar Chandrika*, quoted by *John Bull*, March 9, 1830, in J. K. Majumdar, *op. cit.*, p. 330.
46. B. N. Ganguli, "Rammohun: His Political and Economic Thought," in *Rammohun Roy: a Bi-Centenary Tribute*, ed. Niharranjan Ray (New-Delhi: National Book Trust, 1974), p. 48.
47. *Ibid.*
48. *Ibid.*, p. 49.
49. Extract from a letter to J. Crawford, dated August 18, 1828, in *Selected Works, op. cit.*, p. 297.

## CHAPTER 9

1. *Sambad Kaumudi*, December 11, 1821, in J. K. Majumdar, *op. cit.*, p. 339.
2. *Ibid.*
3. Parliamentary Papers (H. C.) 1831–1832, Vol. 12, p. 151, *Ibid.*
4. Geo. IV, Cap. XXXVII, *Ibid.*, p. 352.
5. *Sambad Kaumudi*, December 30, 1826, quoted in *Oriental Herald*, July 1827, *Ibid.*, p. 358.
6. *Ibid.*
7. *Bengal Chronicle*, quoted in *Oriental Herald*, July 1827, *Ibid.*, p. 359.
8. *Ibid.*, p. 360.
9. *Ibid.*, p. 361.
10. *Ibid.*
11. *Ibid.*, p. 363.
12. *Ibid.*, p. 366.
13. *Ibid.*
14. *Ibid.*, p. 367.
15. Extract from proceedings of the House of Commons, June 5, 1829, p. 370.

16. Extract from a letter to Mr. J. Crawford, *Selected Works, op. cit.*, pp. 297, 298.
17. J. K. Majumdar, *op. cit.*, p. 377.
18. *Ibid.*
19. *Ibid.*, p. 378.
20. *Ibid.*
21. *Ibid.*, p. 395.
22. *Ibid.*, pp. 395, 396.
23. *Ibid.*, p. 396.
24. *Ibid.*
25. *Ibid.*, p. 397.
26. *Ibid.*, pp. 386, 387.
27. *Ibid.*, p. 388.
28. *Asiatic Journal*, September 1833.
29. Sen. *op. cit.*, p. 206.
30. *Samachar Darpan*, September 15, 1832, in J. K. Majumdar, *op. cit.*, p. 391.
31. *Reformer*, quoted in *India Gazette*, January 22, 1833, *Ibid.*, p. 393.
32. *Asiatic Journal*, N. S., Vol. XII, Part II, pp. 1, 93, 169.
33. *Asiatic Journal*, September 1833, in J. K. Majumdar, *op. cit.*, pp. 403, 404.

## CHAPTER 10

1. Mary Carpenter, *The Last Days in England of the Raja Rammohun Roy* (Calcutta: The Rammohun Library, 1915), p. 106; and in Supplementary Notes, *Father of Modern India, op. cit.*, pp. 62–64.
2. Susobhan Chandra Sarkar (ed.), *Rammohun Roy on the Indian Economy* (Calcutta: Rare Book Publishing Syndicate, 1965), xvi.
3. *Ibid.*, i.
4. *Works*, Part II, p. 8.
5. *Samachar Darpan*, March 24, 1832, in J. K. Majumdar, *op. cit.*, p. 482.
6. *India Gazette*, June 13, 1832, *Ibid.*
7. *Works*, Part III, p. 11.
8. *Ibid.*, p. 12.
9. *Ibid.*, p. 12, 13.
10. *Ibid.*, p. 17.
11. *Ibid.*
12. *Ibid.*, p. 18.
13. *Ibid.*, p. 19.
14. *Ibid.*
15. *Ibid.*, p. 21.
16. *Ibid.*, p. 23.
17. *Ibid.*
18. *Ibid.*, p. 24.
19. *Ibid.*, p. 25.
20. *Ibid.*, p. 26.
21. *Ibid.*, p. 29.
22. *Ibid.*, pp. 32, 33.

23. *Ibid.*, p. 33.
24. *Ibid.*, pp. 37, 38.
25. *Ibid.*, p. 38.
26. Vide J. K. Majumdar, *op. cit.*, p. 503.
27. *Works*, Part III, p. 39.
28. *Ibid.*, p. 41.
29. *Ibid.*, p. 42.
30. *Ibid.*, p. 43.
31. *Ibid.*, p. 45.
32. *Ibid.*, pp. 45, 46.
33. *Ibid.*, p. 46.
34. *Ibid.*
35. *Ibid.*
36. *Ibid.*, p. 47.
37. *Ibid.*, p. 49.
38. *Ibid.*, p. 50.
39. *Ibid.*

## CHAPTER 11

1. *India Gazette*, December 17, 1829, in J. K. Majumdar, *op. cit.*, p. 440.
2. *Bengal Hurkaru*, December 17, 1829, *Ibid.*, p. 439.
3. *Sambad Kaumudi*, quoted in *Bengal Chronicle*, January 7, 1830, *Ibid.*, p. 443.
4. *Ibid.*, p. 444.
5. *Bengal Hurkaru, loc. cit.*
6. *Asiatic Journal*, March 1829, *Ibid.*, p. 433.
7. Parliamentary Papers (H. C.), 1831–1832, Vol. 8, pp. 274–280, *Ibid.*, p. 414.
8. *Ibid.*, p. 418.
9. *Ibid.*, p. 419.
10. *Ibid.*, p. 421.
11. *Ibid.*, p. 424.
12. *Ibid.*
13. *Works*, Part III, pp. 50, 51.
14. *Ibid.*, p. 51.
15. *Ibid.*, p. 52.
16. *Ibid.*
17. J. K. Majumdar, *op. cit.*, lxxxvi, vii.
18. *Government Gazette*, November 1, 1830, *Ibid.*, pp. 461, 462.
19. *Ibid.*, p. 463.
20. Parliamentary Papers (H. C.), 1831–1832, Vol. II, pp. 685–686, *Ibid.*, p. 468.
21. *Ibid.*, p. 469.
22. *Ibid.*
23. *Ibid.*
24. *Ibid.*
25. G. Chester and A. Sargent for Board of Customs, Salt and Opium, January 26, 1832, *Ibid.*, p. 474.
26. Parliamentary Papers (H. C.), 1831–1832, Vol. 8, p. 69, *Ibid.*, p. xci.

27. B. N. Ganguli, in Niharranjan Ray (ed.), p. 48.
28. *Ibid.*, p. 65.
29. Asok Sen, "The Bengal Economy and Rammohun Roy," in Joshi (ed.), *op. cit.*, p. 113.
30. *Ibid.*, p. 115.
31. *Bengal Hurkaru*, June 20, 1832, in J. K. Majumdar, *op. cit.*, p. 486.
32. *Samachar Chandrika*, quoted in *Samachar Darpan*, July 7, 1832, *Ibid.*, p. 490.
33. Rajat K. Ray, "Introduction," in Joshi (ed.), *op. cit.*, p. 17.
34. Vide N. K. Sinha, *The Economic History of Bengal 1793–1848*, Vol. III (Calcutta, 1970), p. i.
34a. H. R. Goshal, "Industrial Production in Bengal in the Early Nineteenth Century," in *Readings in Indian Economic History*, B. N. Ganguli (ed.), in Sen, *op. cit.*, p. 125.
35. *Ibid.*, pp. 127, 128.
36. Rajat K. Ray, *op. cit.*, p. 18.
37. Asok Sen, *op. cit.*, p. 127.
38. Hiranmay Banerjee, *The House of the Tagores* (3rd, edn; Calcutta: Rabindra Bharati, 1968), p. 16.
39. *Ibid.*
40. Rajat K. Ray, *op. cit.*, p. 18.
41. *Ibid.*, pp. 18, 19.
42. Asok Sen, *Ibid.*, p. 133.
43. *Ibid.*
44. Appeal to the King-in-Council, *Selected Works, op. cit.*, p. 99.
45. *Ibid.*

### CHAPTER 12

1. Letter to Mrs. Woodford of Brighton, *Selected Works, op. cit.*, p. 293.
2. *Ibid.*
3. Letter to Mr. William Rathbone, in Mary Carpenter, *op. cit.*, p. 87.
4. *Ibid.*
5. *Monthly Repository*, June 1831, Vol. V, N. S., pp. 417–420, *Ibid.*, p. 92.
6. *Ibid.*
7. *Ibid.*, pp. 95, 96.
8. *Ibid.*, p. 98.
9. *Ibid.*, p. 122.
10. *Ibid.*, p. 123.
11. Collet, *op. cit.*, p. 322.
12. Mr. Robert Montgomery Martin, *Court Journal*, October 5, 1833, Collet, *op. cit.*, p. 324.
13. Mr. Southerland, *Ibid.*
14. *Ibid.*, p. 356.
15. *Indian Mirror*, July 15, 1872, *Ibid.*, pp. 355, 356.
16. Dr. Lant Carpenter, in Mary Carpenter, *op. cit.*, pp. 151, 152.
17. Private Journal of Dr. J. B. Estlin, *Ibid.*, p. 166.
18. *Ibid.*, also in Collet, *op. cit.*, p. 363.
19. *Ibid.*, pp. 170, 171.

20. Collet, *op. cit.*, pp. 365, 366.

## CHAPTER 13

1. Charles Heimsath, "Rammohun and Social Reform," ed. V. C. Joshi, *Rammohun Roy and the Process of Modernization in India* (Delhi: Vikas, 1975), p. 152.
2. *Ibid.*, p. 153.
3. *Ibid.*
4. *Ibid.*
5. J. L. Houlden, *Ethics and the New Testament* (London: Penguin Books, 1973), p. 9.
6. Harmon L. Smith and Louis W. Hodges, *The Christian and His Decisions* (Nashville: Abingdon Press, 1969), p. 14.
7. *Works*, Part II, p. 63.
8. *Ibid.*
9. *Ibid.*, pp. 63, 64.
10. *Ibid.*, p. 64.
11. *Ibid.*, p. 68.
12. *Ibid.*, p. 72.
13. *Ibid.*, p. 18n.
14. *Ibid.*, p. 146.
15. Nikhiles Guha, *op. cit.*, p. 18.
16. *Works*, Part 11, pp. 144, 145.
17. Guha, *op. cit.*, pp. 14, 15.

## CHAPTER 14

1. *Works*, Part II, p. 63.
2. *Ibid.*, p. 66.
3. *Ibid.*, pp. 69, 70.
4. *Ibid.*, p. 70.
5. *Ibid.*
6. *Ibid.*
7. Rev. Wiliam Adam, *A Lecture on the Life and Labours of Rammohun Roy* (Calcutta: Roy and Co., 1879), pp. 22–25, in Collet, *op. cit.*, pp. 126, 127.

## CHAPTER 15

1. *Works*, Part II, p. 47.
2. *Ibid.*, p. 53.
3. *Ibid.*, p. 99.
4. *Tuhfat, op. cit.*, p. 25.
5. *The Trust Deed*, Collet, *op. cit.*, Appendix IV, p. 277.
6. *Tuhfat, loc.cit.*
7. William James, *The Varieties of Religious Experience* (London: Longmans Green and Co., 1947), p. 330.
8. *Tuhfat, op. cit.*, pp. 1, 2.
9. James, *op. cit.*, pp. 333, 334.
10. *Ibid.*, p. 335.
11. *Works*, Part II, p. 1.

12. *Ibid.*, p. 16n.
13. *Ibid.*
14. *Ibid.*, p. 92.
15. *Ibid.*
16. *Ibid.*, p. 105.
17. Paul Tillich, *Theology of Culture* (New York: Oxford University Press, 1959), p. 133.
18. *Ibid.*, pp. 133, 134.
19. *Ibid.*, p. 134.
20. *Works*, Part V, p. 3.
21. *Ibid.*, p. 59.
22. Ibid.
23. *Tuhfat, op. cit.*, p. 24.
24. Erich Fromm, *Man For Himself* (New York: Rinehart and Winston, 1964), p. 8.
25. Ibid., p. 9.
26. *Tuhfat, op. cit.*, pp. 3, 4.
27. *Ibid.*, pp. 2, 3.
28. Fromm, *op. cit.*, pp. 10, 11.
29. *Works*, Part II, pp. 48, 49.
30. *Bhagavad Gita* VI:41–43.
31. *Ibid.*, III:3.
32. *Ibid.*, III:42.
33. S. Cromwell Crawford, *Evolution of Hindu Ethical Ideals* (Calcutta: Firma K. L. Mukhopadhyay, 1974), p. 42.
34. *Works*, Part II, p. 52.
35. John Roth, *Freedom and the Moral Life: The Ethics of William James* (Philadelphia: Westminster Press, 1969), p. 42.
36. Letter to the Minister of Foreign Affairs of France, Paris, in *Selected Works, op. cit.*, p. 317.
37. *Works*, Part II, p. 5.
38. *Ibid.*, p. 71.
39. *Ibid.*, p. 72.
40. Crawford, *op. cit.*, pp. 223, 224.
41. *Works*, Part II, p. 177.
42. Joshi (ed.), *op.cit.*, p. 55.
43. Crawford, *op. cit.*, p. 225.
44. S. Radhakrishnan, *The Hindu View of Life* (New York: Macmillan, 1965), p. 54.
45. Vide Crawford, *op. cit.*, p. 228.
46. *Bhagavad Gita* II:47.
47. *Works*, Part II, p. 70.
48. *Bhagavad Gita* III:20.
49. Mahadev Desai, *The Gita According to Gandhi* (Amhedabad: Navajivan Publishing House, 1977), p. 182.
50. *Works.*, Part V, p. 3.
51. *Ibid.*
52. *Ibid.*
53. *The Dhammapada*, tr. P. Lal (New York: Farrar, Strauss, Giroux, 1972), p. 83.

54. *Mahabharata* 13, 113, 9.
55. *Mahabharata* 12, 260, 22.
56. *Bhagavad Gita* XIII:27–28.
57. *Mahabharata* 5, 39, 72.
58. *Works*, Part V, p. 4.
59. Sir Brajendra Nath Seal, "Rammohun Roy, The Universal Man," in *Father of Modern India, op. cit.*, p. 108.
60. Letter to Mrs. Woodford of Brighton, in *Selected Works, op. cit.*, p. 293.
61. *Ibid.*
62. Heramba Chandra Maitra, "Rammohun as Re-Constructor of Indian Life and Society," in *Father of Modern India, op. cit.*, p. 204.
63. Vide Collet, *op. cit.*, p. 255, and editorial footnotes.
64. Convocation address by Shri K. R. Narayan, Vice-Chancellor, Jawaharlal Nehru University, at the Tata Institute of Social Sciences, Bombay, May 5, 1979.
65. *Ibid.*
66. *Ibid.*
67. In "Persecuting Indian Christians," by Vivek Sengupta, *New Delhi*, May 14, 1979.
68. *Narayan, loc. cit.*
69. *Works*, Part V, Preface.
70. *Works*, Part II, p. 140.
71. J. Moltman and M. D. Meeks, "The Liberation of Oppressors," *Christianity and Crisis*, Vol. 38, No. 20, 1978, p. 312.
72. *Ibid.*
73. *Selected Works, op.cit.*, p. 154.
74. *Ibid.*, p. 148.
75. *Works*, Part I, *op. cit.*, p. 7.
76. *Ibid.*
77. *Selected Works, op. cit.*, p. 156.
78. *Ibid.*
79. *Ibid.*
80. *Ibid.*, p. 157.
81. *Works*, Part I, pp. 3–4.
82. *Ibid.*, p. 4.
83. *Ibid.*
84. *Selected Works, op. cit.*, pp. 154, 155.
85. *Ibid.*
86. *Ibid.*
87. *Ibid.*
88. *Ibid.*
89. *Ibid.*, p. 156.
90. Renuka Ray, "Introduction," *Role and Status of Women in India* (Calcutta: Frima K. L. Mukhopadhyay, 1978), p. 1.
91. *Ibid.*
92. Manashi Dasgupta, "New Women in Old Society," *Ibid.*, p. 71.
93. *Ibid.*
94. *Ibid.*
95. *Ibid.*
96. *Ibid.*, p. 70.

97. M. K. Pardhy, "Cultural Diary," *Poona Herald*, April 8, 1979.
98. Speech of Earl Warren, Chief Justice of the United States, at Jewish Theological Seminary of America, 1962.
99. *Selected Works, op. cit.*, p. 157.
100. Aleyamma George, "Status of Women and Education," *Role and Status of Women in India, op. cit.*, p. 100.
101. Gita Mukharji, "Status of Women and Education," *Ibid.*, p. 108.
102. Aleyamma George, *Ibid.*, p. 103.
103. *Selected Works, op. cit.*, p. 163.

## CHAPTER 16

1. Hank Wittemore, "The Legend Who Captures Legends," *Parade*, December 3, 1978, p. 10.
2. *Ibid.*
3. *Ibid.*
4. F. Max Muller, "The Greatness of Rammohun Roy," *Father of Modern India, op. cit.*, p. 177.
5. *Bengal Herald*, January 17, 1841, in J. K. Majumdar, *op.cit.*, pp. cv, cvi.

# Bibliography

Ahmed, A. F. S. *Ideas and Social Change in Bengal 1818–1835*. Leiden: E. J. Brill, 1965.

Ballhatchet, Kenneth. *Social Policy and Social Change in Western India 1817–1830*, London: Oxford University Press, 1957.

Banerjee, Hiranmay. *The House of Tagores*. 3rd ed. Calcutta: Rabindra Bharati University, 1968.

Basham, Arthur L. *The Wonder That Was India*. New York: Grove Press, Inc., 1959.

Basu, A. N. *Indian Education in Parliamentary Papers*, Part I (1832). Bombay, 1952.

Bearce, George. *British Attitudes Towards India 1784–1858*. London: Oxford University Press, 1961.

Brown, A. T. *Half-Lights on Chelsfield Court Lodge*. Liverpool: Private, 1933.

Carpenter, Mary. *The Last Days in England of Raja Rammohun Roy*. Calcutta: The Rammohun Library, 1915.

Chakravarti, Satis Chandra, ed. *The Father of Modern India*. Calcutta: Office of the Rammohun Centenary Committee, 1935.

Chand, Tara. *History of the Freedom Movement in India*, Vol. II. Delhi: Ministry of Education, Government of India, 1967.

Chapman, Gerald. *Edmund Burke*. Cambridge: Harvard University Press, 1967.

Collet, Sophia Dobson. *The Life and Letters of Rammohun Roy*. Dilip Kumar Biswas and Prabhat Chandra Ganguli, eds. Calcutta: Sadharan Brahmo Samaj, 1962.

Crawford, S. Cromwell. *Evolution of Hindu Ethical Ideals*. Calcutta: Firma K. L. Mukhopadhyay, 1974.

Das, Piyus Kanti. *Raja Rammohun Roy and Brahmoism*. Calcutta: By the author, 1970.

De Bary, William Theodore, ed. *Sources of Indian Tradition*, Vol. II. New York: Columbia University Press, 1964.

Desai, Mahadev. *The Gita According to Gandhi*. Amhedabad: Navajivan Publishing House, 1977.

Embree, Ainslie, T. *Charles Grant and British Rule in India*. New York: Columbia University Press, 1962.

Fromm, Erich. *Man for Himself*. New York: Holt, Rinehart, and Winston, 1954.

Grant, Charles. *Observations on the State of Society among the Asiatic Subjects of Great Britain, particularly with respect to Morals and on the Means of Improving it*. Printed privately, 1797.

Guha, Nikhiles, tr. *The Complete Songs of Rammohun Roy*. Calcutta: Writers Workshop, 1973.

Hastings, James, ed. *Encyclopaedia of Religion and Ethics*. New York: Charles Scribner's and Sons, 1925.

Hoby, James. *Memoir of William Yates of Calcutta*. London, 1847.

Houlden, J. L. *Ethics and the New Testament*. London: Penguin Books, 1973.

Howell, A. *Education in British India*. Calcutta, 1872.

Howells, George. *The Story of Serampore and Its College*. Serampore: By the author, 1927.

Howse, E. H. *Saints in Politics: The Clapham Sect and the Growth of Freedom*. Toronto: University of Toronto Press, 1952.

James, William. *The Varieties of Religious Experience*. London: Longmans Green and Co., 1975.

Joshi, V. C., ed. *Rammohun Roy and the Process of Modernization in India*. Delhi: Vikas, 1975.

Lal, P., tr. *The Dhammapada*. New York: Farrar, Strauss and Giroux, 1972.

Majumdar, Jatindra Kumar, ed. *Raja Rammohun Roy and Progressive Movements in India*. Calcutta: Art Press, 1941.

Majumdar, Ramesh C. *Glimpses of Bengal in the Nineteenth Century*. Calcutta; K. L. Mukhopadhyay, 1960.

Majumdar, Ramesh C., H. C. Rayachaudhuri, Kalinka Datta. *An Advanced History of India*, London: Macmillan, 1960.

Mill, James. *The History of British India*. Abridged by William Thomas. Chicago: University of Chicago Press, 1975.

Mukherjee, Amitabha. *Reform and Regeneration in Bengal 1774–1823*. Calcutta; Rabindra Bharati University, 1968.

Mukherjee, S. N. *Sir William Jones: Study in Eighteenth-Century British Attitudes to India*. Cambridge: Cambridge University Press, 1868.

Nag, Kalidas, Burman Debajyoti., eds. *The English Works of Raja Rammohun Roy*, Vols. I-VII. Calcutta: Sadharan Brahmo Samaj, 1889.

Obaide, Moulavi Obaidullah El., tr. *Tuhfatul Muhwahhiddin*. Calcutta: Adi Brahmo Samaj, 1889.

Parekh, Manilal C. *Rajarshi Ram Mohan Roy*. Rajkot: B. Keshub Chunder Sen, 1927.

Radhakrishnan, Sarvepalli. *The Hindu View of Life*. New York: Macmillan, 1965.

Ray, Niharranjan, ed. *Rammohun Roy: A Bi-Centenary Tribute*. New Delhi: National Book Trust, 1974.

Ray, Ajit Kumar. *The Religious Ideas of Rammohun Roy*. New Delhi: Kanak Publications, 1976.

Ray, Renuka, *et al. Role and Status of Women in Indian Society*. Calcutta: Firma K. L. Mukhopadhyay Limited, 1978.

Roth, John. *Freedom and the Moral Life: The Ethics of William James*. Philadelphia: Westminster Press, 1969.

Sarkar, Susobhan Chandra, ed. *Rammohun Roy on Indian Economy*. Calcutta: Rare Book Publishing Syndicate, 1965.

*Selected Works of Raja Rammohun Roy*. Delhi: Publications Division, Ministry of Information and Broadcasting, Government of India, 1977.

Sen, Amiya Kumar. *Raja Rammohun Roy: The Representative Man.* Calcutta: Calcutta Textbook Society, 1967.

Sharp, H., ed. *Selections from Educational Records, Part I: 1781–1839.* Calcutta, 1920.

Singh, Iqbal. *Rammohun Roy.* Bombay: Asia Publishing House, 1958.

Smith, Harmon, L., Hodges, Louis W. *The Christian and His Decisions.* Nashville: Abingdon Press, 1969.

Smith, Vincent A. *The Oxford History of India*, Percival Spear, ed., 3rd. ed. Oxford: Clarendon Press, 1958.

Stokes, Eric. *English Utilitarians and India.* Oxford: Clarendon Press, 1959.

Stutley, Margaret and James. *Harper's Dictionary of Hinduism.* New York: Harper and Row, 1977.

Teignmouth, John ed. *The Works of Sir William Jones.* Delhi: Agam Prakashan, 1977 (Reprint).

Tillich, Paul. *Theology of Culture.* New York: Oxford University Press, 1959.

*A Treasury of Favorite Poems.* New York: Avenell Books, 1978.

Wasserstrom, Richard ed. *Today's Moral Problems.* New York: Macmillan, 1975.

Wilkins, Charles. *A Translation of a Royal Grant of Land by one of the Ancient Rajas of Hindostan, Asiatic Researches*, I, 1788. *Worship and Service Hymnal.* Chicago: Hope Publishing Company, 1957.

# Index

257

DATE DUE